ARCHITECTS

EXPERTISE

**CULTURES AND
TECHNOLOGIES
OF KNOWLEDGE**

EDITED BY DOMINIC BOYER

A list of titles in this series is available at cornellpress.cornell.edu.

ARCHITECTS

Portraits of a Practice

Thomas Yarrow

CORNELL UNIVERSITY PRESS   ITHACA AND LONDON

First published 2019 by Cornell University Press

Library of Congress Cataloging-in-Publication Data

Names: Yarrow, Thomas, 1977– author.
Title: Architects : portraits of a practice / by Thomas Yarrow.
Description: Ithaca : Cornell University Press, 2019. | Series: Expertise | Includes bibliographical references and index.
Identifiers: LCCN 2019008031 (print) | LCCN 2019008900 (ebook) | ISBN 9781501738500 (pdf) | ISBN 9781501738517 (epub/mobi) | ISBN 9781501738494 | ISBN 9781501738494 (pbk.)
Subjects: LCSH: Millar Howard Workshop. | Architectural firms—England—Stroud. | Architectural practice—England—Stroud. | Architects—Professional relationships—England—Stroud.
Classification: LCC NA997.M55 (ebook) | LCC NA997.M55 Y37 2019 (print) | DDC 720.92/2—dc23
LC record available at https://lccn.loc.gov/2019008031

For Joe and Chantal Conneller

And to the memory of Gresham Dodd

Contents

ARCHITECTS

BEFORE THE BEGINNING

Starting with Friendship

Tomas has been a persistently interesting presence in my life. We first met at about age four, though neither of us remembers this. Our parents were friends before we were. He has a quiet charisma emanating from a desire to embrace what he doesn't know. He has always been naturally curious and speaks with the slowness and deliberation of someone aware of how little he understands about the world, even the parts of it that relate to his area of expertise: architecture. During the period of my fieldwork he is in his late thirties and has a beard and slightly unkempt hair.

My first day of research is also the first time I visit him in his new house. He tells me about it before we get there, excited by it as a space but also ambivalent about living in it. He had scoped out the building a while ago: a Victorian corrugated tin prefab in need of complete renovation and extending. It had a dilapidated romance. He had put in an offer but was outbid. Somebody else bought it, employed another local architect, and completed the renovation. Soon, Tomas learned the completed house was for rent, arranged to see it, and "fell in love." This was galling; he was an architect living not just in the creation of another architect but in the house he had coveted and imagined converting to his own design.

It's uncanny seeing familiar possessions rearranged in this unfamiliar space. The new context makes me see them afresh, like a museum to the life they objectify: a huge ultra-real oil portrait of his grandfather; photographic self-portraits by an artist friend; a partly decaying architectural model; some "joiner" photographs taken by his father (also an architect) in the fragmented photo-montage style pioneered by David Hockney. It occurs to me that his minimal-ist design aesthetic is in an uneasy relationship with the untidiness generated through the various creative projects he has on the go. On display shelves, mixed with ceramic sculptures made by his artist partner, Anna, are various bits and pieces of remote-controlled models, the remainders of an obsession going back to his early teens. Bluntly speaking, it's a bit of a mess! Anna is imminently expecting twins, their first children. A cot (crib), buggy, and baby-bouncers have already been acquired, objects that are strange harbingers of lives to come. "In about two weeks my life is going to be totally different, and I just can't imagine how!" Tomas reflects, as we sit talking over late-night drinks.

Some of the things in his house elicit specific memories, others the houses that have provided the stage for earlier periods of his life: the traditional Cotswold terrace house where his parents still live in a neighboring village; the down-at-heel grandeur of a shared student tenement in Edinburgh; and the various houses he has rented in his adult life, in general progressively bigger but always inhabited with what I have found a strange lack of interest or attachment for somebody so interested in buildings. I wonder aloud if this might be a way of avoiding the professional judgments of fellow architects, or because he is more interested in the process of design than in the outcome, or even the fear of failure? His own more prosaic explanation may not be the whole truth but conveys another: "I've never made enough money to buy or build the kind of house I want to live in!"

There is another dimension to my sense of uncanny. Seeing his life through the professional vision of an ethnographer, I find myself analyzing and objectifying it in a way that is doubly disconcerting: I am aware of seeing him differently, and aware of his awareness of this. This book is the outcome of an exploration with, and of, a friendship. To borrow an architectural term, this friendship is the "negative space" at the heart of the book. The idea for the project emerged from it. The "field" in which I explored these questions was profoundly shaped by it. During and after fieldwork, the friendship gave me access to thoughts shared with a level of intimacy and with understanding born of conversations stretching decades back. With trust came access to people, places, and working environments that might otherwise have remained off-limits. As open and generous as other people in the practice were, and even though many independently would become my friends, it was their knowledge of my friendship with Tomas that shaped the possibilities and constraints through which my research unfolded.

If the friendship made the book possible, the book also made the friendship differently possible. An interest with him, about the world, became more an interest in him and his world. In some respects research involved exploration that enriched and deepened the relationship, allowed me to explore the daily reality of a significant part of his life, previously only glimpsed through his summary descriptions of it. In others the process of critical reflection seemed to introduce an asymmetry, even a distance. Conversations about his work displaced conversations we might have had, ones more interesting to him because less directly about him.

A Note on Structure and Approach

The book is written with a broad range of readers in mind. This section, an explanation of the book's structure and narrative approach, is followed by a brief overview of my conceptual orientations, inspirations, and points of departure

(Approaching Architectural Practice). Depending on your interests, these sections may be read selectively, or not at all. Either way, they are a prelude to the main account, which begins with Part One.

This book describes the lives of ten architects working at Millar Howard Workshop (MHW), the practice that Tomas codirects. Specific as these lives are, they also speak of the difficulties and rewards of creative endeavor, of the meaning of work and its relationship to lives beyond, of friendship, of efforts to live good lives where contradictory imperatives make this hard, and of what it means to claim to know with authority.

I have written as an anthropologist, an approach oriented to understanding other people's lives on their own terms, what they do and think in their everyday lives. It is an orientation that seeks to illuminate the manifold complexities and intersecting concerns through which lives are lived, without reducing these to singular explanations. More specifically my approach is ethnographic in the sense described by Les Back. It aims to be "an augmentation of the real . . . turning up the background, enlarging the unremarked upon and making it remarkable."[1] The book contains descriptions of architectural practice, attuned, focused, and understood through ideas drawn from a range of literatures but does not assume a readership with prior knowledge of the concepts and perspectives I build on. For reasons I elaborate below, I have either folded these ideas into my descriptions implicitly or placed them in notes at the end of the book. I hope this enables a wide readership to follow the account, while allowing academic readers to see how it builds on existing work.

Oriented by a commitment to ethnographic description that stays close to the unfolding moments of architectural practice, the account is structured episodically. It is mostly ordered around events, situations, and conversations. Collectively these episodes are intended to evoke the experience of architectural practice. They are loosely themed but not resolved as a chapter might be. Overall they trace the teleological logic of design, from conception to plan to building, but complicate and trouble the flow, showing how everyday working practice unfolds along specific, less linear trajectories, as architects move between different projects and phases. In the office one thing happens after another, sometimes connected but often in unresolved adjacency.

As far as possible I have tried to emphasize the logic of these happenings on their own terms. I hope that any loss of thematic clarity comes with the gain of a better understanding of architectural practice as a space of intersecting interests and complex negotiations. The structure is consistent with an understanding of architecture less as a series of abstract principles or technical competencies than, as Donald Schon describes of professional practice more generally, "an artful practice of the unique case."[2] Focusing on these cases and this art, the point is to highlight how knowing happens through doing; how what these architects know relates necessarily to where, when, and with whom. Replicating my own process of research, analytic reflections are closely related to the moments from which they arose, rather than as a connecting logic over and above them. Consistent with the architectural practices I observed, some of these descriptions are more resolved than others, just as some are more extended.

Throughout the text, I include photographs as a parallel strand of the description. Deliberately untitled, they are related to but not simply illustrative of the adjacent written accounts, an invitation for readers to make their own connections. Since the images were often germane to my textual descriptions, one might even think of the text as a series of extended captions. I took the photographs during research, initially intended only for my own purposes as an aide-mémoire, an accompaniment to my written field notes, focusing especially on things I found difficult to convey in words: gestures, facial expressions, bodily comportment, the spatial contexts and choreography of these social encounters. I took them hastily with my camera phone, juggling notepads and recording equipment, sometimes during interviews or with my mind on other things. I hope their technical deficiencies are compensated, at least to some degree, by an immediate proximity to these moments. Though framed by my interests, they captured more than I knew or was able to see at the time: details familiar to the point I stopped noticing them; spaces, tools, and materials that become more visible when you take the focus of words away; fleeting gestures visible only when the action is stopped.

As a final component of my portrait of these architects, I share with the reader some of their conversations. Entitled *Listen*, the conversations were self-recorded by their participants after my fieldwork ended, as responses to first drafts I shared but on topics of the architects' own choosing: issues they found interesting, frustrating, compelling, and wanted to collectively explore. I have edited the transcripts lightly and added contextualization, where the meaning seemed to lie beyond the transcribed word. Otherwise I have tried to leave them unanalyzed: a chance to eavesdrop, to hear what captures their imagination, the texture of the language they use among themselves, as they seek to explain themselves to themselves, half aware of the digital recorder and an unknown audience of possible listeners.

Throughout the text, I have used the actual names of architects, as they wished to appear, other than "Roisin," a pseudonym. The names of all other people, of sites and of projects, are pseudonyms.

The remainder of this section is a brief explanation of how and why I have removed some of the academic armature that scholars generally expect to find. Readers with no such expectation may wish to skip forward. The next section, an account of my approach and the inspirations behind this, may also be passed over if you are more interested in the lives of architects than in how I have tried to make sense of these.

Architects' comments on early drafts were not encouraging. "A bit dense," as one of them put it; "my eyes slightly glazed over." Another used architectural imagery to highlight a linked problem: "It's as though you've constructed a building and left the scaffolding on," he remarked. The "academic scaffold," by which he meant conceptual reflections and theorized arguments, seemed a distraction from the descriptive passages he found most engaging. The metaphor of scaffold is drawn from his own professional practice and is also a reflection of the sensibilities that orient it. Architects, at least in this practice, spend a lot of time discussing "precedents," drawing influences and inspiration from other designs, but in the final instance they are clear: a building cannot be explained; it has to speak for itself.

Admittedly from a very specific readership, these responses stayed with me, made me question how and for whom I was writing, and provided the stimulus for an experiment in ethnographic form. The analogy of text and building breaks down in various respects but got me thinking: What would a description look like if conceptual engagements with other scholars were treated as "scaffold": enabling the construction of a descriptive object in which readers can imaginatively dwell, even and indeed because the conceptual framework is not visibly on show?

The imagery of "scaffold" is suggestive of the way in which a framework is needed to structure an object, in this case descriptive, being integral to the process of construction but ultimately invisible.

On the analogy of scaffold, the first plank I have sought to remove is *theory*, in the specific sense of externally derived explanatory frameworks of a singular kind. "Writing is an exercise in humility," writes Nigel Rapport:

> Theory is proud in its claims at comprehension. But theory would nevertheless appear to be the principal means of *misrecognition*—not the reverse—in its making of the other into an object whose point is to prove that theory's assumptions. Academia would seem prone to theoretical pride: trafficking in coherent stories and plausible interpretations. But . . . this is to bring an artificial order to a wild world.[3]

By implication his target is "grand theory" and its claims to what Boyer et al.[4] elsewhere characterize as a "monopolising epistemic authority," an inherent asymmetry of knower and known.[5] Rapport advocates the antidote to this, in writing that "eschews theory for a return to the everyday."[6] Arguably, he presents the relationship between academic theory and everyday life in overly binary terms: all descriptions must "tame" to some degree, simplifying even if only enough to bring particular forms of complexity into focus; all are oriented by more or less stated interpretive approaches, ideas drawn from other scholars or examples, that open up ways of seeing, even as they may close down others.[7] Marilyn Strathern's insistence that "theory" and "description" occupy the same conceptual plane highlights how good descriptions arise through the comparative lens of other people and places, and how, in turn, other people's ideas and practice must force us to rethink our own.[8] "Theory," from this perspective, is not a fixed set of ideas, but the conceptual "remainder" of the descriptive act: the ways in which concepts are changed and extended in the act of describing particular circumstances, and the broader implications that expand from the specific case. Still, the thrust of Rapport's argument has resonance in the current moment: pulled toward the assumptions and expectations of fellow professionals, anthropologists, like other academics, are routinely drawn into explanation that moves away from the concerns that animate the lives of those we seek to understand.[9] Even those approaches emphasizing the interdependence of theory and description have more often emphasized the theoretical implications of descriptions than the descriptive implications of theory.[10] My account moves in the other direction: scaling back argument as a frame and focus of description, I hope to amplify understanding of the complexity of architectural lived reality, to give more attention to those aspects that remain specific and inchoate, to dwell in architects' own explanations of what they do and why, and so to refuse the kinds of exegesis that would render these details as epiphenomena of my own explanatory theory.

Second, and relatedly, my approach involves the deliberate attenuation of explicit *argument*. Focusing on Godfrey Lienhardt's ethnography of the Dinka, Michael Carrithers elucidates some of the elements that made the classic monographs of the middle of the twentieth century so compelling:

> Lienhardt devotes his effort throughout to the knotty labour of finding the most felicitous way of characterising the Dinka themselves, rather than adopting the established conceptual coinage of professional anthropology or engaging argumentatively with established professional opinions. He leaves us to infer his understanding of those other voices and how they might err.[11]

His point echoes Rapport's, though he also makes another: the vivid qualities of Lienhardt's writing were as much a function of what he did not say as what he did. Literary theorist Wolfgang Iser develops this point discussing Virginia Woolf's exposition of the role of readers' imagination in the work of Jane Austen:

> [The reader] is drawn into the events and made to supply what is meant from what is not said. What is said only appears to take on significance

as a reference to what is not said; it is the implications and not the statements that give shape and weight to the meaning. But as the unsaid comes to life in the reader's imagination, so the said "expands" to take on greater significance than might have been supposed; even trivial scenes can seem surprisingly profound.[12]

Imagination works through language as an interplay between explicit and implicit, revelation and concealment. Many good examples of this interplay exist in ethnographic writing, Lienhardt's included, alongside a number of more recent accounts, but the general shift to explication and argument have tended to leave less implicit. I hope that a less conceptually "scaffolded," less argumentatively focused text might in this way lead to a richer and more evocative account of architectural practice because, as it were, readers are given more imaginative space to provide their own images.

A third and final form of textual attenuation, also linked, relates to *analysis*. In her introduction to *Women and Wanderers*, Strathern explains: "In [Reay's] book analysis remains very largely off stage . . . , and the pride of place is given to descriptions of people's doings, as they apparently occurred, in story-like form." Comparing this to ethnographic writing of a more conventional kind, she notes: "Much ethnography is seemingly written of the moment. Yet the moment in which the ethnographer writes is also turned to the ends of exposition, and conveying a sense of immediacy has to compete with that. The trade-off between immediacy and reflection, between what is observed and what is analysed seems inevitable." If observation and analysis are inherently connected, Strathern highlights how minimization of the latter has amplifying effects with respect to the former: without the framing post facto analysis of the observer, description captures quick changes from moment to moment, replicating the unpredictable qualities of social interactions: "an element in any 'encounter' is its unpredictability: people try to guess what will happen, watch how others behave, see how this or that person will react. The dynamic of the relationship makes everything for a moment unknown." Analysis of course is needed, among other reasons to spell out what is meant from what is said (or not), the more or less proximate contexts through which words and actions acquire significance, what is specific and what is more general in any given interaction. Beyond these contextualizations, connections, and comparisons, I have sought, in places, to explain what is happening and to reflect on how these circumstances are of more than local interest. Rejoining my preceding point, however, I have tried to keep explicit analysis to a minimum: staying close to the moment, anticipating readers' own connecting analysis, opening out in multiple directions from the immediate circumstances described.

Approaching Architectural Practice: Between the "How," "Who," and "What" of Knowledge

Centrally this book is about architecture as a way of knowing the world in order to shape it. Relatedly it is about the way in which the architectural self both shapes and is shaped through these ways of knowing. Rather than focusing on knowledge as a set of abstract propositional claims, technical competencies, and overarching philosophies, I am interested in the various daily practices through which knowing takes place. The forms this takes are many, and so, accordingly, are the literatures that inform my account.

In the office of MHW is a large bookshelf. Along with technical guides and manuals, an extensive library contains many of the canonical works that include discussions of the key conceptual strands that have shaped the professional practice of architecture both historically and more recently. One way of thinking of this book is as an account of how these principles and approaches are put to work in the daily lives of architects, the myriad forms of application, interpretation, and extension that render them relevant to specific contexts and circumstances. I draw selectively on these architectural literatures to illustrate and exemplify the broader conceptual frameworks in which these architects' own explanations arise. In other words, architectural scholarship figures in the book as an extension of "the field," rather than as theories or explanations of it.

Almost two decades ago Garry Stevens wrote: "The little sociological work conducted on architecture falls into three broad areas: studies of practice, historical theoretical studies, and gender studies. The entire literature could be read in a day."[13] His and subsequent accounts have expanded understanding of the social life of professional architects considerably, but even today the field is relatively small. A quick reader might not be able to read it in a week but would probably get the gist. Mostly driven by a critically deconstructive agenda, these accounts have a focus significantly different from my own more ethnographic account, in which the primary interest is in the everyday practical negotiations of specific individuals. Even so, these works have generated insights about the professional practice of architecture that I build on. In particular, Jeremy Till's *Architecture Depends* and Russell Ellis and Dana Cuff's *Architects' People* relate to the central themes of my book and have helped me understand the broader field in which these practices take shape.

Among this sociological literature, ethnographic accounts of architecture remain scarce, perhaps for the reasons noted by Dana Cuff in *Architecture*,[14] the first, now classic, study of this kind: access is often difficult, and architects can be resistant to the kinds of representation that might challenge their own presentations of professional practice.

Most directly my account is influenced by ethnographies highlighting, as Albena Yaneva puts it, "architecture in the making."[15] Her work,[16] along with other ethnographies of architecture,[17] provides direct inspiration, revealing how architects know things through doing things. In line with ethnographies of design practice,[18] these accounts challenge the ideal of the creative individual, showing how ideas are produced—as people relate to other people, including through interactions with designers, clients, and others; and through their interactions with tools, materials, sites, and places. As various authors have stressed, these media do more than simply represent the already existing ideas of designers:[19] they are ways of creating and transforming these. Design and creativity are not, from this perspective, subjective projections from the mind to the world; architects know the world by manipulating and transforming it, and their own ideas are extended in the process. More generally, accounts of creative practice in anthropology (for example Murphy's *Swedish Design*, Wilf's *School for Cool*, and Pandian's *Reel World*) and beyond (particularly Sennett's *The Craftsman*) provide critical insights into the dynamics through which people shape and are shaped through acts of making. The key point I take from these books is that *what* people know is necessarily a function of *where*, *with what*, and *with whom* they know.

Further inspiration comes from approaches focusing more directly on the "who" of knowing, including some from early, more straightforwardly sociological, perspectives on architecture. Written from a socially constructivist perspective, Cuff's pioneering work from the 1980s has less to say about the tools, materials, and places through which designs are shaped. Even so, it provides inspiration, playing close and thoughtful attention to architects' narratives of their personal and professional lives. Cuff does not use the phrase, but as an extension of Yaneva's "architecture in the making," this attention might be characterized as a focus on "architects in the making." In particular, Cuff highlights how they realize and imagine themselves through various forms of narrative. Lily Chumley's 2016 ethnography of Chinese design classes,[20] Anand Pandian's account of Indian film production,[21] and Eitan Wilf's work on jazz[22] variously highlight how creative activities implicate the self, personally, professionally, and as a specific way of framing the relationship between these domains. More broadly, accounts of life history and personal narrative tune attention to the various ways in which people are constructed through the stories they tell about themselves.[23] This focus is consistent with Boyer's calls to "humanise the expert."[24] Against the grain of much recent work he explains: "The expert may occupy or perform a 'social role' as a particular kind of 'modern subject,' but foremost s/he is enmeshed in all the complexities anthropology acknowledges human life to entail. . . . The anthropology of expertise needs to push harder in every direction to make experts not solely the creatures of expertise that the ideologies and institutions of intellectual professionalism encourage us to recognise and make visible."[25] Inspired by his and other ethnographic accounts of expertise,[26] I seek to show how architects are not straightforwardly creatures of knowledge; how they live lives with all the complexities, contradictions, and dilemmas of people who have been the more traditional focus of ethnography. Relatedly, anthropological research[27] helps to foreground the everyday ethical dilemmas these architects face as they seek to negotiate the contradictory imperatives that frame their work.

Situated between these approaches, the book seeks to connect the "post-human" impulse to interrogate the more than social nature of these interactions, with a humanist orientation to architecture as a way of being in the world. At the intersection of these perspectives, I highlight how architectural practice involves various forms of relationship between the "how" and the "who" of knowing. Descriptions explore the relationship between what is said and done: how words are ways of doing things,[28] and how everyday happenings are verbally narrated as a way of meaningfully reflecting on that practice.[29] While suspicious of the essentializing discourses of individual creativity and sympathetic to thinking that challenges this, I aim to avoid the reduction of being to doing, and so, in terms outlined by Tom Boellstorff, to consider how things work through how they are, and how they are through how they work.[30] This is consistent with a focus on the various ways architects attribute explanatory value to ideas of creative individuality, and on how this ideal is realized as manifold practices and orientations.

Whether focused on what architects do, or on who they are, the thrust of existing work on architectural practice focuses centrally on design and creativity: how architects engage with other people, materials, and places as ways of designing structures that are "innovative," "original," or "novel." Incidental to these accounts, and often entirely absent, are the more ostensibly pragmatic concerns of implementation, particularly those that preoccupy architects in the later stages of design and then during construction. Seeking to illuminate these important but less studied elements of practice, this account is informed by interdisciplinary literatures on expert knowledge,[31] professional practice,[32] and bureaucracy.[33] Collectively these help to highlight how "implementation" is never straightforwardly procedural, involving negotiation, improvisation, and interpretation— myriad specific ways in which existing principles, plans, and procedures are practically elaborated in relation to specific cases. Ethnographic accounts of building and construction[34] inform my understanding of processes that are at once central to architectural practice and largely offstage.

Taking inspiration from these various approaches, I use the term "practice" in specific but encompassing terms: as what people do, think, and say in their everyday interactions. This is not to foreground the concrete in contrast with the abstract, the specific in contrast with the general, or action as opposed to structure, but the ways in which life involves movement between these tendencies. My use of the term in some respects overlaps with architects' own understandings of their daily work as a movement between contradictory interests and tendencies. Both these definitions are distinct from architectural understandings of "the practice," a term that refers more specifically to the organizational context in which architects professionally work.

Part 1

THE OFFICE

ARRIVAL

Tomas picks me up from Stroud railway station to take me to the office of Millar Howard Workshop (MHW), where his architectural practice is based. It's the first hot day of the year; suddenly summer is here. On the way we tour through the center of town. Victorian buildings have a faded grandeur hearkening back to the town's heyday when the woolen industry brought prosperity to Stroud. Boarded-up storefronts, charity shops, and discount stores sit next to high street chains. Though Stroud is in the Cotswolds, a place synonymous with an English pastoral idyll, it is not quite of it. We proceed along the valley bottom, following the railway, the canal, and the stream, the infrastructure of a nineteenth-century economy of a bygone era. The woolen mills closed long ago; some factory buildings remain derelict while others have been converted to serve an economy that now revolves around services, retail, and small-scale manufacturing: garages, a bike shop, a craft brewery, artists' studios, some light engineering. The money now resides in the surrounding villages, whose population of retirees and commuters is growing, a wealthy demographic from which most of Tomas's clients are drawn.

A short distance beyond the town we take a sharp turn, down a single-lane road arriving at a rail crossing. The crossing is manned twenty-four hours a day, but the road leads only to the office. Tomas gets out to ring the bell. We wait some time for a train to pass. As the attendant slowly shrugs on a flash jacket and descends the wooden steps of his cabin, Tomas observes, with the eye of an architect, that the design of the crossing is "a perfect example of form following function." Crossing the tracks feels "like crossing into another world." He likes the sense of being "cut off," an understanding that seems consistent with a romantic ideal: the physical separation literalizes an idea of architecture as a creative, imaginative activity, distinct from the more pragmatic activities of building, and the wider world we are leaving behind. This image is partly true, because it is made to be so. Architects detach themselves from aspects of that world, to construct a space whose imaginative possibilities are partly an artifact of their separation from sites, buildings, and clients. At the same time, it is a profound simplification of what that work involves, enmeshed in this wider world with all the contradictions that entails.

Beyond a humpback bridge, the offices of the practice are in a converted mill, a functional Victorian three-story structure that must once have seemed strikingly modern but which has since acquired the romance of age: rusted tin roofs, stonework cracked and eroded, hard angles softened by subsidence and weathering. Three floors up, we are slightly out of breath. The dark corridor opens out onto an airy open-plan office that occupies the whole of the top floor. The office employs ten people. Each has a desk, designed by Tomas, constructed and built out of OSB, a cheap construction material that they have filled, sanded, and waxed to expose the texture of layered woods. "It takes a lot of time and money to make something look this cheap!" Tomas jokes, highlighting a central paradox of their work: much of it is about the complexities and difficulties of making buildings that seem simple; deceptions are practiced in the name of "honesty." On the walls are photos of the projects the practice has completed since it was founded ten years ago. A distinctive visual grammar to their buildings is noticeable at once: simple structures, mostly built of wood and stone. The photos trace an evolution in their projects' scale and scope. Older projects include a tree house, a small private chapel, and interior renovation projects; more recently the practice has mostly taken on larger projects, including new-built domestic houses, large extensions, and work for commercial organizations and charities. Among the early projects I notice a decking structure with Japanese joints, a small commission from my parents that Tomas and I worked on during the summer before I started my PhD. In total, there are over a hundred buildings.

The material culture of the office hints at complexities I will come to understand but not master. A long, open bookshelf partially divides the space and houses books on a range of more or less pragmatic perspectives on the building process: on the theory and philosophy of design; on building controls and regulations; on drystone walling and tree house architecture.

The material culture of the office reveals some of the practices involved. At the end of the room is a table of models, mostly redundant and partially broken. Next to this, a large yellow oval table provides a space for meeting clients, planners, and consultants, and is where the team's own meetings and design "crits" are held. Desks are littered with sketches, plans, computer printouts, and samples of various kinds of building materials: stone, window profiles, a section of rolled-steel joist. Computer screens flick between e-mail correspondence, the "precedent" images that locate and inspire design, and the various computer-modeling packages through which ideas are realized as various kinds of digital object. Family pictures and the artwork of children are pinned up around the architects' screens, reminders of the personal lives that animate this work. Shelves at the ends of desks contain an ever-expanding record of the processes that sustain the endeavor: minutes of meetings, regulations, correspondence—the documents that create, regulate, and define the architect's relations to others involved in creating these buildings.

How do all these processes come together to create the buildings displayed on the walls? This book sets out to answer that question, and in doing so poses others: What kind of person does this work require? How do architects imagine and create designs? And how are these then realized as buildings? Most centrally this book seeks to provide a specific and situated answer to a deceptively simple question: What is it like to be an architect?

SPACES BETWEEN

During an audio diary, Tomas reflects on the difficulties of occupying, in his words, "the space between." He is talking specifically about the space between a plan and a building, the endless decisions, negotiations, problems, and reconciliations that emerge in the effort to translate a plan into a physical structure. In his account it is an anxious space but also one where profound enjoyment and reward can be found. His reflections can be generalized to a larger truth about the nature of architects' working lives. Much of what this book explores involves architects' efforts to occupy spaces that are, literally and conceptually, "between."[1] Configured through these interstitial spaces, the work of design and construction involves daily contradictions that are encountered in specific forms, reconciled in particular moments, and never fully resolved.

The contradictions are various. At their core is a broader tension that has been central to architecture since its inception as a formalized profession and discipline: architects find themselves operating between enlightenment ideas about the benefits of rational, standardized knowledge and romantic ideas about creativity residing in the unique and specific qualities of individuals.[2] Architects at MHW attempt to create buildings that have "integrity." Their efforts to do this make them aware—sometimes painfully so—that they do this in a context that militates against it, pulling apart the elements they want to keep together. How do they reconcile commitments to holism, the sense that design should be a unifying if not universalizing force, with the fact of practicing in a society characterized by a complex division of labor, specifically as part of a construction process that requires the cooperation of specialists who know the world in profoundly different ways?[3]

Various ideals are simultaneously at play in contradictory ways.[4] Even to the extent that design is paramount (it rarely is), there is little consensus about the principles that should guide this. Pointing to a distinguishing feature of the profession, Donald Schon notes the cacophony of voices that confront the practicing architect: "For a student of the field—and perhaps even more for a student *in* the field—the multiplicity of voices is confusing"[5] Among other tendencies, schools are formed around a "return to tradition" and around stylistic innovation; they may aspire to purity, simplicity, and craftsman-like use of materials; or alternatively to exploit technological possibilities; to react against the vernacular or to seek to develop it. Even within the office of MHW, where common orientations prevail, design involves truths that can be difficult to reconcile: truth to materials, to structure, and to place, among others.

"Business! What a dilemma! If you try to please people, you become corrupt and sell yourself; if you do what you feel you must do, you cause displeasure and create a void around yourself."[6] So spoke Le Corbusier, pioneer of modernism, on the difficulties of the business of design and construction. Beyond considerations of "design philosophy," of *what* it is they should be making, are different orientations to the practice of design, of *how* it is they should do this: creative individualism, the idea a design must honestly express the vision of an individual, is situated alongside a "collaborative" ideal, urging responsiveness to the views of colleagues and clients. In the absence of any strongly determined model of professional practice, the question of which should prevail remains an open one, determined in specific moments of design practice. While many in the office resist the idea that architecture should serve the interests of capitalism, they practice in a situation in which well-designed buildings are unaffordable to all but the most affluent. The fact that most of their clients are well-off does not always sit easily with a vision of architecture as a socially progressive force.[7] A commitment to clients can be justified on commercial or social grounds but either way can be hard to reconcile with a sense of a higher calling: to architecture as a kind of art that, however defined, aspires to truths of a more transcendental kind.[8] The difficulty is not simply that there are many different ideals of professional practice. More profoundly the ideal of "professionalism" involves a kind of conformity that often sits uneasily with the creative and artistic ideals that are also important.[9]

Architects work within a professional context that institutionalizes a division between architecture and building, separating the "creative" work of design from the "practical" work of construction.[10] Though architects at MHW recognize their compilicity with this system, they are also critical of it. Much of their work emerges in the interstitial spaces within and between these oppositions, sometimes finding ways of connecting these, other times seeing virtue in keeping them apart.

On another occasion, Tomas, somewhat at a loss to summarize his approach, characterizes the aspiration as "a truth to tension." Reduced to an abstract principle, the phrase is empty, even a cliché. Yet he gives it substance by the way he lives by it: realizing it as specific ways of seeing, doing, thinking, and knowing. "Spaces between" engender tensions, which are not just problems to be overcome through the application of known procedures, techniques, or professional competencies. Tomas sees them as points of resistance, challenges and provocations to himself and the profession he works within. He tries to dwell within them, regarding them as opportunities to find things out. Tomas's formulation of a "truth to tension" is not a finding or description, but a starting point or principle by which he aims to orient his work and life: a way of trying to make better buildings, more satisfying working practices, of improving himself as a designer, and knowing himself better as a person. In other words, it is a principle of improvement, an aspiration, even as he remains to some extent agnostic regarding the means by which "success" can be judged.

Tracing these tensions, as he and others encounter them, I approach architecture as a way of being in the world, involving technical competencies, forms of knowledge, and professional conduct, but not reducible to these elements.[11] Architects in the practice see their job as a kind of vocation, stressing how their working life involves ways of thinking and acting that are inextricable from the life they live beyond their work. The question of how to be a good architect is tied to the broader questions of how to live a good life. As much as this book is an account of architecture, it is also an effort to understand the emotional, ideological, and personal dimensions of this work, and the lives that make sense of it.[12] I use the term "practice" in a specific but broad sense, to refer to the myriad forms of thinking, acting, understanding, being, and knowing that emerge as movements between things in tension. (These ideas are developed above in the section Approaching Architecture as Practice.).

UNDERSTANDING ARCHITECTURE

In an effort to understand, I spent an extended period living and working with the ten MHW architects. Guided in part by the things they found interesting themselves and in part by what seemed interesting to me, I did what I could to explore the contours of this world.

Sometimes my efforts were more interventionist than others. I spent a lot of time in the office, listening to and watching what was going on, an activity that the architects came to jokingly term "snooping." Sometimes these engagements were planned, but often opportunities arose serendipitously. A meeting came up, and I decided to go along. A problem emerged with a building or design, and I listened to ensuing discussion. Issues arose and required a resolution. "Tom might be interested in this . . . ," and so I would join them.

Offices are awkward places to linger without a clearly defined role. Much of what happens takes place in mostly silent exchanges between people, keyboards, the mouse, or with pencil and paper.[13] In an architectural office a lot of the activities require the kind of concentration that can be achieved only in silence. Architectural knowledge involves practices that, being tacit, are difficult to do while articulating what is being done. For long periods of time the quiet of the office was punctuated only by the sounds of this activity—mouse clicks, intermittent bursts of typing, a brief conversation triggered by an e-mail, or the occasional interruption of the phone. How was I to understand the nonverbal (if not silent) aspects of this knowledge?

In my efforts to understand their work, I involved myself in what they did. Part participant, part observer, and lacking their architectural training, I found it hard to see and think in the ways required to design, still less to operate the tools of their trade. Even so, they encouraged me to have a go. Through efforts to learn I became my own informant, divided between thinking about what I was doing and trying to record, reflect on, and understand the nature of this thinking. My mistakes led others to verbalize the tacit conventions from which my work diverged and so were ways of understanding. Sometimes I watched others in the silence of their work, myself mesmerized by the movement of pencil on paper, lines on a screen, scissors through card. In response to my promptings, people attempted to verbalize what they were thinking, even as they acknowledged the difficulty of doing so. More was verbalized in ad hoc meetings undertaken as part of the ebb and flow of projects and in the weekly design reviews. Knowledge was glimpsed through the everyday controversies that throw into doubt routine ways of thinking and acting. Feeling often that I was in the way, I tried to compensate for my clumsiness by attempting to make myself useful. I helped write a manual, explaining the process for clients, contributed some text to their website, and did bits of research to help various projects along. I was surprised how quickly people accepted my presence and even seemed to cease to notice it.

During fieldwork my responses were recorded, ordered, and explored through notes I took as I listened and observed, sometimes facilitated by an audio-recorder and in the fieldwork diary I wrote up every morning. Additionally, I wrote a blog on the practice's website. Documenting my initial thoughts and findings opened these up to scrutiny and helped to develop them. I was keen to think *with* rather than *about* these architects as much as possible. Their knowledge is not just an object of my own; their thinking has participated profoundly in the ideas at the heart of this book.[14]

What architects say and what they do are never entirely the same thing,[15] but neither are they entirely different. Throughout my time in the office I spent a lot of time contemplating this relationship: How do architects talk about what they do? How do they reflect on their own working practices? And how, on the other hand, do they practice what they say? How are their ideas and understandings realized through everyday encounters with materials, tools, places, and other people?[16]

Toward the end of my time in the office, I undertook a series of recorded interviews with each of the practice architects. I used these interviews as an extension and culmination of other conversations, and of everything else I had seen, as a way to explore what I thought I had understood. These happened first seated on the bench by the mill, and then, as winter drew in, in their cramped strip-lit kitchen. Spatial detachment from the day-to-day activities of the office was accompanied by a more reflective tone.

My focus was the office, but its boundaries were porous. Clients, builders, and consultants sometimes came in for meetings. The architects went out on regular visits to building sites, to survey and assess project sites, to liaise with planners, and to meet with other building consultants. Car journeys provided good places to talk and the chance to witness the last-minute preparations for meetings. Additionally, I undertook interviews with clients, builders, planners, and other building professionals.

Understanding takes time. Over the months I saw different things: the many stages that take place in the movement from site to idea to building; the use of various design tools; the emergence and resolution of assorted kinds of problems; the ways these problems are specified and resolved through negotiations with other people—clients, planners, and other building professionals. The company itself developed and changed: work-experience students came and went; new projects started; one of the junior architects left to continue her training; the two directors started a new property development venture. As time wore on, my relationships deepened and developed, allowing different kinds of conversations and new sorts of knowledge. People told me more about themselves and what they did. Time was important to see more of the various elements of these architects' working lives but more profoundly to transform my own understanding of what I saw. Some insights crept up gradually in the dawning realization of what was going on. Others appeared to come all at once: a comment or interaction that made suddenly evident a new appreciation of how things work.

Why look at only one architectural practice? More precisely, why look at only some aspects of the working lives of those who inhabited that practice, at one period in time? The poet Kavanagh suggests part of an answer in his insistence that "to know fully even one field or one land is a lifetime's experience. In the world of poetic experience it is depth that counts, not width." The geographer Robert MacFarlane has articulated this well in his defense of parochialism. If all lives are lived in particular ways, places are lenses, not perimeters. They open up vision rather than restrict it: "The general is the broad, the vague, the undiscerned; the universal, by contrast, [consists] of fine-tuned principles, induced from an intense concentration on the particular."[17] The approach I take is, in this broad and expansive sense, unapologetically parochial. I want to dwell on the particularities of architectural practice in *this* practice even as I seek to show how these particularities provide a way of exploring themes of more universal interest.[18]

A PARTICULAR KIND OF PRACTICE

Unlike the practices on which architectural critics and indeed ethnographers have tended to focus, MHW is not famous. Employing ten architects during the period I did my work, the practice is slightly smaller than the U.K. national average of just under fourteen.[19] In their mid-thirties, the two directors are relatively young, as is the staff profile of the practice more generally. All are in their twenties and thirties, with the exception of David, the father of Tomas. This youth is something they often present as a virtue, making representational capital through coupling that word with others with which it is popularly associated; "dynamic," "creative," "innovative," "fresh," "original" are words that feature on their website. As a small-to-medium-size practice, MHW rarely takes on projects with budgets of less than £100,000 and is mostly focused on large domestic extensions and renovations, one-off new builds, and small public buildings. The firm's projects involve close working relationships with individual clients, planners, builders, engineers, and other building specialists contracted as consultants when needed. Design and then construction work involves regular site visits. Involvement in these various aspects of the process of design and construction is at one level a necessity for a practice of this size. At another level they see these working practices as a virtue tying into a broader philosophy. Unlike larger practices where specialism and fragmentation are more common, the company takes pride in aiming to connect processes of design and construction, celebrates the "ownership" of projects by individual architects, and aims to keep organizational structures flat.

Although MHW is not famous, it is often described as "successful." It is regularly mentioned in the local press and has had projects featured in national professional journals and popularly focused design magazines. Its work has been acclaimed through various professional awards, including the Royal Institute for British Architects' (RIBA) regional award for the South West of England, a distinction annually afforded to around ten buildings by area. One of MHW's projects was the subject of *Grand Designs*, a prime-time national TV program that is also popular around the world through subscription television. Locally and in particular professional circles the firm is "respected," a term that is often used when others refer to MHW. A local planner I talk with tells me they are one of the few local architectural firms doing "interesting work"; clients often explain a choice to appoint them, describing a "design ambition" that is rare among others in the area. The directors are asked to sit on local committees; within the Stroud Valleys, they are well known on the broader arts scene. They contribute to a RIBA working group for small practices and are gaining a reputation for their innovative approach to contracts and fees.

Designed by Tomas, the physical layout of the office reflects an ambition that it helps to accomplish. Desks are indistinguishable from one another, on a level, arranged in two rows with no discernable order or hierarchy. Facing toward their screens, architects are oriented away from the distraction of others, but with a half crane of the neck all are immediately visible. With minimal movement and without raising their voices, they can hold conversations in all directions. A table for meetings and design reviews is circular and open to the room. Vision and sound are more or less unimpeded.

In these ways and others, the office embodies an aspiration for a lack of hierarchy that has a range of other practical consequences. As an ideology it informs a commitment to listen, to respect other views, to conduct conversations without an assumption that the more experienced colleague is right, and to delegate tasks and responsibilities broadly. These ideas are reflected in various quotidian, mostly unremarked on ways. Responsibility for making tea and coffee circulates among staff regardless of status or role. Conversational turn-taking characterizes most spoken interactions, questions directed in both directions. On Fridays there is a communal lunch, where all bring food to share. Even so, this ideology is not quite the whole story. When new clients call or e-mail, it is one of the directors who responds and who then goes to the initial meeting. Larger projects will generally be overseen by an architect with more experience. Though design input can come from any direction, it is more usually the voice of the more experienced that carries weight. Input into projects comes from all sides but most routinely from the directors, who spend much of their time circulating among the others, perched on desks, gesturing at screens, or sketching over plans. Part II qualified architectural assistants, those who have completed undergraduate and master's degrees but have yet to pass the Part III course that qualifies them as a professional architect, may take the lead with small projects. However, their work will be overseen and officially signed off by another who is Part III qualified. In practice the initial key design moves are more often made by those with more experience, while more of the detailing gets done by those who are less experienced. Differences in pay are small relative to most professions, but not inconsiderable.[20] The ideology of "informalism" in fact takes a subtle form, as conversational and interactional expectations that initially take architectural assistants some time to learn (see Listen: First Impressions).

Likewise, a commitment to holistic design, the ideal of this as a joined-up creative process in which there is individual "ownership," informs practice in a range of ways. Architects will normally see a project through from start to finish, but delegation does take place, specialisms are recognized, and tacit hierarchies inform the distribution of tasks.[21] The directors are keen to involve others in company decision making, but strategic direction comes mostly from them. On a daily basis it is they who are responsible for the management and running of the company. In an open plan office this happens through whispered conversations about such matters as cash flow, management of work flows, decisions about which projects to take on, and a range of staffing-related issues. I realize only retrospectively, with regret and embarrassment, that my account describes very little of the work of the office manager, Marianne. This oversight of mine could be partly a reflection of the way her role is defined in the office: Central to almost all forms of coordination and administration, from time sheets to billing clients, her work is almost invisible when done well. With a background in arts administration, she is the only one in the office trained outside of architecture. "They speak a totally different language," she remarks on one occasion, smiling.

In the various ways I have outlined, and others that will become apparent, MHW is not a "normal" or "representative" practice. Yet the industry structures its professionals inhabit, the economic and planning constraints they deal with, and the construction field with which they engage are typical of those faced by most practicing architects in the U.K. Since many facets of architecture, planning, and construction take increasingly globally standardized forms, broader professional parallels should also be apparent. Even as the practice of MHW is particular, it therefore offers a perspective on the wider dilemmas and negotiations inherent in the work of professional architecture.

OPENINGS

When I first started to share my writing, Tomas confessed that he found some of it hard to read. He wished he had said things more eloquently. He was sometimes aware that in putting things into words, he was not completely comfortable with his own position. Thoughtful but, in his own words, "not a theorist," he worried about sounding naïve if his words were abstracted from the practical contexts through which they arose and were intended to make sense of. Other interviewees, reading their interview transcripts side by side, became newly aware of different perspectives on this work. Even though they expressed discomfort and sometimes harbored doubts about the possible impact on their reputations, the collective thrust of their comments was to urge me further in the direction of "truth." David responded, having read some early drafts, that the process seemed overly sanitized: "What about all the endless doubts, the anxieties, the sleepless nights?!" he wanted to know. Realizing this more difficult content was missing, I tried to write it in.

Sometimes ethnography reveals forms of truth of which the subjects of research are not themselves aware. My own account of architects describes and explains what they do in ways that make their practices more explicit. Reading drafts and hearing my thoughts on their work, they were sometimes kind enough to say my work was "interesting." They used the term with more and less conviction, but their engaged reflections led me to believe this was not *only* a platitude. Vocationally disposed to interrogate their own working practices, they were thoughtful enough to see how a description of what they do afforded possibilities to reflect on this. To the extent they were engaged, this was not because my descriptions and thoughts contain surprising revelations but rather because they present in slightly more explicit terms the contradictions and complexities that are anyway integral to their working lives.

A lot of writing about architecture, by architects and by others, has had a critical thrust, seeking to unmask the reality that lurks beneath the appearance of idealized self-representations. Architects may claim to be progressive but are really part of a capitalist system that has socially regressive consequences.[22] Architects talk about novelty, but beneath the appearance of formal change the profession is radically conservative.[23] Overt concerns with aesthetics are in fact the mechanisms by which architects perpetuate their own elite status.[24] These points are important as counterpoints to professional narratives of architecture as emancipatory, progressive, benign, and disinterested. Frequently, however, architectural critiques uphold an overly stark opposition between truth and fiction, reality and representation, the tangible matter of the world and ways of thinking about this.[25]

When such oppositions are presumed to be beyond the consciousness of those involved in the process, architects seem, at best, dupes of a system and, at worst, as cynically exploiting this in the service of their own self-interest. By contrast, I seek to open up this world through tracing the fault lines, contradictions, and conflicts that lie *within* practices in which the distinction between appearance and reality is often quite explicitly moot. From this perspective I explore the protean and indeterminate qualities of a "reality" that for the architects described in this book is never fully resolved, being always in the process of becoming something slightly other than what it already is.

LISTEN: FIRST IMPRESSIONS
OF THE OFFICE

Martina and Laura recently joined the practice, following three years of training at university. They have not known each other for long but through the common experience of being new have quickly built a close relationship. Together they discuss the transition from university to working in a practice as architectural assistants.

> MARTINA: My first impression, when I started, was, yes, it's all very different for me, because I'm not English [she is from the Czech Republic]. So it was like a culture shock on the one hand, and on the other side it was so hard. So many things I needed to get in my head. It was really difficult.
>
> LAURA: I think I was the same, the first week. You're just exhausted from trying to juggle all of these things that you didn't realize were a part of architecture, like having to send an e-mail for the first time. It's really stressful. They don't teach you this sort of thing at university. And having to work with other people, not on your own.
>
> MARTINA: With the e-mails, I wasn't quite sure about the level of professionalism.
>
> LAURA: . . . And how do you speak to people in the office, as opposed to clients, as opposed to consultants, and how much information do you give different people? I'm still not sure. It's quite a difficult thing to gauge if you haven't done that before.

MARTINA: Yeah, somebody asked me to do something, and I had no idea how to do it, but I really didn't feel comfortable to ask, so then I spent lots of time trying to find out.

LAURA: Googling, yeah! [*They both laugh.*]

MARTINA: And then I didn't find the answers, so I asked, and it actually was much easier and made sense. So now I know I can ask, but in the first weeks I didn't.

LAURA: It's really scary to ask for the first time, and then you realize it saves about four hours, because someone knows the answer in the office, and no one minds answering.

MARTINA: Yeah, it's the thing of what is normal, what's not normal, and then you realize that everyone asks everybody, so you just start to feel comfortable asking.

LAURA: No one knows everything. It's never the same person giving the answer. So collectively we're much more useful to each other than if it's just you on your own trying to find out things. What other impressions were there when I first got here?

MARTINA: When I was designing when I was a student, I wasn't really used to working in a team. We had some team projects but not so many, and I know it's so much better to work in a team: it makes everything quicker because you can ask. And especially with the design process, when you get stuck you just don't know what to do and there is always somebody who comes and brings a new point of view, and it shifts you further. So that's what I really like and makes the design very much quicker and faster, and I can see progress I would never be able to do on my own.

LAURA: At uni[versity] we didn't do group projects very much either. It was all about your design and your process, and then here there was a lot more collaboration, but there's also loads of trust between everybody, which I didn't really have at university.

MARTINA: And lots of respect.

LAURA: Yeah, and everyone has a valid opinion if they choose to contribute it.

MARTINA: That's really encouraging actually, because I remember my first week I was just, oh, I'm so stupid, I don't want to ask silly questions, and now I don't feel like that, which I really like.

LAURA: Yeah, it's so different from architecture school in such a good way. It's really scary, but then it's such a better way to work: not in isolation, and as part of a group of people who all have similar ideals. Do you know what I mean?

MARTINA: I know what you mean. . . .

LAURA: . . . But it's really difficult that we're always working with some project architect and we are his assistants. It depends on which stage the project is, but there are projects that we do detailed design, and so it's something that someone else designed before, and you are actually supposed to make sure his idea has some detail, but you can't really understand the idea. So it's something very new for me, and I find it very difficult. It takes me a long time to really understand a project.

MARTINA: That is hard, to jump into someone else's brain. It's like there's a big gap where normally you would have thought everything through, and it's just missing, and you're muddling your way back to work it out. It's difficult, because you're second-guessing how somebody else came to that conclusion as a designer. That's quite hard work. Also because we're always working as an assistant, and we talk about this sometimes, but when we jump between projects and it takes you a minute to switch project heads. So like you'll spend two days working on something, and then the next day you'll come in and you'll have to put the other thing behind you and then try and remember where you were a week ago on that project. It's always this readjustment.

LAURA: Especially with someone else's project, so then there's like a different thinking you can see in the design, and you have to swap to it. Like when you compare Phil and Rob—you just can't really compare them.

MARTINA: Yeah, you can see the design is different instantly, and even the way that it's been drawn or set up or—

LAURA: Yeah, so then you have to swap your thinking to the other person's thinking.

MARTINA: Yeah, you do, you have to put, like, your Phil hat on!

LAURA: This is really difficult!

MARTINA: I don't know how long it takes me when I have to do that, but it's not quick. Half a day? It's fine until you have to swap again. But I think that's just adjustment, and partly because it's not your own design, and then it's difficult to know when do you take ownership, when do you start making decisions.

LAURA: Exactly—to know which decision you're allowed to make and which you are not.

MARTINA: And how much you can change the original. I often find myself thinking "oh, maybe it should be like that," but then I don't necessarily have the experience or the construction knowledge to make an argument for it. So then it's difficult, because it's just an intuitive feeling that it should be a certain way with nothing real to back it up.

LAURA: And finding arguments is generally very difficult, to just explain a design. It's just so difficult to express.

Part 2
LIVES

BETWEEN PERSON AND PROFESSION

What is the relationship between the personal and professional life of an architect? How do architects' working lives relate to the lives they live outside work? What kind of person does it take to be an architect? And what kind of person does architecture make people become?

I am talking with Rosy at a crossroads in her life. Having just spent two years working for the practice as an architectural assistant, she is about to move on. She has plans for the summer—music festivals, an architectural camp designing and making a building—and then back to university to continue her studies.[1] Beyond that she doesn't really know.

I ask her how she came to be an architect.

> Well, if I start from the very beginning, when I was little I drew my mum a picture of the old lady who lives in a shoe, and I drew her in a slightly more architectural version, as far as a five-year-old can, of the old lady living in the shoe—kind of saying, "If you lived in a shoe this is what it would be like." My mum said, "Oh that's the sort of thing that an architect does." When you're little you grasp onto these things.

The experience is specific to her, but the presentation of career choice in early childhood experiences is common. It seems to underscore a sense of the profession as an underlying calling.

Over a decade later, her degree choice was based in part on indecision and uncertainty, keeping options open through a subject that seemed broad. It was also based on what she retrospectively characterizes as ideals: of how architecture would allow her to be the "renaissance person," who draws knowledge together and is drawn together through this as a more complete, well-rounded individual; and of what it would allow her to do: "I guess I still had this romantic idea, [that] architecture's all about making amazing things and creating wonderful spaces for people to be in that revolutionize people's lives."

The reality was different. Architectural training takes a minimum of seven years in the UK, with a basic structure established during the heyday of modernism in the 1950s. As a whole it involves an oscillation between elements oriented toward creativity and practicality, art and profession. A three-year Part I degree, often loosely informed by the Bauhaus ideal, is less about imparting skills, knowledge, or even creativity than freeing students from the preconceptions that stop them from being able to design. The image is of a self that must be demolished before rebuilding can commence. At university the tutors gave Rosy little support and direction. The competition was overwhelming. The workload was relentless. "I think it's seen as a necessary process, this martyrdom of architecture students, and you hold this placard 'I have suffered,' you know, 'I've earned this because literally blood, sweat, and tears have gone into this.' I've cut bits of my fingers off with scalpels, I've not slept, I've cried more times in my three years at university than probably the whole of the rest of my life combined, you know." At the end of her degree she felt "emotionally drained," "disillusioned," uncertain what the future held: "I buried my head in the sand for a couple of months, thought I hated architecture and it probably wasn't what I wanted to do with my life." She experienced an "existential crisis," feeling unresolved about what architecture was and what her life might be in relation to it. She didn't like the person it had made her become, lacked confidence, wanted to get out.

The experiences are viscerally specific and evidently raw, but the language of sacrifice, doubt, and crisis are not hers alone. The architectural theorist and practitioner Jeremy Till observed the following about architecture students when he was a first-year tutor: "Three weeks into their course, at the end of their first project, you see them gathered at the foot of the building, eyes smudged with tiredness, bad hair, three-day-worn clothes. But far from being ashamed of these afflictions, they wear them as badges of honour."[2] The "honour" is in the demonstration of commitment to an art and vocation. What doubt there might be for Rosy and others is not likely a straightforward rejection of that vocation, based as it is on an idea that architecture requires a profound questioning: of the self through architecture, and of architecture through the self.[3]

For Rosy a sense of failure results from a tension between an idealized version of an architectural life and the realities of a course far removed from her original ideal. As her experiences led her to question the ideal, so the vestiges of that ideal caused her to question herself. Did she have the necessary commitment? She decided to continue. Family and friends played their part, but mostly it was the thought she didn't want to give up on the ideals that drew her in before she knew what it was like to work as a practicing architect: "So I was like, right, I'm going to go and work in architecture, figure out whether that's what I want to do with my life, and if it's not, well, then I'll have to reconsider."

She took a job as Part I assistant at MHW. A relic of the nineteenth-century pupilage system, and a form of apprenticeship, architectural training requires a year in practice as a prelude to the Part II master's degree, where trainee architects develop theoretical understanding and are encouraged to specialize. Rosy's views, as she speaks to me just before beginning her Part II, may be partly inflected by the wistful nostalgia of her imminent detachment from what she's been doing. Even so, the enthusiasm is palpable as she relates the tangible satisfaction of see-ing buildings constructed, and the fulfillment of a more collaborative way of working. How does she see the relationship between her work and her life now?

> I think it's one of those things that once you're in it it's a vocation, it's definitely a way of life. I'll be walking round with my friends and I'll be looking up and going, "Oh, look at that roof detail," and they're like, "Oh, you are such a weirdo, why have you noticed that? Everyone else is looking at that pretty window display over there." It grabs you and it affects you, because it's such an overarching thing and you have to be in control of all these different elements all at once. It's very hard to then switch that off and not be seeing them everywhere, which I think is a good thing.

Later she expands on this point. "If you see it as just a profession, then you design really badly. . . . I don't really see how you can just see it as a profession; it sort of grabs you." Architecture as vocation becomes an animating and compelling force that is lived, breathed, and exuded. Not just a kind of work but a way of seeing and thinking—a part of who you are, a way of life.

This sense of vocation represents a blurring of personal and professional selves that is widely celebrated. While the self may be discovered and uncovered through the profession,[4] architecture develops through the selves that are sacri-ficed to it. Rosy exemplifies this through an anecdote from university:

> I went in to my tutors one day and told them, "For the last week I've done nothing but dream about my project, I cannot get away from it, it's everywhere, I'm having nightmares where people can't get out because the fire escape's in the wrong place." They were like, "Oh that's a good sign, that means you're really into it, that's how it should be." It does make it slightly hellish at times because you can't get away from it, but . . .

Her voice trails off, but the implication is clear—good architecture involves an obsessive commitment that comes at a personal cost. Accounts of the personal costs are demonstrations of vocational commitment.

The anthropologist Michael Jackson has written that "a tension always remains between the selves we construct together and aspects of our selves that cannot be made over to the public sphere, calling conventional wisdom into question, resisting recognized roles, refusing to fit in or swear fidelity to another sphere."[5] He suggests there is a universal struggle between aspects of ourselves that pull away from the public realm and aspects that engage and identify with it. At one level, the vocational ideal Rosy alludes to involves a blurring of these horizons. At another level, the distinction remains salient. "Switching off"—leaving time for people, interests, and activities outside work—is a way not just of protecting personal sanity, but also of achieving perspective. Sometimes the best thoughts come when she stops working and is thinking about something else—when the solution to a problem can pop into her head: "It's generally in the shower. I do my best thinking in the shower," she reflects. The insight that occurs outside working hours is born of the perspective of distance this brings. Rosy explains: "You have to say 'no, I'm going home and I'm not thinking about it'; it's got to be quite a conscious thing if you decide not to think about it."

QUESTIONS OF VOCATION

Now in his sixties, David reflects on his architecture and his life from the other end of his career. He remains an affiliate of the practice but is now semiretired, mostly working on his own to the extent he continues to do so. As in Rosy's life, there are questions about the relationship between his life and work, and even some doubts, but David's are more directed backward than forward, more about what he has done than what he will do.

He is seated in the extension to his home he designed himself, an oak-frame and glass addition to a traditional Cotswold cottage overlooking a wooded valley. A design developed from a life—the distillation of the influences, dispositions, interactions he is about to narrate—and that now contains that life. Dana Cuff suggests that "like the results of a personality test, a building reveals a self-portrait of its maker."[6] The reverse is also true, buildings being ways in which architects try to physically construct what they want to become.[7] Whichever way the construction process works, I'm struck by the shared characteristics: David and his house have a quietness and calm, considered and understated. The complexities are not projected outward but concealed beneath the surface.

The father of Tomas and a friend of my parents since before I was born, David is no stranger to me. I already know some of his story. As the conversation develops, I am also surprised by how much I do not know. Initially it seems strange to be talking in the context of an interview. I am aware of feeling self-conscious, asking questions to which I think I already know the answer with a formality that seems artificial. I sense David may be similarly self-conscious, though he professes on a number of occasions to enjoy being interviewed—"a chance to pontificate," as he jokes self-effacingly, and then more seriously, "It's nice to be able to reflect on the things we"—he means architects—"often take for granted." He speaks with the authority of someone who is used to speaking and to being listened to but is open about his doubts. If elements form part of a received biography, told on other occasions and for different purposes, the pauses, sometimes very long, are moments of reflection and inquisition: as though he is questioning the relationship between the story he is telling and the life to which it refers, wondering if they are in alignment.

How did he come to be an architect? I wonder. He tells me. "Probably not unusually it was fortuitous and not particularly rational or conscious. . . . My father had always wanted to be an architect, but he used to enjoy playing music too much, and didn't study hard enough, and so he ended up being a window dresser. But he had quite an interest in buildings—less formally architecturally, more just visual sensibilities. He used to like color and line, all of which I think he taught me." David came from a "semi-working-class council estate" in Manchester, did well at school and, in an era of generous funding, got a place at Cambridge University. He went to study pure mathematics and theoretical physics but decided to change degree at the end of the first year, in part driven away from his initial course by the realization of "the brilliance of others" and feelings of his own inadequacy, in part drawn toward architecture through a girlfriend studying at the Architectural Association (AA):

> The AA in 1968 was an absolute hotbed, a ferment of ideas really. . . . There were people talking about the beginnings of conversations about self-sufficiency and alternative energy. I just walked in and thought it was the most wonderful environment I'd ever seen. There were people lounging around on beanbags, and there was color, and there were lots of beautiful people I suppose, in that London sixties sense. But predominantly, also, an atmosphere of being run collaboratively with students, student democracy, a kind of anarchic environment. I thought "well, this is what I want!" I suddenly just decided impulsively this was really what I wanted.

The appeal of architecture was as much the social milieu around the course as the degree itself. He started back at the architecture school in Cambridge, inspired by the possibilities that architecture seemed to open up. Cambridge was less radical than the Architectural Association, but still there was a sense of architecture in transition and a desire to challenge orthodoxy. This sometimes led to clashes between tutors and students:

> There was quite an air of rebellion in the studios generally. Some of the people who were very good at drafting would show buildings that were

almost invisible behind an enormous foreground of vegetation and people. They would draw lovely drawings of old ladies and children in pushchairs and beautiful bushes and trees, with a very withdrawn building behind it which was almost unbelievably modest, and that was the message that was being put across: "Far be it from me to be so arrogant as to impose a building on these people! What is important is the community, is people, ordinary people, old ladies and children and mothers and fathers and dogs and things." The cardinal sin was arrogance or assertiveness.

Taking inspiration from Buckminster Fuller, the maverick American modernist and polymath, David was less interested in buildings as objects of design than in a holistic understanding of architecture as a way of intervening in social, political, and ecological problems—"design in that broadest global sense." Architecture could be about everything, from global energy flows and whole settlement systems to the design of chairs. In his first year he did various projects, following the things that interested him: a chair that folded out of a sheet of cardboard; computer-oriented approaches to design, using the university mainframe computers; a technical study of day lighting; a project to take a disused gasometer (a gigantic cylindrical tank to store gas) and propose how it might be used for housing; an audit of the architecture school looking at the psychological warmth of different places in the building and representing these by color coding. Although David had left behind the formal study of physics and mathematics, his understanding of these disciplines became central to his approach to architecture. That approach was shaped by interests and knowledge from beyond the discipline as narrowly defined. Architecture made sense of these interests and gave them new impetus.

In his final year, with a new tutor, his work began to change. "Suddenly it was all about aesthetics, about space, about color, form." It wasn't an approach he related to. "I lost the plot, really. I sometimes didn't finish the work in time, so I'd put half-completed drawings up. At the same time I had a sense in which I felt it was beneath me to some extent. I had a rather arrogant approach. I remained passionately interested and engaged, but it didn't always bear fruit, and I wasn't going to worry if it didn't. There was almost an arrogance, that if the creative thing didn't come through, then so be it." Commitment to the creative process was more important than where it led or what resulted from it. Indifference to the outcome of this process went hand in hand with a commitment to that ideal over and above the assessments of his tutors.

David graduated with a third-class degree, the lowest pass in UK higher education. It was a failure in one sense that, in another, was a vindication of this singular commitment. After a year spent helping a friend build an extension, he went to the Architectural Association to study for his Part II. His disillusionment deepened with an architectural profession that seemed to value words over building, a professional "jargon" directed at fellow professionals more than to the world beyond. At a time when other architects were starting to build careers, setting up architectural practices and working toward the Part III qualification that completes an architectural training, David chose a different, more practical path. He spent a short period designing high-street banking halls while working in a graphic design studio, then a year designing and building an extension: "working with our hands again, but in a very primitive way, with no machines and lots of wheelbarrowing; a rather minimal pottering around, building brick walls for not particularly notable extensions."

Why take this unusual path? "I didn't have the ambition, really. It was almost a penance, 'this is what is most real and it's down to earth and justifiable.'" The path was inspired by the holistic and eclectic design philosophy of thinkers he encountered during his studies, even as it represented a rejection of the professional interests that shaped that education. The holistic approach of Buckminster Fuller resonated with the eclecticism of Charles Eames, whose talk at the Architectural Association gave particular inspiration: "[Eames] talked about the design of Indian water-carrying jugs, he talked about soap films, he talked about the typography, and this was music to my ears; I loved it. He said 'follow your dreams, follow your passions, let yourself be interested in things, forget the labels, you don't need to call yourself an architect.'"

Interests shaped within an architectural degree engendered a sense of vocation, an ideal of self-discovery that led beyond the profession. Working with his hands was a response to a kind of professional disillusionment. Building work appealed because it seemed "real," "very normal, very ordinary, very conventional." Over time the work brought disillusionment of a different kind: "it was nothing innovative, nothing you'd want to make a foundation of anything bigger." Looking back, he is critical of a "lack of ambition," of "a lack of a sense of direction." Only half jokingly he seems obliged to apologize: "I'm sorry if this is all terribly disappointing!" The sense of failure is relative to his understanding of what an architectural life could be, of having fallen short by his own ideals.

Then for David, a moment of epiphany led to a radical change of direction. In the maternity hospital in 1979, as he waited while his wife gave birth to his eldest son, Tomas:

> I picked up a magazine that was about home computing, the first home computers. Pre-PC, pre–Sinclair Spectrum—it was really out of the

States, 1978; it was what people were doing, hobbyists, and I latched onto that like a drowning man. I thought "that's what I want." In the same way that initially I had been very taken by the AA, '68, ten years earlier, suddenly I was now prepared to throw all the architectural experience up and chase after computing.

The sense of vocation that grew out of his architectural training again found realization in the possibilities he saw beyond it.

The excitement I somehow didn't find in architecture I found in that. So the instinct for excitement was all very healthy, but it found a different outlet, and somehow it didn't worry me because it was consistent with that old Buckminster Fuller approach, which is a holistic one.

Though he left the profession, the discipline continued to reside within him: "I carried my architecture into my computing life."

The same sense of vocation that drew David away from architecture in the late 1970s drew him back over two decades later: "The world I was in, in computing, having started off as a typical start-up thing with almost the Google myths of the toys and the pizzas and all of that—suddenly I found myself in the context of large multinational companies with traditional management hierarchies and everything." He enjoyed the intellectual challenge of solving computing problems but had moved through promotion to the point where the role was increasingly managerial. As the creativity and excitement of computing had started to wane, David began to wonder if architecture might provide renewed possibilities for self-realization and creative fulfillment. His son, Tomas, whose interests in architecture had been sparked by his own, was by this time starting to practice as a professional architect, leading to conversations that renewed enthusiasm in David. They collaborated on a couple of small projects, including the extension to his own house. Another extension for a friend helped him to see the particular appeal of domestic architecture:

What was really persuasive for me was the fact that their youngest child was just born around the time that they were planning to move in. I was suddenly acutely aware that for this little baby this house was going to be its first environment, its world. We all remember our early world, wherever that was. We all know our first little early world, and somehow it's highly significant, it comes into your dreams. I just found it enormously touching to think that something that at one moment was on your drawing board, was just a twinkle in your eye as a design, was the next minute going to be a child's whole world. I know it's somewhat sentimental, but I found that really quite attractive, and it mainly motivated me to think more about domestic architecture and having ambitions to do it on a bigger scale.

Over four decades after leaving formal architectural training, he returned to undertake his Part III qualification, working as part of a practice set up by his own son. The RIBA magazine ran a small feature on him: it was the longest time that any architect had taken to qualify!

Architects in the practice are trained into a profession but embody an ideal that goes beyond a narrow sense of professionalism. David's account makes evident how truth to a personal vision of architecture may lead to a rejection of, or at least ambivalence to, architecture as professionally instituted and practiced. If architectural practice is often imagined as a way of creating, uncovering, and complementing the self,[8] it engenders forms of self-exploration and questioning that can lead in a range of other directions.

In William Stafford's poem "The Way It Is," he writes,

> There's a thread you follow. It goes among
> things that change. But it doesn't change.
> People wonder what you are pursuing.
> You have to explain about the thread.

Biographical narratives are forms of stabilization: they make explicit a "thread," give some form, a sense of solidity, to what U. A. Fanthorpe characterizes as the "permanently rickety elaborate structures of living."[9] The architectural self is seen to have an essence that is not straightforward or fixed. For those at MHW, the effort to "be yourself" involves questioning that self, in a process that, as they see it, is unending. Individuality from this perspective is more like a logic of change, a method of engaging with oneself and the world, than a fixed set of traits. In David's narrative it is particularly clear how what is stabilized is in a sense a recurring need to question: a kind of logic of destabilization.

LISTEN: THE GREEDY PROFESSION

Laura, Megan, and Sam are talking among themselves about the job they all do. Although at slightly different stages, they are all in their twenties. Threaded through their discussion are ambivalences about the profession: Why is it so compelling? Why is it so difficult? they wonder together:

> LAURA: [*Recently joined the practice, a Part II–qualified architectural assistant*]
>
> We're all trained; we all observe things day to day. I haven't yet been on a car journey with one of us where someone hasn't gone "Oh, look at that, look at this," because our eyes are trained to look at spaces or funny kinks in the landscape where there are opportunities, or something's been done and it's not quite working.
>
> MEGAN: [*A fully qualified architect, working for the practice for a couple of years*]
>
> It's like a running dialogue with yourself and with your colleagues, and I think that's really important. You have to create that space for yourself where you're setting the parameters and addressing the questions that you want to be looking at, which you don't necessarily look at when you're on a project.
>
> LAURA: But then maybe if we're training and investing all this time in learning about architecture then that's what you take upon yourself, to just notice these things, and then to bring your

observations to the table. So you're kind of being proactive, but it means that you have to do all the architecting at work and then also in your spare time. So then it means you have to be putting in two hundred percent all the time to be able to do that, and that's a big ask.

SAM: [*Part II–trained architectural assistant, working at MHW while studying for Part III*]

It's time-consuming as well. You love architecture, but you want to have a life outside of it too.

LAURA: Because it can be all-consuming, can't it?

SAM: Yeah, it could so easily become your life, absolutely your everything.

LAURA: God, it's crippling if you start to think about it too much!

MEGAN: Well, all the best architects I know are that sort of person, and it is their everything. You know, they eat it, they breathe it, they sleep it, everything.

SAM: I did that for two years, and that's too long. Two too many years.

MEGAN: But the thing with architecture is it contains everything, which is what makes it amazing.

LAURA: That's what makes it so addictive. You naturally fall into architecture because it contains bits of everything that you like. So it's like the greedy profession: you get to take bits from every bag that you want, but it also means that there's no space for anything else, really.

Architecture can be both rewarding and crippling because it is "all-consuming." It takes a lot and gives a lot because it is "about everything."

PERSONAL VISION

For some people [architecture] can be a profession. It's not ordinary for that to be the case. I think it's ordinary for you to think about it and to look at things in different ways, and when you're anywhere to be thinking "oh, a building here could be really good," or maybe "no building here could be really good." You're constantly forming opinions on things even without realizing it. Anyone who designs something has a constant will to design, and will continue to design when they're asleep, awake, with friends, with partners. It doesn't really stop.

Roisin tells me this during an interview, with a conviction I find unerring. She is in her mid-twenties.

What is the relationship between architects and their life? Roisin's striking phrase, the "will to design," is one way of imaging this: as a kind of vocation or calling, an overarching orientation and compulsion, daily substantiated through countless acts. Lives, architectural and otherwise, are formed not only in this doing but also in their telling.[10] Stories about their lives are ways of constructing themselves for themselves, of critically reflecting on who they were, are, and might become. Biographies are also constructed for others, as "accounts" in the linked senses: of describing a process of personal and professional self-formation and of being accountable for that self, explaining and justifying the form it has taken. Architects' self-narratives are memories not only of the experiences to which they refer but of the previous occasions on which they were recounted:[11] as elements that are more or less explicit components of educational assessment;

as narratives recounted on CVs and in job interviews; as website biographies; for journalists and clients as reputations are built. If tellings are always in this sense retellings, I am struck in Roisin's case by a correspondence between the account she gives during our interview and the one I have earlier read: her statement of "personal vision" elucidated over three pages of carefully constructed prose.

Roisin is now poised to qualify as a practicing architect. This written account, part of the career evaluation, an assessed component of the Part III examination, summarizes what she has learned through the ten years she has so far spent training. She explains in words borrowed from the novelist Arundhati Roy, in *The God of Small Things*: "Not only is another world possible. She is on her way. On a quiet day I can hear her breathing." Architecture, in Roisin's own words, is about "the power to create new realities for places." She likens the process to dreaming, involving a movement beyond things as they literally are. Where does this vision come from?

Her account traces its emergence, chronologically beginning with childhood experiences:

> I remember building with my grandfather, learning the construction of drystone walls at an early age and beginning my fascination with the construction and inhabitation of structures. I climbed trees and built seats in which I could sit and draw, places where I could observe the world as it passed by. I remember watching small garden structures in summer from height, as the growth encapsulated them and being enthralled by the reclamation of nature. I wanted to be involved in allowing for such reclamation to take place.

Another influence was the house in which her grandfather lived, a "magical place" on the West Coast of Ireland, built in the traditional vernacular of the region. It had a niche, a warm inset next to the fireplace, where Roisin remembers being placed during a period of illness. "Its wood-lined walls and soft bedded base made it a wonderfully tactile space to take a nap and recover in. This tactility is something I have been trying to re-create in my work and designs ever since." A close relationship with her other grandfather, a wheelwright by trade, was also formative. He taught her technical drawing and showed her how to sculpt wood. Sitting watching him, quietly fascinated, she came to appreciate the precise and careful movements that characterized his craft, along with his respect for the materials he worked with.

[12] Accounts of early childhood, in architecture as in other domains, make evident personal orientations that prefigure later vocational callings and in this case specific architectural interests. They are invoked as evidence of a self that remains fundamentally concerned with the same basic interests, even as these are shaped,

molded, developed, and expressed: through interactions with other people, through education, and through experience in different working contexts. In Roisin's own telling, from these very early experiences, "a fascination with how things worked physically" developed that has since been "ever present." Chronologically earlier, childhood experiences are also regarded as more fundamental: "original" in the linked senses, as an index and origin of a true self, and as a way of designating the qualities that are unique to it. After secondary school, Roisin started a degree in interior and conservation architecture. Though successful, gaining the highest grade in her year, she realized she had taken the wrong path: "The voice in my head, the childhood me, knew what I had to do." Roisin switched to an architectural degree; she said it was the "childhood me" that called her back to herself.

Architectural education provides a set of skills and approaches that help to realize and express personal capacities but cannot provide the vision itself. At university Roisin learned design and analytic skills, how to explore a design brief, the set of constraints that frame a project, and how to work autonomously. She studied broadly: on metaphysics, the effects of design on communities, geometry and the Kepler triangle, advanced material technology, utopian studies, and photography as an architectural tool. Working as an architect she learned a more practical set of skills: how to manage relationships with clients, coordinating consultants and construction professionals, and using contracts. Photos, sketches, and maps illustrate a chronological sequence of projects: a "complex staircase and design for a staff room"; "model study of a market place"; "elevation study for a competition in Budapest." Projects are narrated as evidence of personal and professional capacities: illustrations of a "vision," traced through the narrative as an underlying connection between these.

The account exemplifies a wider set of understandings about the importance of personal vision, and the development of a distinctive perspective. Roisin locates these in ways that are specific to her: a particular constellation of personal dispositions, experiences, encounters, and training, which describe and explain a personally distinctive approach. At the same time the account takes shape through narrative forms that are not entirely her own, constructed, as Carol Greenhouse puts it in relation to biographical testimonies of US high court judges, "from the outside in."[13] Roisin tells the story anticipating its assessment by fellow professionals. It is a way of making the personal public.[14] Her efforts are shaped through collective efforts in the office: of questioning, commenting, criticizing, and editing. The resulting text delimits the parameters of a personal vision, through the parameters it narratively creates: coherent and singular, the vision is individuated as distinct from the influences and inspirations of others. A connecting strand of continuity is teased out through time and space. Text and person are assembled through each other.[15]

LISTEN: MYTHS OF ORIGIN

September 16, 2015. Tomas is in the car, on his own, heading into work. The recorder clicks on. He sends me this, along with a series of other audio files, reflecting on various elements of his work. I can hear the morning in his voice as it croakily comes to life and the traces of a cold:

> So I've just been listening to the radio on my way into work and just heard something really interesting that I thought I'd just get down while it's in my head. It was about the role of myth in human cooperation. . . . If you look at successful large businesses, they all have a kind of myth and a story at their heart. It's that myth that helps consolidate all those people together, for a common good or the organization. I think I relate to that with our practice. There's a story or a myth behind the practice that people hang on to, that isn't necessarily based on a truth or anything rational but is more about a narrative which people can join in on. It's also interesting because some companies might have a story that they fix on, that they lock down and then carry on with. But with us our narrative kind of needs to evolve, and it's interesting to consider how important that might be to the business. And that was it. All right!

The car crunches over gravel, then comes to a halt. The tape clicks off.

DESIGNING AND MAKING

The office bears the trace of other times and places. As I experienced it in 2014, the room contained ten architects, then involved in the construction of four buildings, with numerous other design projects at various stages of completion. When I visited two years previously, there were still only six architects, working in an office in the house of Tomas's codirector, Tom, in an extension he had himself designed. The practice had moved there a couple of years before, having outgrown an adapted garden shed at the end of Tomas's rented cottage. Freezing in winter and too hot in summer, the shed was where they first set up office and where they subsequently took on their first employee. These details are themselves part of a story I hear recounted on a number of occasions. They are factually correct but convey a narrative truth beyond this: of sacrifice, and of rapid change from humble beginnings that is a source collective pride. Alongside this are ambivalences, anxieties that the progress won through hard work has nonetheless been accompanied by changes about which they are more ambivalent.

Tomas is himself amazed at the transformation that has taken place. He describes the business as "an organism," with "a life of its own," and confesses to being unable to explain exactly how it developed. In the practice there are various stories, "myths" of origin, as Tomas characterizes them. As individuals are shaped through the narratives told about them, so organizations are realized through collective stories of self making. As is more generally common of architectural organizations,[16] the biographies of the practice directors are central to these collective stories.

MHW cofounder Tom Howard, like Tomas Millar, grew up in Cotswold villages within a couple of miles of where they now work; they are nearly the same age. Though they did not know each other as children, their early years both provided paths to the same place. They first met in Edinburgh, as first-year students in architecture. Their shared experiences lend the practice story a sense of destiny and roots them in the place they work. Family connections to the area tie into accounts of their architecture as a kind of "contemporary vernacular," arising from and responding to a place they each know well.

Tom describes how an interest in making developed before an interest in architecture:

> I always loved making things. From when I was a child growing up I had a workshop. I went through school, and I always loved spending most of my time in the workshops. I got to looking at university and vaguely looked at various types of engineering and boat building, but I felt most of them were a bit narrow, and I just felt architecture seemed to be the most interesting, broadest, all-encompassing degree. So, yes, I went for it.

At university he encountered and rejected an approach that seemed to separate a theoretical discourse about buildings from the practical activity of making. He is not alone in the practice in this "practical" emphasis, nor in seeing the development of his approach in part through a critical rejection of his education.[17] It is telling that he talks about this, mostly to emphasize a distance from it, describing two subsequent experiences as particularly formative. After completing Part I, he went to work in Sri Lanka. Seeing good architecture in a completely different context, he reflects how "the otherness in that experience shone a light into my own impression of what we were doing here. It was only seeing a stark contrast that helped provide a sense of perspective and insight into what I thought was important about what we do [in Britain]." These insights informed an "instinctive" approach to architecture, which he now knows so well that he finds it difficult to articulate: "[It's] just about the experience of moving through a space and what delights, what you need functionally, and making the most of a place: something very rooted spatially and experientially." His emphasis on "experience" as a way of designing relates to the way he traces his own development: more through practical personal experiences than ideological or conceptual inspiration.

During the first year of his diploma, while he was studying in Finland, there was a second "big epiphany." A term with wider currency, it captures the sense of intellectual development, not as a gradual accretion of knowledge or skill but as a sudden revelation,[18] an event or experience that makes apparent a previously unrecognized truth and orients life in a different direction: "I was the only person for whom English was their first language, and so you couldn't really talk about your work. It just had to talk for itself." The experience led him to reflect on the relationship between architecture and language more generally: "I always think architecture has to talk for itself. It shouldn't need to be explained. Sometimes you might learn something interesting through an explanation of it, about a history that adds a layer of interest, but certainly I felt like an awful lot of what we were doing at Edinburgh needed so much explanation it became fairly irrelevant. It was so self-referential."

Tom is highly articulate during the interview, as he is in the practice. Although he talks a lot, in ways that have significant consequences for the organization of work within the practice, he downplays the role of theoretical language and an overreliance on explanation. He emphasizes what he sees as the subsidiary role of words: as practical means to the ends of building and as elements of experience that they can never fully capture. In this respect he marks a distinction, his own and of the practice as a whole, from the intellectualism and jargon of academic architecture discourse in terms that also connect him to a long-standing tradition in architecture: when the leading modernist architect Mies van der Rohe said "Don't talk. Build!" his sentiments arose from a very different tradition of thought but privileged a similar ideal: of words as incidental and even incompatible with architecture as a primarily visual and material medium.[19]

Tom is gracious in his answers, but even so the interview is short. He is in a hurry, pushed for time as usual, but the brevity of these responses seems to make a further point by implication: that the real stuff of architecture is elsewhere.

When people ask Tomas about his approach to architecture, he likes to explain it in relation to a formative period spent on an island in British Columbia, Canada. On Hornby Island, many houses were self-built by the people who then lived in them, as part of a counterculture that revolved around making. As a small child, he spent time living there with friends of his parents. During the remainder of his childhood, the memories remained vivid and drew him back in his late teens. He spent some time helping to build a wooden house and learned how the process of building could itself be a way of designing. Tomas saw how construction without qualified architects could have interesting results. Structures emerged from the lives of those who made them, exploiting unanticipated possibilities encountered through the process by which they were made. He left "understanding that space could be that exciting," and resolved to make architecture his life's work.

Tomas tells me all this, aware he's told me before. "It's difficult to tell how much this is a narrative that I've developed." He is conscious it is a simple and romantic story, and though he returns often to it, he is also suspicious. Is the memory of the experience, or of its many subsequent retellings? Does the story explain the path his life and career have taken? Or is it a retrospective projection, a justification more than explanation, of the kind of architecture he now practices? Tomas is not alone in seeing the artifice in a self-narrative in which he also, at some level, believes. Whether or not the story is entirely faithful, it conveys a truth beyond itself, anchoring his own approach, and by extension that of the practice, in personal experience.[20]

Interests in the relationship between design and making developed further at university. He describes how, as a student in the mid-1990s, he sensed general disillusionment among tutors and fellow students with the kind of architecture that had been produced in the preceding two decades. Architecture had become "pretty dire," in the postmodern forms of pastiche that characterized many buildings in the 1980s. Even the better architecture produced by "stars" such as Norman Foster and Richard Rogers had a high-tech focus and approach that seemed to sideline the element of making.

> When we were at university, [the element of making] was something that was really played upon, of exploring architecture in that sensual way, which encourages a directness. That then has a logical development to actually engaging with the final product rather than just the drawings. I really enjoyed doing my dissertation, which explored the gap between drawing and building. There was something that felt really true about that in acknowledging that there's a difference between the two, and that something happens between the process of drawing and the final product that has a bit of alchemy about it almost. And so directly engaging in that gap, by actually becoming a builder, was an interesting thing.

Much of what Tom and Tomas have subsequently done, together and with others, has involved an effort to live with and work through the "alchemy" that emerges in the gap between designing and making: between a drawing and a building.

Both trace the genesis of this approach primarily through their own experiences, though these efforts are situated through a wider context. The "disillusionment" Tomas describes has given impetus to a range of interconnected if disparate approaches to architecture, self-consciously marginal yet increasingly widespread, including respect for making and the craft of building; attention to the material and sensual qualities of structures; the rise of "eco-architecture" and "sustainability." Linked to this, an emphasis on context responds to the a-contextual approaches that characterized modernist and postmodern architecture, including through renewed interest in the vernacular and buildings that respond to place, and an emphasis on design that is collaborative and socially responsive.[21]

BUILDING FRIENDSHIP

Tom and Tomas trace the genesis of their interests in making through different personal experiences but also through their subsequent involvements in each other's lives. A friendship that developed, in part, out of a common interest in making was given impetus through a practical exploration of these ideas. Tom explains: "We both realized we lived near here, had long holidays, we both liked making things, and we probably had very similar architectural sensibilities. We both liked and valued similar things, so we ended up building a tree house for someone."

After completing Part II, some architects take a year or two before embarking on the final stage of training, completing a series of practical assignments while working for a practice. Tom and Tomas were inspired by the projects they had done together and felt mutual disillusionment toward mainstream professional architecture. They decided to set up a business together. In Tom's words: "After all that [time at] university you just want to go out and try a few ideas and do some things right at the coal face rather than join a big treadmill of some career progression. . . . It's a great freedom being able to do that rather than just getting a job." Tom's narrative echoes those of others in the practice, as indeed in the broader professions of design, highlighting a tension between creatively oriented work and financially oriented work.[22] Their rejection of the profession is seen to be consistent with a vocational commitment to a more experimental, creative ideal. The collective aim was to find a way of working that would relate design with making. Both Tom and Tomas were attracted to the idea of work and life away from the constraints of professional employment.

They were based in London at the time, and many of their first projects came through friends and family, then by word of mouth, one job leading to another. Their ambition related more to a way of working than to the final outcome. Committed and interested in the process, they found excitement in the uncertainty. They took on everything from kitchen fitting to house renovation. Unwittingly they were laying the foundations on which the practice would be built: as much as they were constructing buildings, they were constructing a common approach. Through working with materials, they learned from them, acquiring basic skills in joinery and masonry as they went along, through experimentation and mistake.

Professional biographies commonly render working lives as a series of choices and decisions.[23] They highlight professional selves in control of themselves and their destinies, that are conscious and know what they are doing. These kinds of narratives are sometimes apparent among the architects I worked with but are complicated by an emphasis on experimentation, making, and the role of serendipity. Tom and Tomas describe their own careers as they describe the development of the practice in precisely these terms: they are led by a process, take leaps into the unknown, realize only retrospectively where they were going. Accurate characterizations as these may well be, they are told to make something apparent: individual and organizational selves that are not fully in control of themselves, that make a virtue of recognizing possibilities within the unanticipated and unplanned.

So it is that both describe how new projects were taken on, their grasp often deliberately exceeding their reach: excitement and interest always in the interstices of known and unknown that construction involved them in. New and bigger projects posed problems and questions that were a stimulus to creativity and to the acquisition of new skills. They consulted friends, manuals, and the internet for answers to the questions thrown up through the process. Though projects started out with a plan, they were happy to depart from initial designs and actively sought opportunities to do so. Making led them to see unanticipated possibilities. The realization of ideas challenged the designs they had started with: possibilities were apparent only on-site. Even failures can be seen as positive elements of this experimental approach—the contingent problems of specific projects that vindicate the overall commitment to this ideal of practical creativity.

Both are wary of overintellectualizing a period of their life that was driven more by interest and fun than by a grand plan. But as much as their struggles with plumbing and electrics were practical, they saw these as instances of a bigger struggle to connect head and hand, disconnected through the habits, professional structures, and working norms that divide architect and builder.[24] Reflecting on this period of work, Tom is explicit about this:

If you read Ruskin and Morris, they would talk about that link between the head and the hand. I think it's a massive issue politically now for school-leavers [young adults completing compulsory education]; somehow our culture suggests that a desk job is what everyone should strive for, and an architect is someone who should be off up an ivory tower somewhere, that architects and builders, and architects and engineers, are always somehow absolutely at odds, and I just don't see that at all. I think it should be much more connected than that, and certainly that's what we were trying to do.

As the arts and crafts movement of the nineteenth century responded to the disconnection of head and hand in an age of industrial mechanization, so Tom and Tomas saw their efforts as a response to the disconnections of the twenty-first century construction industry. Their narratives have a romanticism that echoes several recent theorists of craft,[25] but for them this diagnosis is less a conclusion than a starting point. Put another way, their idealism takes a pragmatic form.

As they acquired a set of skills and a way of working, they also built a relationship. Their friendship involved a common way of working, even as the point of connection was partly an ability to work through their differences. Tom reflects on the dynamic that developed: "We were both quite happy to be called an idiot by the other one. I think we had an appreciation for a similar kind of craft and making in architecture. We both loved making things, building things, working with wood, getting our hands dirty. And maybe both had a slight reluctance to go and work for anyone else."

As much as the friendship was built on common interests, it sharpened their differences as a set of complementary skills and roles: Tom more affable, assertive, charming, gung-ho, instinctive; Tomas more cerebral, obsessive, reflective, meticulous; Tom's draftsmanship complemented by Tomas's fluency in computer-aided design (CAD). Both from solidly but differently middle-class backgrounds: Tom, privately educated, his parents more establishment; Tomas sent to state school by left-leaning parents.

STARTING TO DOUBT

Stories of how the practice came to be are also an account of what the practice now is, a way of articulating aspirations for what if might become. The story of friendship and making has a simplicity that continues to speak to these architects: that design and making are linked elements of a process that is interesting and creative because it is unpredictable, experimental, and sometimes leads to failure. Tomas explains the rationale for describing the practice as a "workshop," and the enduring appeal of the story that supports this:

> When we started we actually weren't architects; we were quite keen to differentiate ourselves from that. So it was a way of contacting with that making. The thing is, now, when talking to people and selling the practice, I still go back to those design-build days, because it was such a good story. People just got it. They'd go "What do you do?" and I'd say "Well, I'm an architect, but I also build," or "We're builders but trained as architects." . . . And people would instantly then fill in the gap; I wouldn't need to explain any more. People would go, "Oh that's great, because architects are known for maybe not being that practical," or "That must mean that you understand costs or construction more," or that "you've got a practical head and you're not going to suggest ridiculous things."

Tomas recognizes the practical utility of this narrative, which persists in various guises, in promotional material and on their website, as conversations with existing and prospective clients, and even in efforts to articulate a shared vision within the practice. He is also aware there is more to the story.

After a couple of years in London, Tomas and Tom relocated to the Cotswolds, moving back to the place where they had both grown up. In an area of relative wealth and strict planning laws, they found a niche, producing designs that clients liked and planners approved with unusual regularity. The business grew, their reputation spreading by word of mouth, helped initially by a network of friends, family, and more distant connections already established through childhood association with the area. The scale and number of projects started to expand. Pragmatic elements played a part in shaping the decisions they took. Having spent their twenties in education and then in relative poverty, they now began to acquire family commitments and the need for steady incomes. While they hoped to bring design and building more closely together, professional structures and regulations militated against this aspiration: electrical and plumbing work required certification via qualifications they didn't hold. The work became too much for them to manage alone. They took on others to help with the design. As the scale and complexity of their buildings increased, it became necessary to appoint others to undertake the construction.

Tomas describes this reorientation as part of a growing awareness of what he came to see as the problems inherent in their approach: "There was a point I remember starting to doubt—having been really into the design-build idea, starting to doubt it a little bit. I realized the projects I was most happy with were the ones that were most designed from the outset." If making involves indeterminacy—a space in which possibilities open up through the interplay of relations between people and materials—this same indeterminacy can also create problems: "You can make bad judgments, . . . which are just led by 'Oh, it would be easier to do it this way.'" Tom relates how their own skills began to constrain the process: "One's own capacity—and perhaps craft, knowledge—limits what one can design. . . . So I think we got to a point where we were stunting the creativity of the projects." Working in a more conventional way had pragmatic and ideological benefits: generally more profitable and less risky, it also enabled the practice to expand the scale and scope of their designs. What, then, has become of the ideology they started out with? "It's something we talk about endlessly," Tom concedes.

Partly through choice, partly caught up in processes beyond their control, if not also their consciousness, Tom and Tomas soon found themselves as directors of a successful architectural practice, implicated in the very structures they had set out to challenge. As directors of the practice, what they now mostly create are the conditions for other people to make things: relationships between people, organizational infrastructures, strategic decisions and contracts. The frustrations of a working day dominated by e-mail correspondence and day-to-day office management are sometimes accompanied by a sense of personal diminishment that prompts nostalgia. Tom reflects wistfully, "When it's a hot sunny day, and I'm sitting in front of a computer, you think 'God, I'd love to be up on the roof.'" If such nostalgia is partly a reflection of an unresolved tension that remains in their work, it does not, as they see it, offer a viable or satisfactory resolution to these conditions. "I definitely miss it, but I'm not sure that I would want to go back there now."

Now rarely involved in construction work, they continue to stress that making is inherent to their own design practice. Tomas makes this point explicit:

> Something that sometimes frustrates me, say for building a model, people think, "Well let's wait until we've got the design and then build the model." As if you finalize all the design, somehow, in your head, or maybe a drawing that encapsulates the whole design, and then you just make a model of it. Whereas through exploring that gap again, by making the model, you change the design. So different ways of interrogating a design, through drawing or modeling or . . . computer modeling or even building, are different ways of revealing things.

Rob, another of the architects in the practice, makes a similar point. Architecture, as he sees it, is not "just about pushing lines about"—the representation of a concept, idea, or image that already exists—but should be "an exploration of the physical world in whatever medium." Different media are not just a means of expression; they afford different possibilities for exploration and experimentation through different kinds of making.

Perhaps unsurprisingly, the architects find it difficult to say anything definitive about the nature of what they do and recognize only too acutely the incompleteness of the narratives they tell about "the practice." Even to the extent that those in the practice share a commitment to making and design as aspects of one another, there is a complexity to these commitments that does not resolve in any straightforward way. Perhaps it is inevitable that a process driven by a commitment to exploit the uncertain and unpredictable will always result in a situation in which stories about the practice exist in unresolved relationship to the everyday practices in which they engage. One might also put this the other way around: if there is a candid honesty in Tomas's admission of the lack of fit between story and reality, an acknowledgment of its "mythical" status, there is also an interest in how that gap can be exploited as a way to question and reconfigure what they do. Narratives about the practice are always in one sense behind the practices they explain, even as they are also in another sense ahead: as aspirations that shape present and future possibilities.

Individual and organizational self-constructions involve an artifice and art, most obvious in their externally oriented narratives, but also there in myriad everyday presentations of self. In constructing themselves in these singular, explicit terms, they may become newly aware of themselves, realize they have capacities they were unaware of. The narrated self can also lead to uncertainties and doubts: of whether this is really who they are. And the projected self can in this way undermine the more complex, less resolved form they might more "genuinely" imagine themselves to be. Not all such tellings are fully or always believed, even, maybe especially, by those who tell them.

REFLECTION: ARCHITECTURAL LIVES

In *A Fortunate Man*, a vivid and moving account of a medical general practitioner working in a rural part of England in the 1960s, John Berger describes the lived realities of a vocational ideal. Despite numerous routine difficulties, Sassell, the focus of the account, "is nevertheless a fortunate man doing what he wants. Or more accurately what he wishes to pursue. Sometimes the pursuit involves strain and disappointment, but in itself it is his unique source of satisfaction. Like an artist or like anybody else who believes that his work justifies his life, Sassell . . . is a fortunate man."[26] Architects at MHW might be similarly characterized as fortunate in doing what they wish to pursue. They believe their work justifies their life, or that in principle it should: they draw value from it, being satisfied, or at least hopeful, it has a benefit to others, beyond the financial opportunities it affords.

Even so, these accounts point to a striking difference in the kind of vocational ideal involved. Unlike medical practitioners, architects are also concerned with the question of how their life justifies their work. The architectural theorist Dalibor Vesely describes this as the profound question that all architects must face: How can we be ourselves, in a way that is of broader benefit to others?[27] The personal lives of architects at MHW, who grapple with these questions, are not just a residual remainder of their working life, those things they happen to do and think once work is done. Neither is this something that must be actively and decisively separated, in the way that scientists might imagine subjectivity as an inhibition to objectivity.[28] Rather, personal lives are explicitly made present in the stories they tell about themselves, among themselves, and for others. More simply put, biographical narratives are an object of professional interest and are integral to architectural working identities.

Being a good architect is understood to involve more than the ability to embody a set of skills, conventions, and professional dispositions. Ideas about the importance of such a vocational ideal relate to the notion that good design emanates from and expresses something that is personal, unique, and original. Architecture, as they see it, involves the search for truthful relationships to the world, which necessarily involve a truthful relationship between the architectural and personal self. Architects at MHW sometimes talk of the profession as a form of self-exploration. They hold to the importance of developing approaches that respond to personal "passions." Through exploring and understanding architecture, they explore and understand their own lives and come to understand these in slightly different terms. A good architect is never *only* an architect. Personal narratives focus on relationships between the *who* and the *how* of knowing; they make explicit a more general concern to connect epistemic truth with personal self-conduct.[29]

Even if these vocational ideals are not always—or even ever—exactly realized, they orient the specific trajectories that lives can take. They frame doubts sometimes directed at themselves, sometimes at others: that the necessary commitment is not really there, that the job becomes routine, or that the passion has gone. In the retrospective accounts of their lives, the architects at MHW describe moments of "drifting," "lack of direction," and "uncertainty," alongside moments of "epiphany," "self-revelation," "excitement," and "momentum." Doubt may take more or less profound forms but is to some extent a vocational hazard connected to the ideal of architecture as a mode of questioning.

Some architects stress the professional ethos of architecture more than others. Either way, the relationship between these personal and professional identities remains ultimately unresolved: enthusiasm waxes and wanes; architecture becomes too consuming at times, while at other times careers stagnate; personal events mean that work takes a backseat and becomes a job, a way of earning a living. Other bits of life enhance and diminish the energies that architecture consumes or expand to take up the slack that disillusionment produces. Sometimes that disillusionment is the wellspring for something positive, even if what this is becomes evident only retrospectively. Crises lead to revelation, force reflection and reevaluation, and provoke a renewed sense of purpose and possibility. If the vocational ideal is relatively straightforward, the specific question of how to personally occupy it is anything but.

Part two has focused on architects in the making: on individual and collective selves as explicit objects of interest, on the way in which these are made through forms of expression that are primarily linguistic. Although these narratives are also shaped through practices, they take the form of interviews, conversations, reflections, documents, and presentations that are mostly set apart from the everyday work of design and construction. In the following section, I trace how these selves are implicated in the more routine practices of imagination and design. In these practices, understandings of architects as creative individuals exist alongside other understandings about the nature of imagination and where ideas come from. Architectural selves are constructed and reconstructed through myriad daily conversations and interactions, mostly too routine to notice or remark on: as forms of comportment and bodily control, through conversational turn taking, the choreography of meetings. If these are ways in which the architectural self is corporeally and ideologically given substance, the ideal is also more and less subtly deflected through these everyday performances: extended to different contexts and concerns and remade through them.

Part 3

DESIGNS

A FEEL FOR PLACE

Where do ideas come from?

I ask Tom. "Yes, where do they come from?" he asks himself, giving the question some thought. "A lot of my ideas come when I'm wandering around a place. I've gone to see a client or I'm there surveying. Just being in a place, trying to work out where I want to be, what I want to be looking at, what I want to not be looking at or be protected from, what I want to get rid of. Yes, definitely, a lot of it comes from just sitting, being in a place."

Architects make visits as part of the process of understanding the brief, the constraints to which they must respond, and then they sometimes return during the early stages of design.[1] MHW is a small practice working mostly within the immediate locale, so its architects make frequent visits to sites, a necessity that is also a choice. They see their designs as a contemporary response to the vernacular of the region and present this as an explicit critique of a globalized construction industry whose local effects are felt in homogenized buildings and ersatz "locality." Some see this way of working arising from a specific affinity to a place in which they grew up and have lived. Still more specifically they emphasize site-level particularities as both necessitating and stimulating creative response.

Although I never heard the connection explicitly made, this emphasis on place can be situated as part of a long tradition of architectural thinking; a romantic nineteenth-century emphasis on genius loci, the spirit of the place, emerged as an anxiety about the homogenizing effects of mass development, just as the 1960s saw a flourishing of interest in place-based architecture as a response to the perceived excesses of modernism as a concern with universal principles.[2]

These contexts help to explain why the architects at MHW think place is important, but not how they elaborate this importance. Focusing on the specific dynamics that develop through a series of site visits, in the following sections I explore how these commitments to place are given practical substance: in the terms developed in part one (above), how design both emerges from and shapes a *space between* architect and site.

I first met Megan when she and Tomas came to visit me five years ago. Then doing her master's degree, she was in a romantic relationship with Tomas that later became a friendship. Amicably separated, she joined MHW a couple of years ago following her Part II, recently becoming a fully qualified architect. Unlike many of the others in the practice, she is not originally from the area. Even so, she professes a personal enthusiasm for it beyond her more cerebral commitments to a place-based architecture.

She and I are on our way to visit the site of a possible new project. It's a short drive from the office, through the outskirts of Stroud, where industrial estates and a council estate give way suddenly and surprisingly to the verdant Slad valley. The site is close to where the author Laurie Lee grew up, a place that was the inspiration for much of his writing and which is now difficult to see other than in relation to this bucolic idyll. This is not just a testament to his own romantic vision but also to subsequent legislation intended to conserve this: the valley's status as an Area of Outstanding Natural Beauty is partly owed to this literary association.

We drive slowly along a single-track road with drystone walls and ancient-looking hedgerows. The brief is still extremely vague, but Megan describes what little she knows: the clients, a couple, are both well-known artists, based in London. They bought the site, a small parcel of land previously used as a market garden, to use as a weekend retreat. Ramshackle and partly derelict agricultural buildings were part of the appeal but have since been found to be "unconsented." The clients made contact with Tomas, looking for a planning consultancy with a view to gaining retrospective consent. They also have plans to convert one of the existing buildings as a new studio. It is unclear whether MHW will be commissioned to do this, but Tomas is hopeful that a positive initial response might help to convince the clients. The aim of today's visit is to take some pictures, take some measurements, and "get a feel" for the site. Megan uses the phrase repeatedly. As is usual for these initial visits, she has already done some preparation: looking at maps, locating the site and trying to understand the topography, researching the planning history. This helps to frame her understanding of the site but, she claims, cannot substitute for the experience that comes from a visit: "You can only properly understand a place by experiencing it firsthand." How does this understanding happen?

We park by a gate. Megan has a bag with the few tools she needs: tape measures, a notepad and pencil, a printout of the Google Earth map of the site. Her sense of the encounter as "direct" relates partly to the simplicity of these representational tools. "Let's just look around generally," she remarks as we set off, climbing over a rusting gate. We walk down an avenue of trees, on an old driveway now covered with moss. We happen upon the first building, an agricultural shed—corrugated iron and wood—and peer inside. White walls and a wood-burning stove. "Nice, I like it." I ask why: "It has an honesty and simplicity," she explains. Megan is observing things carefully but doesn't say much.

Initial communions with place are often accompanied by a distanced look: intense but unfocused. It is looking with concentration, anticipating interest without knowing exactly where this will be found. Eyes are cast about expansively, head moving up and down, ranging from side to side—actively looking, without knowing quite what for. At this stage architects imagine themselves as a kind of receptor, deliberately permeable and "open," oriented to receive rather than project, "just taking things in," as Megan puts it.

Paths are mown through long grass, thick with butterflies and insects. A chorus of crickets, thousands singing to the same monotonous rhythm, is persistent, insistent, all-pervasive. "I love that," Megan remarks. It reminds her of Africa, her home for most of her childhood and where her parents still live. Her comment exemplifies a broader point: the "feel" of a site is a response that is emotional and personal. Architects are trained to recognize, register, and channel these responses as a way of understanding the site.

Often these initial interactions are deliberately unstructured. Megan is not entirely sure where we are heading. We walk through a tunnel of trees and discover a converted wooden shed, the site's current living area. Megan doesn't have the keys; we peer inside, hands and face pressed to the glass, looking beyond our own reflections. The décor is simple and understated but obviously carefully considered. The kitchen is made from reclaimed wood; the cupboard doors are plywood. There are some deliberately eclectic pieces of furniture and some of the clients' art. Outside, a terrace is made from reclaimed scaffolding. I ask Megan for her impressions: "I love it," she says again. I press her further: "It's not conventional . . . simple . . . modest but highly designed . . . interesting." Though the architect wants to experience the whole site, it is often the details that capture attention. Time is given to peer into a window or to touch an interesting surface. Things are handled, watched, tapped. The claim that places have a "feel" is also an acknowledgment of their tactile and sensory qualities, that the site cannot be understood only by looking.

Even so, architects' responses are channeled in specific ways that are routinely visual. Movements are oriented to position "views" and "perspectives." The site is captured through cameras and sketches that do not simply "record" what is seen but actively structure how the architect sees.[3] As the visit progresses, our engagement with the site becomes more structured: Megan takes pictures of all elevations of the buildings we visit. Then she takes measurements, which are added to sketched drawings of the elevations. We come to the barn the clients want to convert to a studio. Megan remarks on the weathered boards used as exterior cladding: "they're beautiful!" She is taken with their patina and character and likes the thought of a connection between what is there now and whatever comes later. She wonders if they might be reused, perhaps inside, as part of the final design. Megan likes the site and sees interesting possibilities: a relationship to the views across the valley; to the house behind; and to the wood. The visit has helped her to understand the site as a set of spatial relationships and design constraints. But the feel for the place is understood as quality of experience over and above this explicitly conscious understanding.

Schon describes "feel" as an important quality of all forms of expert knowledge. He suggests it encapsulates the sense in which tacit forms of knowledge allow skilled practitioners to know more than they are able to say.[4] At MHW, architects likewise acknowledge their own difficulty in accounting for their interactions with sites, describing these variously as "unconscious," "intuitive," and "difficult to put into words." "Feel" refers in these respects to a self that is only partly conscious of its actions and abilities, to emotions and experiences that elude their ability to explicate them, even to themselves. Feel is a way of being in touch with the site through being differently in touch with themselves, an orientation that requires the deliberate suspension of more critical, more explicit responses. To put this the other way around, the feel of the site, its specific qualities and characteristics, elicits thoughts, emotions, ideas, and inspiration, which they could not otherwise have registered.

As a response to place, design is imagined in part as a process of tracing out this feel: less as a matter of fitting buildings into sites than of unfolding buildings from them.

SITES OF DESIGN

Another site visit illuminates how this happens. Roisin is accompanied by Rob, one of the more senior architects in the practice. The plot has an extensive garden, originally part of the grounds of a bigger Victorian mansion. There is already a house, built in the 1980s. The clients, a middle-aged couple with two children, have acquired the site with a view to demolishing the house and rebuilding. Roisin has been working on initial ideas prior to the site visit. The project is being overseen by Rob. Originally a product designer, he changed direction and retrained as an architect in his late twenties. Though he is deferential to Roisin and respectful of her work, his pronouncements seem subtly to carry more weight. This may partly be an artifact of his greater experience but also manifests itself as a form of distancing from the details of the project: he has oversight in the sense of seeing more through seeing less of these distractions. Both have surveyed maps. Rob remarks on notable trees, conscious there may be tree preservation orders. He is using his phone, held outstretched, to take pictures. He observes the site through its screen, his engagement with the site literally framed by the camera and the photographic conventions that govern its architectural use. "You can never take too many," he observes, joking that however many pictures you take, the crucial view is always missing when you get back to the office. As much as these are personal aide-mémoires, they are also intended to convey the site to others in the office.

Rob and Roisin wander, mostly in silence. They occasionally exchange words, passing remarks on topics ranging from the heavy dew in the long grass that quickly saturates our shoes to a twee 1980s ornamental well, to the beauty of the orchard. Their movement through the site leads their conversation and vice versa. As they respond to what they encounter, their discussion prompts them to walk in particular ways as they look for specific things, wondering connected to wandering.[5] Sometimes they walk together, sometimes apart. The initial plans had focused on the top of the site, but Rob is unsure: "I do wonder if we want to be occupying this top area?" Both peer into the greenhouse, which they take to be Victorian. Old vines are growing out and through the windows and around rusty old mechanisms for opening and closing them. "This is really cool! I feel like it would be nice to keep some of it," Roisin remarks, excited by the possibilities this seems to open up. "It would be a shame to get rid of it." Rob remarks that it has character and atmosphere and wonders if this might provide the basis for a design response without retaining the structure itself. We spend some time looking at the existing house, which has been uninhabited for some time but is otherwise structurally sound. Both agree they dislike it. It is in the wrong place, pushed awkwardly to the side of a large plot, and also out of character.

Stories about place, about what it was and could be, are ways of turning the site into a different kind of object. Conversations articulate shared or divergent understandings of the feel of the site and more or less formed ideas about the design consequences that might flow from this. Sketches are exchanged and discussed. Different possibilities are suggested: an existing architectural detail, an interesting material, a sense of the place that might be "right," or "where the building wants to be."[6] Perspectives bifurcate and align, not only through conversations, sketches, and plans but also through the different paths that are traced across a site. Numerous seemingly inconsequential utterances are ways of willing forms into being ("maybe . . ." "perhaps . . ." "how about . . . ?") as possible worlds are multiplied; other possibilities are closed down or off ("I don't think so"; "it doesn't work").[7] As Keith Murphy has observed in relation to Swedish product designers, words are "suffused with the capacity to move people, to simultaneously bring them together and push them apart."[8] Architects at MHW are trained in ways of seeing and thinking that are partly but not entirely shared. One might have a more developed sense of the conservation issues, while another might be more attuned to the structural or planning constraints. Understanding develops and thickens, as perspectives are layered, ideas explored, and emotions shared. "Feel" is discerned through collective effort. It is made a focus of design through conversations that tack backward and forward: trying to discern what it is as a way of imagining what the building could be; always on the cusp between the actual and the possible.

"What would the view be like from here?" Rob asks. He scrambles up a nearby tree to find the answer. Then he balances precariously, camera in hand, taking the image that conveys the perspective to others. Sometimes new perspectives

are improvised in other ways: climbing on chairs, or upon walls, beating paths through thick undergrowth.

After about half an hour Rob suggests a bit of sketching. He and Roisin take out drawing boards, tracing paper taped over base plans. They work quickly, trying out several possibilities, "not thinking too hard," Rob explains: not wanting to get bogged down in the detail; trying to tap into a feel that is less than fully conscious. Their efforts are aided by the scale at which they are working. Little more is possible than the rough sense of where the building might be and the kind of form it might take. Working in plan both constrains and enables, attuning them to the possible shape and footprint of the building through bracketing detailed consideration of topography.

As they draw, the movement of their heads from the drawing board to the site and back mediates the conceptual movement between the existing site and the possible building. Architects at MHW stress the "directness" of a site visit, but in practice the lack of mediation is only relative. Even in these initial interactions, the site is moved by the architect. Design emerges as a dialogue between plan and place, drawing and site.[9] Possible buildings are coaxed into existence as the "feel" is channeled through sketching. The resulting designs in turn become a way of interrogating the site, of better understanding this feel and of sharpening attention to its possibilities and constraints. A feel emanates from the place, inspires a thought, realized as a quickly sketched design; the design is checked and modified against the physical constraints of the site.

After a separate visit to the site, Tom had initially stressed the need for a design that would respond to the views, but Rob is more taken with the garden itself. He wonders if the views might be a bit of a red herring and focuses instead on the more immediate plot, its feel of containment and enclosure. The derelict atmosphere of the existing garden, with its overgrown greenhouse and orchard, sparks a series of ideas. He talks to me as he sketches, explaining his thought process. His inclination is to "try to push something very modernist." He observes that in the process there is always a tendency to "soften back" designs. You start bold, with a strong conceptual idea, which then tends to weaken as other factors are considered: cost, clients' preferences, the need to get planning permission, and so on.

He outlines a design that is very light, with a permeable structure and a very direct relationship to the surrounding landscape. The site calls to his mind the architecture of Geoffrey Bawa. The mental images conjured by this comparison animate his initial sketches.[10] He thinks aloud as he draws: "Perhaps we could have a very light structure, to blur the distinction between inside and outside? Or a flat turf roof?" Roisin agrees, referring back to the greenhouse. Inspired by its structure, she is also wondering about something very light. Or perhaps even retaining part of the greenhouse itself: "It would be nice to keep a little bit of history." Unlike Rob, her encounter with the site is already influenced by some initial sketches. Even while these designs partly frame a way of seeing the place, the visit suggests possibilities she hadn't anticipated. Where the initial interactions were quiet and deliberate, now their voices are excited, animated.

Just as the feel of place is understood through conversations on-site, so there is a dialogue between these sketched designs and the conversations that are had, as and after they talk. Design is given form as a way of exploring actualities and possibilities of the site through the intersections of words, gestures, drawings, and the various qualities that give these sites their feel. It is for these reasons that architects distinguish and value design work on site as distinct from that which happens in the office.

In a remarkable passage, Dana Cuff and Russell Ellis relate the story of an unnamed architect who told them, "I've dreamed I was a building, and I changed myself in the dream. I've also dreamed I was an element in the landscape. When I'm looking around in a two-story space my consciousness is everywhere." Imagine! Cuff and Ellis continue their own interpretation of this account, "through the bubbling activity of dream life actually becoming buildings, parts of sites and changing oneself! Prospective buildings were animated through him and he experienced their structures by becoming them. Anthropomorphizing the building through himself was a way of establishing a dialogue between the emergent structure and his own evolving ideas as a designer. It became clearer how some architects can seriously say things like 'the building wants to be that tall.' If you are the building, it can have volition."[11]

Architects at MHW never related their experiences of sites and buildings in quite these terms, yet there are clear resonances in their understanding of "feel" as a specific volition in design, as a way of animating the site and of being animated by it, trying to understand and to channel what the site "wants to be."

DRIPPING WITH HISTORY

We are on a site visit to St. Andrew's Church, in Tom's car, a people carrier. He apologizes for the detritus of children's toys and discarded food wrappers, the material culture of a family life I have glimpsed only in relief. Sometimes Tom leaves early or arrives late to work when he picks up or drops off his boys at school. He talks often and fondly about them, even as he acknowledges the trials and tribulations of fatherhood, as part of a life packed with too many commitments: "Juggling too many things." We drive along winding lanes, through the claustrophobically narrow valleys of Stroud, then up onto the tops, where the dark earth of freshly plowed autumn fields exposes a skeleton of drystone walls. This is a familiar landscape for Tom. As we drive he points out places of interest, houses the firm has built and projects that didn't come off, along with buildings and details of architectural interest.

Preparation often takes place on journeys to sites. Ronan, the main project architect, grew up locally and knows the area well. Architects can be said to be in a world of their own in a professionally specific sense: they understand the act of imagining new buildings to require a critical distance from actually existing circumstances. In the case of Ronan, who perhaps inhabits this imaginative world more vividly than others, this manifests itself as a kind of introversion, jokingly acknowledged through office banter. Even when he is talking about pragmatics, his voice has a slightly otherworldly quality. He has the project folder and reads aloud passages that convey the key points. As is common for public projects, the brief has been created through a formal process of consultation, prior to the involvement of the architects. The church committee members have produced a "statement of needs," which forms the basis of the brief MHW has been given: they want better kitchen facilities, the addition of a toilet, good storage, and seating that gives them more flexibility than the existing heavy pews. Tom, himself an active member of the Church of England, contextualizes the project as part of a broader shift: "Medieval churches were the places where everything happened. Then the Victorians made everyone put on a shirt and tie and face the front. Now there's a move to restore a more participatory form of church." He is already starting to form a sense of what the project involves, the kind of problems they will need to resolve, and the approach that might inform this. "What they need is a place that will be fun, flexible, and warm." He thinks there will need to be "lots of doubling up," that "everything needs to do lots of different jobs." It won't be possible to resolve all these needs in one space, so the trick will be to balance these, "doing the best for the most."

Christopher Alexander, one of the key proponents of "contextual architecture," wrote in 1964: "Every design problem begins with an effort to achieve fitness between two entities: the form in question, and its context. The form is the solution to the problem; the Context defines the problem."[12] Such an orientation was central to much of the "contextualist" architecture that followed, framing an interest in design as a response to place. We have seen already how, in practice, form (design) is not just a response to context (site) but a way of understanding it. The relationship between the context and the problem has a similarly iterative quality. The "brief" develops, through interactions with sites and clients, and frames the interactions that architects subsequently have.

As Tom and Ronan wander around the church, they are wondering about the issues contained in the documents they consulted prior to the visit. Where might the toilet be located? How best to design the seating to allow both for the big congregations at Christmas and Easter and the "messy church" where the space needs to be open and flexible? On a number of occasions Tom seems visibly perplexed, face screwed up in uncertainty, forehead furrowed and rubbed. "Nothing seems obvious. It's a difficult brief," he explains aloud, perhaps conscious of my interrogating looks. In his earlier conversations with the church committee, committee members have indicated an interest in undertaking work only to the interior of the church. Tom wonders if it might help to "step back from what has been requested," to think about the building and the problems "more holistically." Any work will need to be externally funded. If they can "tell a story" that appeals to a donor, it might be possible to expand the scope of the work.

We have a look at the entrance to the site. A small lychgate leads to a paved drive that leads, in turn, to the church building. "It's not very welcoming," Tom concludes. His eyes take on a distant look, already seeing beyond what *is* there to what *could* be, a form of mental Photoshopping, as he puts it. He asks Ronan to take notes. "Perhaps we could change the road surface to soften it? And maybe do something with good lighting?" Walking farther up the drive we see the parish buildings, used to prepare food and for meetings. They are housed away from the church with, as Ronan puts it, "their back turned." Ronan and Tom feel the architecture should realize and express a close relationship between the structures. Ronan quickly sketches below the notes he has made: his visualization "punches a hole" in the wall; he extemporizes, highlighting the new relationships that are created, drawing a series of arrows. Will any of this happen? I wonder. "Who knows," is Tom's response, "but you have to start by thinking about all the options and what is best for the site." Both architects see the site through the concerns, ideas, and limits the client has imposed, but the encounter in turn transforms their understanding of these issues. Place and brief are mutually transformed through these interactions, each redefined, respecified, and newly understood in relation to the other.

Even in a public project that starts from a formal client brief, sites are framed by questions and present a series of puzzles that may cause architects to reframe the problems they are set. In an idealized portrayal of architecture, the problem and brief come prior to the design solution.[13] Yet in practice, design is entangled in this process from the start.[14] As much as the design solution may respond to an existing problem that the client or others have set, it can also be a way of reformulating or expanding the remit. A design "solution" allows a re-perception of what the "problem" is. In purely instrumental terms, the authority of architects rests on an ability to control the terms on which problems are set.[15] Ideologically, they see this as part of a commitment to architecture as a form of exploration, in the service of artistic, ideological, and social goals. While architecture must understand the more proximate, more pragmatic problems that others may recognize, it is as much about challenging these framings as responding to them.

The feel for a place can be an animating force that architects seek to exploit through design. Often this feel is distinctively historical, a specific relation between time and space. Inside the church we walk slowly, eyes drawn upward to impressive stained glass and the volume of space above us. As we look around, details are picked out. Ronan's face is not normally prone to overt demonstrations of enthusiasm but it lights up visibly: "incredible murals on the wall!" Tom points to the organ, a dark hulking presence, with an inscription to the person who donated it: "That's a fabulous thing." Their comments are interspersed by long periods of silence, perhaps amplified and extended by the sense of reverence the place instills. Enthusiasm, though obvious, is conveyed in the hushed tones the space seems to require: "lovely sundial"; "gorgeous worn moldings."

The moldings draw the hand as well as the eye. Intricate, cold, massive, they make the past obviously and viscerally present.

Tom comments on this more generally: "The place is dripping with history." By their own admission, neither Tom nor Ronan is deeply knowledgeable about architectural history. The nature of the project will require the involvement of a conservation architect, and their own interest in the building's past is largely tangential to these concerns. Through these interactions, time is unfolded from place, not in the chronological sense of historical epochs or architectural styles but as an emotional response to stories and processes held within its fabric. The appeal is partly in the sense of depth, mystery, and intrigue that comes from not knowing exactly what that history might have been. Seeing the plaque that commemorates the donor of the organ, they speculate with interest: "Who was he?" and "How did it come to be there?" One of them remarks on the distinctive musty smell that churches so commonly have. "Why is that?" A worn step is pointed out, a silent witness to thousands of feet over hundreds of years. "Think of all the people who have walked there," Ronan exclaims, eyes lighting up. The connection is to an unknown population of churchgoers but intimate still. They are less interested in the building's History (capital *H*) than in these more intimate stories. The less they precisely know, the more they are free to imagine. Interest is not a matter of age alone, nor do their assessments straightforwardly coincide with conservation professionals' assessments of historical significance per se. The architects at MHW see little point in preservation for its own sake and are critical of conservationist approaches to the extent these artificially arrest the story of a place. What are the consequences of this orientation to history? What problems and possibilities flow from it?

Tom comments on a contradiction that is central to much of their work:[16] "This is the kind of project where the tension between conservation and development is most acute. Part of you thinks it's wonderful as it is, and perhaps they just need to muddle through. Another part thinks: 'What would it look like if you started from scratch, strip it back and de-clutter it?'" Ronan comments that the space has a quality of permanence that is appealing and seducing but also problematic from a design perspective: "The church is not a museum. It needs to meet the needs of those who use it. I'd like to start from scratch—imagine what the space would be like without anything in it."

Drawing is a way of doing this. Having had a chance to look around, they start to sketch some ideas. Seated on pews, they work in plan, tracing paper taped over base plans, brainstorming different options that quickly accumulate in piles on the floor. The general tension Tom expresses between conservation and development, between a duty owed to the history of the building and the duty owed to its present and future inhabitants, disaggregates as a series of design problems to work through. The pews are too heavy to be moved and so are not practical, but perhaps they can be put on wheels? Or could the wood be recycled? The church needs to be warm to feel welcoming. The most efficient way to heat such a large space is using under-floor heating, which would mean a new floor. The existing one is "nice"—worn and uneven—but probably "only Victorian"; its loss may be a necessary sacrifice for the gain of warmth. If a timber floor was suspended above it, the floor could be retained underneath, original fabric preserved in an intervention that is "reversible." That would be "good conservation practice." More or less explicitly, their initial design responses meld the reconciliation of multiple interests and activities with a consideration of the constraints and possibilities of this existing context.

Linked to the question of *how much* the past should matter is the question of *how*. A "feel" is discerned historically in various ways, including as "atmosphere" and "character," terms that are significant in architects' efforts to relate the past and the present. They entail the idea that the site has a specific integrity, an identity that involves an irreducible individuality—the characteristics that are unique to a place, even as these may be composed of elements shared by other sites.[17] Not all the things the architects see and experience during such visits are equally relevant to the sense of character that emerges. Specific architectural details may be dwelt on, while others are ignored or quickly passed over. We have seen already how a structurally redundant conservatory nevertheless contributes to a "character" that architects seek to carry through in their designs. By contrast, built in the early 1990s, the offices at Wrenswood Hill are still functional and still used, but are seen as an imposition on the space, extrinsic to it and therefore dispensable, bearing little relationship to its surrounding environment. "Straight out of a book," is Tom's response. "This could have been built anywhere." Ideas about character are central to architects' efforts to imagine "appropriate" relationships between the actual and the possible.

Tom and Ronan's sense of the character of the church informs ideas about what should stay and what might go. At the front there is an ornate metal railing, a Victorian addition that both see as "ugly," "out of keeping" with the earlier medieval building and with the aspirations of a more participatory congregation. They are keen to take it out but wonder whether this will be possible on conservation grounds. Might the Victorian society object? Would this be protected by the church's listing? Their own sense of character takes shape in relation to this broader, if as yet largely unknown, legislative context. An altar by the entrance presents a barrier to one of the possible designs. Though this is medieval, a conversation with Ann, a parishioner who let us into the building, reveals that it was moved about fifty years ago. It is of obvious historical significance, but its spatial location seems negotiable. Moving it to the opposite end of the nave could be

seen as a return to its more original setting, Tom suggests. The tension between conservation and development is not just a matter of what to keep and what can go, but also of the extent to which new additions respond to existing circumstances. Ronan notes the presence of the organ as providing the "precedent" for a large volume contained within the space. He wonders if this might make a similarly sized addition seem "appropriate"—perhaps a wooden structure that could house a kitchen and toilet. Is the existing character best preserved by carrying through details, forms, materials, and aesthetics derived from what is already there? Or might this result in a confusing and dishonest fusion of new and old? Perhaps it is better to do something "completely modern," to give what is already there "the space to be itself," as Ronan puts it. Conservation principles are abstractly clear. The question of how to apply these requires elaboration and hence interpretation.[18]

Writing in the 1950s, Ernesto Rogers, a key thinker in the development of contextual architecture, emphasized the importance of *preesistenze ambiente,* or "surrounding preexistences." In a critique of the a-temporality of modernism, he argued that architecture should respond to location in ways that were significantly historical. He cited with approval the author T. S. Eliot's idea that "the present is directed by the past."[19] Architects at MHW are likewise interested in the present possibilities that flow from the past, specifically as these frame two basic questions: How should the past direct the work of design? And how much weight should this be given, relative to other considerations? The questions are general, but the answers are necessarily specific.

SITE STORIES

Architects' responses to place are framed by the actions of other people, and by the legislative contexts in which they operate. Building professionals, clients, planners, and consultants are often met on-site.

Tom explains some of the background of a possible new project on the drive over. He had a call the preceding week from Michael, the father of an old school friend. They had a chat about a couple of building projects. Both sounded interesting, though it is still unclear what they would entail and whether they were likely to be feasible. There is no brief. Depending on today's visit, there may even be no project.

Tom knows the place from visits as a child. Michael and his wife live in a medieval manor house at the bottom of the valley. Michael inherited the estate some time ago. Originally it had comprised most of the valley, including a farm and various cottages within it, but following a pattern repeated across the country, the estate shrank during the early and middle years of the twentieth century, as property was sold off to pay for upkeep, repair, and inheritance tax.[20] Over the past few decades, Michael has been trying to reverse the trend, buying back land and houses, which he lets out individually and as part of a wedding and functions business.

We approach the house from the top of the estate, via a long rutted drive that winds down through mature deciduous woodland. Ian, the planning consultant, has just arrived. He is in his mid-thirties, dressed in a tweed jacket and brogues that convey a solidly establishment trustworthiness. Tom and Ian have worked together several times previously. The tone of their interactions is professional,

but there is an obvious rapport between them. Pleasantries are exchanged regarding work and family before we head to the house.

Michael is in his sixties, wearing baggy corduroys and a thick woolen sweater. His manner is unassuming and kindly. His speech is erudite and considered. As well as helping his wife run the estate, he's a historian, mostly writing books about country houses. We gather around a large old wooden table, piled high with books and papers. Tom asks for news of Michael's son, his childhood friend, now a correspondent for the *Financial Times* who lives in Latin America with a small child of his own.

Michael prefaces his description of two projects with some thoughts on the logic and approach behind them. Both could be ways of helping to make the estate more financially sustainable, but his thinking is not driven only by financial considerations. He has, as he puts it, "a feeling of latent moral responsibility to preserve what is unique within the country." This conservation ethos is partly at stake in his thoughts about how the estate should be run. The holiday rental business arose from the desire to preserve the buildings, generating the revenue that would ensure their sustainability and future survival. Both, as he sees it, involve historically important buildings whose futures are in doubt. He introduces two buildings in turn, describing the historical context of each with the evident knowledge of a historian of buildings. The first is a gasworks dating from the nineteenth century, originally built to provide gas for the manor house. It is now completely ruined, with little surviving aboveground other than a chimney and the remains of some walls. He is not sure how it might be used but has been wondering about "some sort of stone tent." "A creative opportunity," Tom responds. The second is a nineteenth-century barn for possible domestic conversion. There is no real brief, beyond a desire to give the barn a "new life." With this context established, Tom brings things to a close. "Let's go and have a look," he says, face lighting with an enthusiasm that is both sincere and instrumental. He likes this stage of the process, the sense of almost infinite possibility, but is also aware of the strategic benefit of making this interest evident to clients. "We need to really see it," he concludes.

We drive to the barn, about a third of a mile from the house. It is low and long, completely open to the front, with a pantile roof (curved, fired-clay tiles) and exposed wooden beams. Dung-trodden straw and plastic feeding troughs show it is still in use. Tom choreographs the conversation, bringing in the thoughts of others as required. They walk around the building as they talk, conversation elicited by various points of interest. Michael gives the history: built in the nineteenth century, it used to be part of the original home-farm. It was modified twenty or thirty years ago to make it easier for the farmer to use, and a Dutch barn was added to store hay and farm implements. A wall was knocked through to connect these, and some cinder block studwork was added. Tom comments on

the roofline and the way it follows the sloping contour of the hill: "that's what I'd do if I was a farmer! Just follow the line. You don't want to be moving earth unless you have to." He is evidently taken by this haphazard charm—"form following function," a perfect adaptation of a building to a place.

Ian comments "from a planning perspective," a phrase that prefaces most of his remarks. He thinks it will be considerably easier to gain permission for a holiday cottage than for a regular residential unit. This would tie in with the existing business, and so the rationale is more straightforward. He stresses that planning is always about a balance between competing legislation, and outlines some of the relevant context: the government minister has recently introduced legislation that in principle gives approval for barn conversions, so nationally there should be support. However, this principle is complicated by local planning commitments that, as is often the case, give greater weight to conservation than to development.

The fact the barn is located in an Area of Outstanding Natural Beauty involves legislative restrictions that could complicate things further. As we tour the site, Ian points out the hay and agricultural machinery that are being stored in the Dutch barn. Here again is a possible planning issue: "A planner is going to look at that and want to know where the machinery is going to be stored if the barn is converted. They are reluctant to allow conversions if that means another barn is going to have to be constructed elsewhere, a possible blot on the landscape, particularly in an area as beautiful as this."

The linked logics of development and conservation engender a tension that has been central to modern planning since the nineteenth century.[21] These logics are embedded in places in different ways, through various and sometimes contradictory legislation and policy. Is it listed? Is it in an Area of Outstanding Natural Beauty? Is it in a conservation area? Are there tree preservation orders? Are there bats? These are often among the first questions that are asked on a site visit. They are shorthand ways of assessing to what extent and in what ways might existing buildings, sites, landscapes, or habitats determine the nature and scope of the design. Legislation intersects around sites in different ways, creating different possibilities and constraints. The internally contradictory nature of such policies always leaves room for interpretation and maneuver, the space to argue a case.

Ian's perspective occupies the negative space of the planner's vision, knowing how planners think in order to gainsay it. If planning is about a balance between competing and contradictory forces, it can be tipped toward a favorable outcome by "telling a good story." The trick is to provide a strong narrative, "to show that there are more pros than cons." Already he is starting to imagine what this story might be: the context for any application would need to be "the estate as a whole and the unique nature of what you've got here. There's a good story here, about the family connection to the place and an existing business that the building helps to support." The story can be used "to give the building an economic rationale, presenting it as an evolution of something that already exists." Sometimes planners are worried about setting precedents, rejecting proposals if they worry other developments might get through on the back of these. Here, the unique context of the estate makes this less of a problem.

Our tour of the buildings complete, and with the planning context established, Tom comments on the issue: the barn faces the original farmhouse and has a very limited view—onto the road and blocked by the farmhouse at the back. He gestures the other way, across a field of cows, with woods in the distance and the manor house partly screened by trees—"the bucolic ideal! That's what you want to be looking at!" He pauses as they all take it in. "A very special place." Then he wonders aloud how to make the most of this, throwing out possibilities as they occur. He thinks about adding an extension from the back of the barn, in place of the existing Dutch barn. Or might it be possible to reuse this prefabricated addition? Though it is a much later, mass-manufactured structure, he likes the utilitarian, agricultural aesthetic. It seems "appropriate to the context" and provides a "sense of continuity." Working back from the existing site, he tries to make sense of it as a domestic space: the original barn could be used for bedrooms, while the main living space takes advantage of the views and the light. His thoughts are a continuation of the "story" suggested by the planning consultant, a response to the constraints he has outlined. The entire conversation has a hypothetical "what if" tone, but even so a consensus starts to solidify. The narratives of architects, planners, and clients are not simply told "about" places: they are the very means by which these places are made: the meeting makes the barn conceivable as a site, consolidating it as an object of possibility and constraint.

After our visit to the barn, we drive up to the gasworks. Michael gives us some historical context, partly gleaned through a recent excavation of the site by a local archaeological group. The building is Victorian, one of the few of its kind still in existence. Some of the chimney remains, and there is evidence of the original walls, but otherwise there is not much to see. We try to discern a structure, walking among the decaying walls, partly enveloped by shrubs and plants. Then we beat our way through thick undergrowth in an effort to gain a better understanding of the setting At the perimeter of the wood, we see the view to fields beyond, though by the accounts of Tom and Ian this is rather underwhelming. We walk in the other direction along a track skirting the escarpment, glimpsing views down across the valley and back to the manor. "That's where you want to be!" Looking over the woods down the valley, Tom, his mind racing forward, imagines "really stunning, interesting structures up in the trees." Then it returns to the existing reality of the gasworks: "I'm struggling with it." The location is wrong: too enclosed by undergrowth, difficult to imagine a use for the remaining structure, and too close to the

road. He wonders about a "design reason" to link it to another structure away from the road that would take in the views. Could the chimney be used as some sort of oven? Perhaps it could provide the service nucleus for some new structures? He professes to be having difficulty seeing a "natural" link, and Ian concurs: "At the moment it feels forced. It's an uphill struggle to sell it to the planners." All agree that the building is interesting and that its long-term future will best be protected if a new use for it can be found. But these aspirations, and with them the nascent project, already seem doomed by the challenge of finding a "story" that will give it a future. In the absence of such a story, the gasworks remains an interesting place, even a historically significant one, but not conceivable as a "site."

As a response to a specific place, design is imagined as a process of under-standing and recomposing the story of a site. Architects attempt to harness such stories, to use them as an inspiration, and to recompose them through design. Some loose ends are tied off, as others are left loose and new ones are created. Stories are another way in which the actual is connected to present and future possibilities. Many are conceivable, but only some are told, and still fewer become compelling. Though architects are central to this process, these narratives are significantly shaped by a range of other people and are contoured by the specific qualities of the places they occupy.

At MHW, design is understood to emerge in the space between a person and a place—more specifically, in the way this relationship is figured through the pro-fessional vision of an architect and the qualities of the sites that are the object of this gaze. Descriptions of these encounters reveal a two-way process of composi-tion. On the one hand, the architect's response is imagined as a way of tracing out the intrinsic qualities of the site, whether oriented by a "feel," a "story," or a more ostensibly pragmatic set of constraints. On the other hand, it is through the architect's work, often with others, that the site is shaped as a specific object of attention, conceivable as a locus of intervention, as a particular set of problems and constraints. In the terms developed in the first section of the book, design develops in the *space between* architect and site, which is in practice composed of multiple kinds of spaces, formed through interactions between architects and others, involving conversations and various representational technologies. Architect and site are defined and related in myriad possible ways, in these early practices of design.

The remaining sections of part three focus on stories from and about design as it happens in the office. This narrative structure echoes the architects' own sense that design possibilities are shaped by the places in which they happen. Interac-tions, as they see it, are qualitatively different on-site as opposed to in the office.

BETWEEN REALITY AND POSSIBILITY

In the late 1970s, David's life took an unexpected turn when he happened upon an article about the newly emergent area of computer microprocessing. Following "an instinct for excitement," he decided on a change of career. Later, following that same instinct, he returned to architecture (as we saw in part two). He sees a connection between his work in computer programming and in architecture in a particular approach to problem solving—as he puts it, "a willingness to be content with incompleteness." This requires faith, sustaining the patience to continue even when the solution doesn't seem obvious. "Uncertainty becomes your friend—it is pregnant with the solution."

David explains how this belief informs a particular approach to architecture. Physical form is persuasive. Confronted by things as they are, it can be hard to imagine things as they might be. On the initial visit to a site, he tries not to think too much. It's important to understand the constraints, but he doesn't want to be taken in by "the actuality of a real space":

> The space, the real space, constrains you of course. That's the discipline—the real site or the space or the existing building is the framework of possibilities, it's the narrowing of possibility, you've got to accept that. . . . I can actually visualize the spaces better in the abstract, so I don't really need to see the real space, I really don't. I almost prefer not to see it. I find it distracting. It's almost like in music if you had another noise. I know I've got to work with it, so it's important to survey it, it's important to look at it, to at least appreciate what direction the sun's coming

in, just to get a feeling that there's a nice view over there. You get a few lines of power, lines of constraint. But beyond that I prefer to visualize the spaces, because that gives you a freedom.

Architectural training instills the capacity to disengage from that seduction. Architectural imagination involves perceiving, as Murphy aptly puts it, "in the hypothetical mode, purposefully seeing things as if they were something else."[22] When David visits a building or site, he is trying to look beyond what is actually there. Site constraints are often possibilities in disguise, but only if you can see beyond the manifest reality of what is there. Detachment from the real is facilitated by a process of abstraction that is integral to design. Before David starts thinking, he likes to get a space measured up and modeled: "It's only then you start to see the possibilities."

> One of the things I find very difficult is if I go and see a house, or someone shows me and they say what they want to do. I almost perversely don't let myself think too much on the spot. There's an entrancing effect of a real space that is hard to escape. So what I always like to do is get it measured and drawn as an abstraction . . . and it's only when I see it in that abstract sense that I can really get into seeing the possibilities of what could be done. When I'm actually standing in front of the real space, I'm really reluctant to even let myself start thinking about it, in case I make a mistake or miss something or too rapidly try to find a solution. An abstracted plan gives you a detachment. That detachment, it's almost like a Zen, letting go of the illusion. When the drawing is there in front of you, you get yourself a cup of tea and then you sit and look.

David's remarks relate the movement from the actual to the possible, to the shift from site to office. At the desk this "reality" is revealed through its representational transformation. Plans are technologies of an imaginative movement away from existing circumstances.[23]

How to explain the apparent contradiction between this orientation to sites and those encountered in the preceding sections? Partly this is a matter of personal approach, the degree to which individual architects seek to channel or resist the "reality" of an existing place, seeing design possibilities arising from or in distinction to this. In these general terms the "entrancing" qualities of a site can be seen as a stimulus or impediment to the imagination, just as their physically "seductive" qualities can be regarded as imaginatively productive or stifling.

Yet in practice the opposition between the actual and the possible is integral to the negotiations in which all these architects engage across a range of sites and at various stages of design. We have already seen how site visits are characterized by oscillations between more engaged and more detached orientations, and how experiences of the "reality" of place are already highly structured by representational tools architects use—written, spoken, photographic, and so on. Once sites enter the office as representations, drawings, and models of various kinds, this process of oscillation continues. Megan makes this explicit as she describes the design process: "You need to let your mind go in the sketches, and then once you've got that idea, you start working it out in the model. It's a process of bringing ideas into physical form."

Design involves a process of realization: making ideas durable, playing with possibility by amplifying forms, as sketches or as digital and analog models. At the same time imagination works as a movement away from these emerging realities of design, detaching from the physical forms these take:

> It's that process of wondering, considering, exploring different possibilities. It's partly unconscious and partly conscious. The unconscious part is always based on your previous experience and previous knowledge, so you can start to automatically think, "oh yeah, this material," or "well, it's going to have to be this high for a desk or a chair." That automatic unconscious thing relies on your previous experience, and then the conscious part is trying to look for new things, new possibilities, and pulling ideas from that unconscious thing that might work together. You need a sense of not being limited by the constraints there, but then once you've done that, you've got to go back to what you do have, what you do know for certain, and see if it works. So it's this process of building on what you know for sure, what is in reality, and then going off and dreaming and coming back. I think they start to inform each other.

From the architect's perspective this process is accompanied by an experience of design that moves between more and less conscious orientations. From one perspective the subconscious is aligned with a movement beyond the "real": "daydreaming," "playing," "imagining," and "letting yourself go" are all seen to have creative possibility. In Keith Murphy's terms, they are ways of "seeing in the hypothetical mode," being aware of things as if they were something else.[24]

Megan makes explicit how the architectural unconscious is itself a kind of sedimentation of tacitly acquired knowledge. From this perspective, architects seek to move beyond these conventions through more conscious forms of reflection. They do this in an attempt to distance themselves from their own unconscious embodiment of professionally received wisdom, the existing "reality" of their own ways of thinking and acting.

BETWEEN INTUITION AND EXPLORATION

Within the practice there are as many approaches to design as there are designers—in fact, more than that, because the quest for novelty means that the method is never entirely resolved. As architects make a professional virtue of questioning themselves, they likewise make a virtue of questioning their methods. Tom reflects on the development of his own approach:

> I find it's a case of throwing ideas at a site and seeing what sticks, seeing what grows and nurturing it, encouraging it along. Over the years you get more experienced in knowing what's going to work and what isn't, and knowing what drawing or what model is going to be the thing that shows you whether it does or doesn't work, or what brings out the next idea. It's just saying "we've got to get everyone round this, everyone in the studio round this, and have a look." Yes, it's unpredictable. I think it retains its excitement when it's unpredictable. I'm sure there are some jobs where you are slightly reworking an old idea, and architecture doesn't come from nowhere. It's all just a slow evolution of experiences, things you've done before, things you've seen.

The process of design is difficult to explain and never exactly the same. Even so, two broad orientations prevail.

The first of these stresses the "truth" of the process through which the design emerges. Tomas finds this a particularly good way of working and is a strong advocate for this approach within the practice. For him, the best insights tend to come slowly. He demonstrates this through what he says and how he says it: often his voice has a slight hesitancy, long pauses to compose thoughts and reflect on what he has just said. He admits that for an architect he is not fluent at drawing. This has its drawbacks, but also its possibilities.

He has to take time to get into a site—and then a building—through sketching, or more usually at a computer. Design involves a kind of immersion that takes time. If the "right" design suggests itself too soon, he is suspicious:

> If you're having to negotiate all these things, are you using some kind of compass to help you make those decisions, which I think the best buildings do have. But the compass almost evolves with the design. You might think there's something prior to the process, which is going to guide you and leads to something that was predictable at the outset, whereas I find it far more exciting when the process itself reveals the end result.

Having dwelt in the tensions through a process of design, the end result—the "right" design—might, as Tomas puts it, "be full of contradictions," even as it partly reconciles these.

Tomas's description, partly an explanation of a personal methodology that has evolved and developed over almost two decades, has broader resonance among architects in the practice. What he describes as "truth to the process" involves commitment to an approach, regardless of where that might lead. Design requires the time to explore and then to find the solution that is "right," not just because it must understand and then resolve a complex set of variables but also because architects must themselves transform, thinking things never thought before in quite those terms, imagining themselves into a space that has never existed. In this vision, it is not just that the design shifts through a process of exploration. In Tomas's terms, the "compass" of design—the standards by which its honesty, truth, or success are assessed—are shifted by the process. Design as process involves faith, insofar as the moment of resolution is deferred or delayed in the hope of its arrival in an unanticipated form.

Understandings of design as process exist alongside a view of design as "intuition." Milo outlines elements of this idea as he describes his own approach to design, in relation to his personal trajectory into architecture. On a gray autumnal day, he is hunched in a thick duffel coat, against a chilling wind and then an increasingly persistent drizzle that splashes my notepad with tiny spiderwebs of running ink. Eventually we are forced to retreat inside, where, in a corner of the office, it is warmer and drier but less private.

By his own admission he is "not really an architect," by which he means that his approach to design has developed through a series of different jobs, in the absence of formal training. The latter stages of school, when he was in his late teens, coincided with "some difficult moments in life" and "a bit of rebellion." He messed up exams and dropped out of school. Later, a foundation art course gave him renewed inspiration and a sense of purpose. A photography degree followed, but he "lost his way": the course was badly run, and he realized it was not for him. Sharing a flat with architectural students, he was interested and compelled by the diversity and scope of the discipline. He spent a lot of the time he should have spent on his own work helping them out with their projects, making models and discussing architecture. After graduating, he found his way to London, working for an art fabrication company, "designing, fixing mechanisms, and planning and plotting." It was an interesting job with interesting people, but it came to a sudden end in 2008. The recession hit. The art world imploded. He found himself back home, doing "bits and pieces"—some work for his dad, a sculptor, and whatever he could find to make ends meet. Growing up in the area, he had known Tomas as a good friend of his older sister, and through their mutual involvement in local theater productions. They bumped into each other at a party, shortly after Tomas had moved the practice back to the area he grew up in. Tomas was "an interesting character and much admired," and Milo had ambitions to work with him, as he needed work, and as architecture appealed to him. Emboldened by this admiration, and by drink, he was uncharacteristically brazen in his request for work. The practice was small, still in the shed at the end of Tomas's garden, but they took him on, initially to do computer-aided design, paid on a day rate.

Perhaps this unconventional biography explains a slightly apologetic tone in much of what Milo says. Perhaps it is because this "instinctive" approach is not readily articulated through words. Whether by choice or chance, these personal circumstances help to account for a specific orientation to design that he offers less as an advocate than as an explanation of how it came to be: "I'd say I've got a very naïve approach to architecture. I think my design approach is instinctive and very led by what I can get my hands on or what I can see." By contrast to some of those with a formal training, "it's less exploratory," though the approach is not without method:

> When you develop your design reasoning and budget, reacting to site forces or whatever it is, you do your damn hardest to stick to that initial instinct . . . all the way through the design process, even when you're having to factor in the TV and a reversing circle of a fire engine. There has to be a skeleton that's true all the way through. Whether that's a response to views and light, which is one we talk about on-site all the time, or whether it's in the office, or some old rubble wall that you are reacting to or building off. You just have to be rigorous and take some skeletal elements right through. If it's lost you just end up with watered-down design.

"Instinctive" design, in these terms, is about the simple truth of an initial response to a site. The difficulty is in trusting to this response and maintaining it in the face of various pragmatic constraints that can lead to compromise. Often the best ideas emerge quickly, an immediate response to people and place. The "rigor" is in seeing it through, making choices and decisions that stay true to this vision. In contrast with an approach to design as process, there is less emphasis on unraveling, analyzing, and questioning. Design as intuition is a matter of "listening to yourself," "learning to trust a response," "to recognize and then to follow an instinct." Formal training comes with a technical language that Milo is sometimes forced to speak but in which he never feels entirely fluent. It is not so much that he doubts the validity of the approach as he does his own capacity to inhabit it truthfully.

Tom articulates sentiments that resonate with Milo's, but with the confidence of somebody who has known and actively rejected a more analytic approach—if not in general, at least as a personal method of designing. He explains that he thinks more in pictures and ideas than in words, often arriving at an idea, sure it is right, but without knowing quite where it came from. "One of the most sage things my design tutor said on the course was about training your intuition. So, a five-year-old has wonderful intuitive design, but it's about recognizing when you're onto something good and being able to run with it and develop it and also learn at what point you need to change tack or use a different medium to express it; whether you jump from a drawing to a model to a computer to a whatever, a poem."

Though Tom is skeptical of an architectural training that can retard intuition, he acknowledges that it gave him a kind of control: he learned how to "listen" to his intuition and how to express it; when to trust it and when to doubt it; how to hold on to it, in the face of the many pressures that can lead one to question an initial sense of what is right.

"Exploratory" and "intuitive" design relate to different kinds of training, skill, approach, and disposition and come more or less easily to different architects within the practice. They are related, in practice, in various complementary and contradictory ways. At times contrasting orientations drive a design on, while on other occasions personal differences can lead to clashes that cause a design to stall. Those of a more intuitive disposition may struggle to articulate the explicit rationale for an "instinct," and may dispute the need for one. At times the process of explicit questioning can seem unnecessarily time-consuming and even confusing. In contrast, those committed to a more exploratory approach to design may wish for more time for discussion and explicit reflection.

At issue are not just differences of perspective, but the very practices through which such differences are engaged and reconciled. How much time should be

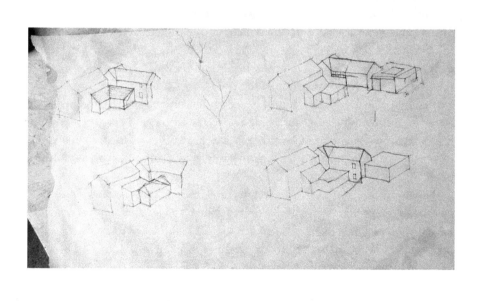

made for discussion and reflection? To what extent should design reviews seek to refine or to question? These differences are relative rather than absolute. The broad contrast between intuitive and process-driven design encompasses several related but distinct contrasts that do not neatly align in the judgments people make or the sensibilities they express. Differences within the practice are more a matter of emphasis than of kind: given that design involves intuition and exploration, to what extent should these respective tendencies prevail? If architecture is formed as a response to a site, to what extent is it useful to trust or to question the initial judgments that characterize the encounter? When does analysis liberate, and when does it paralyze the creative process?

Design involves choices between approaches but also movements between them: sometimes an architect will go with what "feels right," trusting intuition; at other times, that same architect may pause to reflect and to analyze. During a self-recorded discussion, Ronan is talking to Phil, an experienced architect who recently joined the practice, having previously worked for a number of years for a much larger company. They highlight the relationship between these different orientations to design:

> RONAN: Your first, initial, instinctive solution is often more than adequate, and it's actually quite good, but you don't always know why, and sometimes you need to go through the—
>
> PHIL: Well, it takes that time to explore it, and actually question it, and . . .
>
> RONAN: . . . Know why it's the right decision, and that takes time, sometimes, as you say, to go through all of the parameters and double-checking it, and sometimes a new solution does pop out as well, and you go with that.

At times architects will find themselves torn between tendencies: a "gut instinct" suggests one approach, while a more "rational" analysis suggests another. Varied orientations come to the fore in different moments. Someone has a strong intuition that gives impetus to a design. Later it stalls, and the design is moved on through a more reflective design review. Alternative possibilities are evolved through a process of exploration, but one "feels right." Alternatively there is a "hunch" of an idea that might work, but which then needs testing, exploring, or taking apart. Some sites suggest an approach that seems intuitively right, while others call for the exploration of a broader range of options. Then again, the orientation of clients will also be significant in determining how much time is given to the exploration of a brief, and how much explicit justification of the process is required.

ACTS OF DESIGN

Often I watch the architects at work, captivated by the process through which designs develop and evolve. Much of this happens in silence. Eyes concentrate on screens, computer-generated images of more or less realized structures moved and remade through barely perceptible movements of the mouse. The movement of hand on tracing paper seems a more literal relationship—eye-arm-hand-pencil-paper—but the question of what it is that animates the process is no less enigmatic. Asked where their designs come from, architects offer thoughtful reflections but confess their own uncertainty about a process that is both familiar and mysterious: "total magic," as Megan once put it during a group discussion in the office; "something comes from nothing!"

At times, architects' descriptions foreground their own ideas and actions as a driving force of design. Rob explains his own approach, which he connects to the craft ethos that pervades in the practice, a commitment to the exploration of materials that also carries over to his personal life. He is currently renovating and extending the Victorian terraced house in which he lives. Rob distinguishes an emphasis on making and materials from the more visually oriented approach of mainstream architecture. Design, as he sees it, "is not just pushing lines about"; "it's an exploration of a physical world that you may not be doing always in three dimensions, but your mind is in three dimensions—whether you're drawing it on the screen, on the computer, whether you're sketching it, whether you're modeling it, whether you're talking about it, you're imaging a physical three-dimensional space, and I think the mind-set, the workshop mind-set, [is that] you're exploring what that space-object might be." While Rob stresses the importance of materials as elements of this exploratory process, he describes the architect as the ultimate originator of the actions and ideas that drive it:

> The actual materials of that craft—the tools of it—need not be anything but the brain, but we use various methods to record that or track it or control it. So sketching just allows you to spew out an idea onto the paper, and then you can move on from it and try something else, evolve it. The tools that you use are only ever just a record of where we've gone, and they help us to move designs on.

Different design tools enable different forms of exploration and expression. In Rob's account these "track," "record," and "register" a set of ideas that ultimately originate in the brain of the architect.[25] Conception is an action that originates in the architect, even if its effects are registered outwardly. In an understanding that is more widely shared among architectural professionals[26] and designers,[27] the individual is imagined as the locus of creative conception. More specifically this is a divided self, with a brain distinct from yet in control of its bodily appendages.[28] The architectural self is not only made through the stories architects tell about themselves (see part two): again and again it is constructed through the routine ways in which actions are parsed along these lines: subject from object; designer from design; architect from architecture; individual from the world.

At other times, it is the design that is imagined to act on the designer. In an ethnographic account of the architects at the Office for Metropolitan Architecture, Albena Yaneva suggests, "By reacting to models and allowing themselves to be surprised . . . architects can detect the consequences of the model's actions."[29] At MHW, this basic orientation extends to the objects of design more generally. Rosy explains how the process involves a general shift, as details are worked out, elements become fixed, and the building acquires "a life of its own." As the design develops, it exerts an increasing force on what the designer can do with it: "You feed off it, and it feeds off you, and you're creating this—it's like a big organism, really." Organic metaphors of "life" connote the sense in which designs begin to act autonomously from their designers. Elements are fixed in ever greater detail, as the number and scale of design objects increases through the proliferation of models and drawings. As more and more elements are entangled, the building begins to respond to a logic of its own, as distinct from the actions and ideas of architects, including those responsible for its design. For architects, this can be associated with a positive experience of being "led." The design acquires an energy that, in Rosy's terms, the architect "feeds off." Megan makes a similar point during a group reflection on the design process: "Design starts to become an entity before it becomes a building." The architect can "guide it," "steer it," "feed it with energy," but does not in any straightforward sense control it. Extending the analogy, Rosy characterizes it as a "living thing," an essence that retains its identity even as it transforms: "It has to evolve but is there all along." The role of the architect, as she sees it, is not to impose her will on it, but to cajole and respond, drawing out and "listening" to what the design itself is telling her. As with those design interactions that happen on-site, the architect is imagined as a kind of receptor, responding to action that originates outside. Designs also exert themselves more negatively, solidifying in ways that constrain creative possibility. Architects in the practice narrate this as a matter of feeling "trapped" or "blocked."[30]

While different architects approach and experience design in distinctive ways, their accounts point to the personal shifts that accompany specific moments in the design process. Design, as they see it, is an action that they produce and a way of responding to the actions of the objects that result. The process involves oscillation: between a self that is "in control" and one that is "led." At times, this may blur their sense of self, of who they are in relation to what they have made, yet this is always ultimately recovered in the distinction that is made between the subject and object of design, the individual designer and the resulting designs. This relationship is further complicated by the mediating role that is played by a range of design tools. To ask where designs come from, it is necessarily to inquire about the media and materials through which they are formed. What, then, is the relationship between the media and the "message" of design? Between the tool and the architect who uses it?

DESIGN TOOLS

There is a new work-experience student in the practice. Milo introduces her to the office and explains what normally goes without saying, how the design process works: "We have all kinds of tools available to us." Computers are one of these tools: "There is a temptation to use them because they are easy to use and produce drawings that look like architects' drawings." In fact they are tools that have several tools within them. One of these is SketchUp, a 3D modeling program. Milo explains as he demonstrates, quickly drawing a series of 3D shapes that in only a couple of minutes begins to resemble a house: "It is very, very simple, which is a blessing and a curse—it's easy to use and quick, which makes it good for working out volumes and masses." But speed and simplicity come at the expense of precision and refinement. Milo illustrates by rendering a surface with a wood effect: "pretty rank!" he concludes with disgust. Vectorworks is another popular program. Unlike SketchUp, it's very precise: "good for working out details." But that can produce its own problems: "It's easy to get buried in the detail."

In general, computers have become an increasingly central tool of the architectural process,[31] but Milo is keen to stress the benefits of other, more analog kinds of design tools. Pencil and paper are good for sketching initial ideas and for working out problems. There's a creative interplay among mind, hand, pencil, and paper that opens up qualitatively different ways of working. "There's no such thing as a wrong drawing. Drawings help you to express things." Then there are various kinds of physical models. They tend to be slower to make but have a three-dimensional tangibility that is difficult to convey in even the most sophisticated computer program.

Milo stresses the possibilities of various tools but also explains that the same tool has different capacities for individual users: Tom likes to draw; Tomas is more comfortable using computers; Rob originally trained in product design; Milo trained as an artist and photographer and similarly likes to make things. If each tool facilitates different ways of thinking and seeing, the movement between them is an important element of the design process. If a design gets "stuck," the solution often emerges by switching tools. Milo explains: "You work out something using one thing and then go on to something else."

Some tools allow architects to work quickly; others require them to slow down. In general the process of design involves a movement from the former to the latter, with further movements between them. These shifts in the tempo of design are accompanied by a shift in scale: speed of expression is facilitated by smaller, less accurate, and less detailed ways of working. Quick design modes allow them to see "the whole," through forgoing the details. Details are important and can feed back into the overall design concept but are understood to blind the architect to the bigger picture. Tools and media that lack precision are therefore valuable. Hand sketches and the computer program SketchUp are both used in these early stages to explore "massing," the stage at which basic spatial relationships are designed and tested: "just quickly getting your head round it and testing what things look like," as Rosy puts it.

Megan explains how speed of expression is connected to the forms of exploration that characterize the design in its early phases:

> Design sketches all seem to be a really good, quick way of looking at different ideas and options, and also in terms of presenting to clients, because they're not fixed, and you can get the sense from a sketch that it's just an idea and it can change. Whereas when you start drawing things in AutoCAD [another digital design package commonly used], with sharp lines, it starts to become more fixed. SketchUp models are quite useful in terms of quickly setting up different perspectives so you can start trying things out in a quick freehand way.

The shift in speed and scale are not linear. The sequence of tools employed is not predetermined. In the office, it is usual for architects to work between different media: a quick sketch on tracing paper is used to make a computer model to "test" the relationships it develops; fitted to the "reality" of the survey, it becomes apparent that elements of the design do not work. Perhaps the architect then makes another sketch to explore other possible options. Sometimes architects make printouts of their computer models, sketching over them to exploit the different creative possibilities of this quicker, less accurate way of working.

Megan's account of the design process shows how this involves complex and sometimes intuitive shifts between different design tools:

> [I take] a lot of photographs to jog my memory when I get back to the office. The next stage is to start sketching out some options in plan and see how that works, and then possibly go back to site and reevaluate it. They start to iteratively inform each other. So being in the place, freestyle sketching where you're throwing ideas around, and then I'm waiting for the survey to come back, which will be an accurate measured survey of the topography and the existing site. So then I'll take those ideas and put that onto the survey, and some of them might not work or some of them might work actually really well. Then you start bringing these different tools in. Some are more free, and some are records. They start to inform each other. You have to keep going back, juggling between them. And then I'll probably go into a 3D exploration because of the slopes on the site. It's difficult to imagine the reality of that if you don't have something to work with, and it's easier to work things out if it's flat.

Tools exist alongside each other, offering a range of starting points. They are not so much ways of generating different perspectives "on the same thing" as ways of making different kinds of things. Different media result in distinct outcomes (model, sketch, plan), through which previous objects are reinterpreted and recontextualized. The space between these media is regarded as productive, precisely insofar as each raises the question of its relation to the others.[32]

The effect of designs constantly shape-shifting as computer models on a screen can be captivating; designs can quickly seem "too real" and are said to "suck you in." Eyes, as the architects put it, "go." The screen has a hypnotic effect, flicking between scales, views, and options. Sometimes, toward the end of the day, it is possible to see this effect on architects as they emerge from their computer screens: eyes look vacant, exhausted; faces, disoriented, tell of minds still elsewhere. The sociologist and philosopher Richard Sennett suggests that "mentally we need to let go of a problem, usually only temporarily, in order to see it afresh."[33] For architects at MHW, the switch between media is a way to facilitate a movement away from the design object that ultimately brings them back to it: letting go in one sense, they can in another sense hold the design more securely, grasping the object that appears more clearly through their detachment from it.

Through their interactions with design tools, the boundary between the world and the architect shifts At various points in the process, thoughts can seem contained within the imagination of a singular mind, to be latent in the movements of hand and pencil, or as a movement that is detached from the mind that more or less consciously controls this process. The computers architects use can likewise seem so much a part of the way they think that they forget the machine is there. In the process of design, mind, hand, mouse, and screen can seem animated by a single force. Acts of design extend the perceived boundary of the architect beyond the physical limits of the body. It is not so much that the architectural self is dissolved, as that its limits are seen to expand and contract, extended and curtailed by the various media being employed.

DIGITAL ROMANTICS

In the office, computers are central to a range of tasks. The architects' days are mostly spent at screens: checking and responding to e-mail, finding "precedent" images that provide the inspiration for design, researching building materials and new technologies, and most centrally of all using one of a range of computer-aided design packages. Watching them at work, I observe screens flicking perpetually between these programs and tasks. Observing their movements, I find it clear that these architects are thoroughly digital humans, their capacities of thought and action indissoluble from digital technologies that saturate this working environment.[34]

Rosy explains: "It's a dialogue between hand sketching and computer. It's quite important, because you learn—you know, they're each good for different things, so the millimeter-perfect element of it, and [using CAD] you can drop scaled furniture in and know exactly how big it's going to be and that kind of thing, that's quite important, but at the same time that dilutes the creative element of it, and so you need to use both in conjunction with each other."

Most of those in the practice are aged in their twenties and thirties and have used CAD throughout their student and professional lives as architects. Still, digital technologies are often seen as an intrusion into the working life. Nostalgia is frequently evident in accounts of more analog ways of working in a time they never knew. Why, then, does a conceptual distinction between the digital and the analog remain so central to their understanding of these design processes? And how, given the central role of computers, to explain their ambivalence toward working with them?[35]

In the car on the way back from Stroud, Roisin is reacting to the exhibition we have just been to see. Hosted by a local art cooperative, it presented projects by final-year students at a nearby university. Students had been allocated various disused buildings and unused sites, with the brief of developing these for social and economic regeneration. Most of the practice came along—a lunchtime "jaunt," but also a chance to engage with new ideas and approaches, perhaps even to identify new talent to join the practice. Roisin concedes the projects are "technically good," but is critical of a lack of variation in the proposed designs. "Way too much computer render!" she comments, her exasperation reflecting a broader complaint about the ubiquitous use of digital design tools. Others agree. She is critical of the sense of aesthetic conformity this produces: the projects "look the same." Her more profound frustration is that computer-aided design often acts to "deaden the creative process." Later, as I prompt her, she elaborates:

> What was [striking in] those projects for me was . . . the absence of hand drawing and of hand communication, of actually holding a pencil and letting it just go off on a line instead of having something very regimented on a computer and allowing the computer to draw your lines for you. I think that's also the issue with a lot of projects where the landscape doesn't work with the building, because you haven't used your pencil to get that soft line and the soft edge that nature has but a building doesn't.

Resistance to computers is partly a reaction to what they displace: drawing by hand is associated with a particular way of working and is said to produce a different quality of work. As Roisin sees it, design that emanates from the hand is "less regimented," more "natural."[36] By making the process easier, computers can also make it less thoughtful. Having a computer "drawing the lines for you," as Roisin describes it, constrains her own creative capacities. Her thoughts echo anxieties central to the profession since computer-aided design was first embraced in the 1960s:[37] seen as synonymous with standardization and rationality, digital design was imagined to displace the creativity of the human individual. Architect and site were seen as subservient to the determining logic of the computer, the embodiment of voices, judgments, and assumptions from other times and places. Resistance was to control by a seemingly foreign form of expertise.[38]

Roisin is not alone in her insistence that architectural design should constrain the role of digital design in order to retain the human element:

> Computers have a purpose, and that is to compute. They're fine for technical drawings where you have to be very technical, straight edged,

straight lined. But I think for the earlier stages of a design it's a lot nicer to just draw something and draw it fifty times. You don't draw it fifty times on the computer. You never do. You draw it two or three times, that's it. If you're drawing with some tracing paper and a pencil, you'll draw fifty, sixty drawings, and then you'll finally get to something that just feels right.

Each sketch is quick, but designs made quickly are also less precise. Accordingly, sketching is associated with a way of working that leaves more possibilities open for longer.

With your hand you can draw a nice curve, you can draw a nice angle, you can draw nice things. But then the second you take that into the computer it becomes something physical in a physical space and it has this presence and then it's there, and you're like "hmm, how did that get there? Oh well, it's there, so I may as well leave it there."

As the "reality" of the site is sometimes said to "seduce," so in this account is the reality of a computer model. It appears to have a precision and presence, an actuality that, as Roisin sees it, blinds her to other imaginative possibilities. Sketching, by contrast, is regarded as a more thoughtful process: "When you're still within your drawing you're still considering, and I think the second you step into the computer you stop considering in a way and you get onto a more regimented, 'this is now a planning set,' 'this is now a tender set.'" The architectural theorist Horst Bredekamp proposes that drawing by hand is a way for architects to move beyond "articulated ideas," producing lines that "obey their creator but astonish them."[39] In his account the architect is in control even as he or she is deliberately seeking surprise. Roisin's description echoes this understanding of sketching in a contrast with CAD: a kind of design that evades the control of the architect and yet never really surprises. Designs, being "regimented" by the computer, are seen as different in ways that are ultimately always predictable.[40]

Roisin's account of the relationship between CAD and sketching reflects broader discussions of the relationship between digital and analog media. While these media are often used in tandem, architects' sense of the qualities of each are made through a series of contrasts drawn between them. An understanding of computer-aided design as "rational" relates to what Yanni Loukissas describes as "changing notions of human presence,"[41] specifically a novel awareness of the individual architect as a unique locus of creativity. "Working by hand" has a romance, projected from the frustrations of working on computers.

"There are no wrong sketches," Milo asserts. In the practice, architects describe how pencil sketches have personally distinctive styles, errors and imprecisions that remind their author of the "as if" nature of what is proposed. A sketch is a realization of an idea.[42] It presents a possibility that engenders its own caveats: when architects look at their own or others' sketches, they are aware they are assessing a proposition that is provisional. The sketches need to be interpreted, thought about, made sense of.

Celebrations of sketching and disenchanted accounts of CAD both make present a distinction between terms that are often conflated: the digital is not the same as the virtual,[43] if we understand this to mean those possibilities that exist outside or beyond the "actuality" of things immediately and tangibly to hand.[44] On the one hand, these architects ascribe CAD models a "reality" that is associated with a diminishment of virtual capacity: computer-generated images are already resolved, made compatible and commensurate with one another, stabilized as a digital object that requires less imaginative work.[45] On the other, the virtual potential of the sketch is both in the detail it leaves out and the incompatibilities it creates. Imagination is needed to fill in the details and connect the gaps.

Critiques of digital design voiced by the architects at MHW should not be heard too literally as an outright rejection of the media. They represent a way of being attentive to the limitations of digital design in relation to the other tools and media through which designs take shape. Digital design is said to bring problems but also possibilities. It has different capacities in the hands of different people.[46] Martin, a Part II qualified architect in the process of working for his Part III, explains this via a contrast between the two directors of the practice:

> Tomas uses the computer the same way Tom uses the sketch paper. He opens it up and says, "windows here, let's have a big oversailing roof here and a bit of a plinth here and the patio there," or something. He's very good at using the computer as a sketch tool. He's got a unique take on that, that we don't. Whereas Tom is really good at sitting down in the evening and getting a bit of paper and then he'll work it out.

For some, hand sketching is associated with a fluency and freedom that for others is more readily associated with the use of CAD.

In the late 1970s, David's decision to forsake a career in architecture for one in computer programming was partly informed by a digital utopianism of the time:[47] the thought, within and beyond architecture, that a digital revolution could open up a more equal society and more sustainable environmental future. Drawn to computing as a medium of experimentation, he developed a facility with code that now informs his use of CAD. While critical of particular pro-

grams, he is resistant to romantic dismissals of digital design that equate the technology with how it is routinely used:

> I don't often work anymore with pencil and paper. I think an architect's business is to create buildings, not drawings. I know a lot of people would dispute that: at times it would seem as if the intention was to create a beautiful drawing, and the building then comes across as an extra. But although it's satisfying to do a nice drawing, it's the building that's going to be the test of whether you've been successful. So if my drawings are a bit sterile because they're done on the computer, well then too bad.

Design tools, digital or analog, are means to the end of realizing something else: a building. While they may allow different creative possibilities, David sees no deterministic link between media and outcome. In the office, critical orientations to digital design exist alongside more celebratory understandings of the creative possibilities that computers open up: more vivid realizations, a better ability to explore beyond the manifest reality of a site.

Architects narrate the virtual potential of these media in different ways but share a sense of the qualitative difference between digital and analog ways of working. Also shared is an understanding of the productive potential of working between these. Martin describes how the process of design involves a fluid movement between media: "We use a variety of mediums. You can do a quick Photoshop visualization of where it is. You can use SketchUp to make a 3D thing. You can then rotate around and get a good idea of the form. You can labor on a computer a bit. You can just do a hand sketch." Virtual possibilities arise as architects work between and across media, realizing designs that operate together more as a collection than a system. The difficulty and the possibility are in imaginatively reconciling what ultimately remain distinct: different starting points that require and enable reinterpretation of the "reality" to which a design responds. In this final analysis, resistance is less to any specific media than to the systemic collapsing of these differences. Much of their design practice emerges in the imaginative spaces between digital and analog media.

BETWEEN ARCHITECT AND CLIENT

Rob is trying to describe the attributes that make for a good architect:

> I'd say it's quite selfless from a designer's point of view, in that a good designer should really just be a vehicle that responds to the client's wishes, even if the client doesn't know what they want. So you're quite often teasing those ideas out of them and pitching your own ideas for them to grab hold of. I think that's very difficult, but quite key to recognize, the client as the ultimate designer.

These are attributes of good design that are commonly expressed in the practice.[48] They emerge by explicit contrast to the "egotistical" approach of celebrity architects, the linked images of architect as all-seeing expert and as "artist hero":[49]

> It's said in history that the best thing to do is for the client to give the architect a load of money and then go on holiday for a year. And I think that might create one fantastic building, but the next one that an architect did, if it was exactly the same process, you very quickly run out of ideas or start doing stuff that wasn't very original because you're only drawing on your own likes and desires rather than the client's point of view.

Clients, in Rob's description, are not a constraint on the personal creativity of the architect: they represent a creative opportunity, disrupting the assumptions of architects, introducing ideas into a process that can otherwise become circular and repetitive.

If good architecture is a matter of understanding the client's view, this has implications for the kind of person architects should strive to be:[50] In common with others in the practice, Rob emphasizes the virtues of "selflessness" along with a range of associated personal traits: a lack of ego, sensitivity, modesty, and the ability to admit that one is wrong. Personal opinions are deliberately suppressed, so that the architect is able to register and respond to others' ideas. As a general philosophy, the approach is not particularly distinctive; indeed it could even be seen as a cliché of recent architecture.[51] As a practice it is not easy to do.

The approach does not involve a literal translation of client opinion, but a commitment to take such opinion seriously as the starting point of design. Roisin describes this in relation to the importance of "knowing the person":

> When somebody explains something to you, there's a number of ways of actually interpreting that. And with couples it's really interesting, because one person says something and the other person doesn't think that. In that initial time when you speak to somebody, there's a tension there, if there's something that's not quite right for both of them. I think it's important to unravel those things and question what is the brief for both of them combined, and then you can start to work out special spaces for either of them or both of them, depending on what kind of characters they are. It's a bit weird, but we do have to think in that way, I think. It's important to understand relationships and people to be able to actually do this initial bit and get the right brief, and then question them, make sure that that's what they want. If somebody says they want an extension to their house, do they want an extension to their house? What is the purpose of this thing, what's this project going to bring? Then I guess, from that, thinking about what's feasible on that place or in that site, or if that is the right site.

Clients may hold contradictory opinions, may disagree with one another, and are often unsure what they want. The process of drawing out these understandings requires interpretation and skill. What clients do not say may be as revealing as what they do. Judgment is also needed to triangulate between the different elements that compose a brief: to what extent should clients' explicit wishes be taken at face value? How do these relate to the possibilities that architects may see within the site? Questioning clients is important to understand them: probing beyond what they see to try to understand what they really think, provoking them to be explicit about elements of their lives they may have given little conscious thought to.

Client attitudes are not just drawn out discursively. Often clients are encouraged to create actual or virtual scrapbooks, visual collages that are used to convey preferences in relation to architectural styles, materials, use of color, and décor. Revealing in their own right, these are then part of a dialogue that is simultaneously visual and verbal. Scrapbooks are discussed in meetings, preferences explored and interrogated, responded to verbally and then through subsequent designs.

Initial client meetings are often held on-site, frequently the client's house, in order to better appreciate the relationship between the client (or clients) and the space in which the project will take place. Martin explains: "It's funny, because it's kind of intuitive and you don't really think about it. But you look around the house and you *see.*" Furniture and décor give clues to existing aesthetic sensibilities. Evidence of domestic routines and ways of using space may be obvious to the architect, while too obvious to the client to put into words. During these visits, the architects are observing these unarticulated signifiers of attitudes and ways of life, and also seek to make this explicit through questions and conversations. "Where do you normally eat? Do you do a lot of cooking? Where do you take your coats off? Where do you sit when friends come round?"

Architectural interventions are, by definition, responses to spatial problems. During these visits architects are also attempting to understand awkward relationships between people and place. Sometimes a response will help to draw this out: "the kitchen seems quite disconnected from the rest of the house"; "it seems you spend most of your time in the living room, but it's dark, and the best views are on the other side." In these early interactions, the architect attempts to animate and amplify a client response, and then to be receptive to the understandings that arise.

Often the initial meeting will involve one or both of the directors, though the detailed design work will be undertaken by others. Martin explains how clients are made imaginatively present even in the absence of direct interaction.

> Sometimes you don't meet the clients, so we have a filtered version from [the directors] Tom and Tomas of what they're like. So it's hard for us to say, because we haven't physically met them, but generally we do pick up on aesthetics, character. And we all have quite a good picture of what Tom or someone means when they say that. So I think we use a kind of coded thing in the office to get to the nub of what the client's like.

If selfless design involves a commitment to see from the client's point of view, differences between the architect's own life and the life of their client must be imaginatively overcome. By virtue of their education and training, architects occupy a social position that they mostly self-define as middle class. However, those in the practice are predominantly in their twenties and thirties, poorly remunerated relative to other professions, and particularly relative to their clients. Most live in modest-size rented accommodation. The worlds they imaginatively occupy during their professional lives as designers are not those they occupy in their personal lives. On one occasion I am watching Ronan, working on the computer to detail a new-build house. He lives in a small terraced Victorian house and describes, as he works, the suspension of disbelief that has to occur: imagining yourself into the mind-set where you, as a couple, are occupying a five-bedroom house, and the way you might use that space. "It's sometimes difficult to think yourself into how you would want to use that much space, but you have to try."

David highlights how selfless design forces architects out of a professional discourse and the circularities this can entail:

> It's the language and the conversation one has with clients, the interior-to-exterior interchange and interface, that I find more interesting than the interior dialogue [with other architects]. So "tectonics" and "massing" and things like this [he is referring to architectural terms with broad currency, and which are routinely used within the office] I find, well, I can take it or leave it to some extent. The conversations I find most stimulating are those that I have, say, with a client, because I think you can bring something to the situation which is really unique and which is what you've spent all this time thinking about. The conversation one has between architects is kind of dispute, controversy, and whatever, whereas the language you have with a client is almost therapeutic. They're asking you to help them. They're not interested in whether it's "tectonic" or not, but they might be very interested in the outcome, in terms of the house they are going to live in.

The approach is, as David sees it, "therapeutic," in a number of linked senses. The architect acts as a kind of therapist for the client, understanding the client's life in order to improve it through design. Self-fulfillment for the architect derives from the validation that comes from the feeling of having, however modestly, contributed to allowing the client to live in different and more fulfilling ways. At the same time, the imperative to design for others, to see the client as the ultimate arbiter of a building's success, disrupts the assumptions of professional architecture.

Initial interactions carry through to a set of design practices, in which the architect's efforts to understand are the basis for an architectural response. This involves a qualitative shift in orientation: from passive to active. But the shift is only relative. Designing selflessly, architects sees their own actions prefigured and configured by the ideas and actions of their clients.

When these architects describe this selfless approach to design, they recognize they are describing an ideal that is not always, or even ever, fully realized. Megan tells me how the ideal of commitment to the client can be compromised by the practical constraints of commercial design:

> What would be nicer would be to be in a place where you're exploring things for yourself, and what you would do there and what you really do believe is the best thing, and then having the means of communicating that to the client, obviously bearing in mind their requirements and tastes and so on. And it's that thing—we had that phrase in the consultation of going on a journey together and discovering things that neither of you necessarily knew were a priority or a possibility, so it's like finding that together. But often it feels quite distant. On some projects I've never spoken to the person, I've got no idea, and all I know is what the director has told me that they do and don't want. So where's that process of going on a journey and finding something together?

During early interactions there are various reasons why an architect's understanding of a client's attitude, approach, and aesthetic sensibilities may be less full than the architect might wish. Clients may be unable to articulate what they want. Sometimes there are misunderstandings. On occasion clients change their mind—their circumstances change, or their views shift as the design or even building evolves. Frequently clients are internally conflicted, unsure, or indecisive. Couples might start a build with intractably different visions of what they want to achieve. There are also structural constraints to understanding client views. Budgets and hence time are finite. It is not always possible for all those involved with a project to meet the client directly. Architects in the practice also recognize that personal limitations play a part: not all are equally good at eliciting and then registering what a client wants. The "chemistry" with clients may not always be good.

Even where design is oriented by a selfless attitude, it can result in a response that is at odds with what clients anticipate or imagine that they want. Roisin describes how this might play out:

> The projects I work on I really imagine, "Okay, that family is going to live there. How are they going to live there?" and then try and work out the design based on that and what we think would be best for them. Because often somebody will say to you, "Oh, I don't want that like that," "Oh, I'm not sure about that." Then you just have to do it and say we really believe that this is the best design that we can possibly have, and it's funny how sometimes that's received, but often in the end it does materialize into something that's really amazing. And then the clients are like, "Right, okay, yeah, we know what you were saying." I think you

have to trust in yourself sometimes, trust in what you would have liked to see if you were to have your own place. What would you imagine is the perfect thing to have in your home?

As I discuss the design process with Tom, he tells me that "design is giving people what they need and pretending it's what they want." He is joking, but the comment—an architectural witticism with broader currency—has a kernel of truth.[52] He elaborates this himself: "It's a challenging interaction. Clients can tell you what they think but not what to draw." Designs, as he sees it, are produced as part of a dialogue with a client. They must recognize and respond to what the client says and thinks, but should not be beholden to this. Though the opinions of clients are important, an overly literal response is unlikely to produce a good building.

On another occasion Tom distinguishes selfless design from the idea of consumer choice. In advance of a client meeting, the architect doing the detailed design work has put together a number of possible designs that he has labeled as "options." As Tom flicks through the draft, he is keen on a number of the designs but emphatic in his dislike of the way they are presented: "These are not 'options'! I hate that word!" Architects, as he sees it, should believe in their designs and persuade their clients of this belief. During an interview, Martin highlights a potential conflict between the views of clients and commitment to the principles of good design: "We're not compliant architects, 'Oh, you want this, therefore we'll draw it up.' We're very good at going back to first principles in design, and does this really work, is this what you need, have you thought about this?" In such contexts, the architect may push a client, in the conviction of the need to persuade the client of a design that is "right." Architects in the practice acknowledge the pressure to cede to client opinion and the compromises that are sometimes required, but they stress, in the final instance, that commercial imperatives and "client choice" should not override all other considerations.

What these architects describe as "selfless design" does not connote the erasure of self but the ideal of a self that is open and receptive. The process of design involves interactions with clients, in which the architect's own orientations oscillate between different dispositions. Reception is a prelude to a more active form of projection, in the form of a design. A more receptive orientation may then again prevail during subsequent design consultation meetings. At times, architects see themselves as conduits, channeling, directing, and responding to the client through design. At other times, the actions and ideas of the architect are sharply delineated from those of the client, as contrasting and even conflicting perspectives. Selfless design is not incompatible with the notion that good design involves moments of solipsistic thought, the creative freedom that comes from "cutting off" from the places and people to which the design responds.

LISTEN: CHANNELING OR IMPOSING IDEAS?

Three of the architects are discussing the relationship between architect and client.

> MEGAN: It's tricky to work out how much to just channel what a client wants or to come up with an idea that we feel strongly about. Would that just be arrogant? And what is our role, actually? Who are we representing?
>
> TOMAS: Are we helping them channel their ideas and design, or are we imposing our design and ideas on them? What do you think, Martina?
>
> MARTINA: I think it depends on the project and on the client as well. For example, on one of our recent projects the client had a different opinion, and then we came with an idea that was so strong for them, and they decided they liked it. But sometimes I think it's really being arrogant, I think there is no general way to do it. It always depends. Well, it also depends on the site and a lot of other factors as well. So you need to be feeling something altruistic. What is the best thing in this situation for everybody: for the place; for the surrounding people; for the clients? I think it always depends on lots of things. What do you think, Tomas?
>
> TOMAS: I wonder if there's something about being real and truthful—to a client and to a set of needs. If you're doing a library for

a school, maybe having something that's an inspiring place to learn and read and hang out does call for something that's a bit different: like a little amphitheater or something, that encourages performance, and isn't just a library with a set of desks that people can read at. Whereas maybe on someone's house, making a fancy façade just for the sake of a façade being fancy. . . . And it's like, "to what end? To what is that being truthful?" I suppose that's what I quite liked about your design, Megan [on a recent project]: it was being truthful to the site, and it was kind of saying "let's acknowledge both the woods and the rest of the land" by pointing these two things equally in their directions. I don't think it's just design for design's sake.

MEGAN: But also I think the other thing was, this project in particular, they're based in London, and it's not just about this site for them; it's about balancing different aspects of their life.

MARTINA: And I think there was also some kind of tension in the building, with these two opposite buildings they were creating, and maybe she just wants to create something very peaceful so that she can just concentrate on her work. She wants to have it clean just to work there, so the building is just a cover.

BETWEEN ONE AND ONE ANOTHER

Design emerges through interactions with clients. It is also centrally shaped through interactions with others in the office.

The "Friday review" is the weekly slot where designs are discussed by the whole practice. During one of these sessions, Ronan is presenting ideas he has been working on. He starts by explaining the brief, which is simple: there is a house at the head of a wooded valley; the house doesn't make the most of its site and isn't well adapted to the needs of the clients who live in it, a middle-aged couple with older children. He notes, in passing, that they own the local builders merchants, a detail that is not elaborated but, in the absence of a fixed budget, seems intended to convey the likelihood the budget will be generous. He illustrates the site with plans and maps, gesturing and pointing as he talks. As he describes what he shows, he shuffles and rearranges papers, moving between a map of the site, plans of the building, and images of the site. What Ronan shows through this description is a building on a steep slope, "marooned" at the edge of a large plot. The views are "fantastic," but windows and rooms are configured so that the views are rarely seen. The existing building is "uninspiring." Ronan shows us some of his ideas. My untrained eyes focus on the elegant tidiness of his pencil sketches, but Ronan doesn't see this: looking at his plans and sketches, he is looking at an idea that doesn't quite work, a solution he can't yet see.

Tom picks up where Ronan has left off, engendering a collective sense of excitement. Voices are raised in animation: "So what are the options? Shall we just brainstorm?" The modus operandi of the exchange is itself negotiable: "Shall we draw it or talk it?" Tom asks. In fact, the ensuing interactions meld both seamlessly: discussion is mediated by Tom's drawing. Quick pencil lines act as a focal point, condensing different ideas and responding to things being said. Conversation generates drawing; drawing elicits conversation.[53] These sketches and dialogues are oriented by what Robin Evans terms "the principle of reverse directionality": to make real what is not, rather than to represent what already exists. Discussion weaves abstracted spatial terminologies with considerations of various kinds of pragmatic constraint, speculation about what the client wants, and analysis of various elements of the site—financial, topographical, the existing structure, the client's brief, and so on. There is talk of "the language" and "grammar" of the building, the "tectonic" approach. Ideas are turned over, suggestions multiplied. Sometimes an idea gains traction—a thought is exciting, and others see possibilities: "nice," "I like it." Alongside this, there are moments of doubt. Someone sees a problem with an idea, or there is disagreement as to whether something will work; ineffable shifts in conversation help build a collective sense of what is possible and what is not.[54]

Ronan's various proposals are discussed, assessed, and analyzed. Taking these apart, conversation identifies elements that might be developed, but also problems. There are different views but no strong consensus. The conversation draws in different opinions but seems to lack direction. Voices collide—people talking together, words overlapping, the thread difficult to discern. The process of sketching helps to move conversation on, but without obvious purpose. Some designs are abandoned halfway through, as their limits become apparent. Designs are literally cast off, half finished, as piled-up scraps of tracing paper—redundant before they are finished. Tom's pencil is the main point of reference, focusing eyes and eliciting ideas; others also sketch sporadic responses of their own.

The common understanding that designs are made through "breakthroughs" may be a misleading characterization of this longer, more complex, more quotidian, indeed more collaborative process of negotiation.[55] Ideas do not emerge all at once, but through a gradual process of realization: conversations, sketches, and models, through which possibilities bifurcate and focus. Even so, the process is never straightforwardly cumulative: profoundly transformative insights can arise in a moment, and not all moments are of equal significance.

Nothing more than a suggestion by Rob: "Could the road come up from here instead?" he wonders, tracing a line on the plan. A sentence and the gesture of a finger on a plan. There is evident excitement as new possibilities build. Their sense of breakthrough reflects and produces a qualitative shift in the way they interact. Suddenly all are speaking, quickly, excitedly, as if animated by a single force. Sentences begun by one and ended by another—words and thoughts lined up along the same trajectory. Tom is sketching quickly and with obvious purpose—abstract shapes in planned form; arrows to indicate relations between spatial elements. A few lines and some conversation, and suddenly there is broad consensus. Endless details will need resolving, but broad agreement has been reached. "That's good," "Brilliant."

Quickly the assembled architects disperse back to their desks. Ronan remains to tidy up the plans and drawings that are scattered on the desk. Intended to make things happen, these images are also a document of what has happened,[56] a record of the meeting and a source to which Ronan will return as he further develops the design.

I wonder if he might feel a sense of wasted effort. He's been working on plans for days, time that now seems pointless. But he is sanguine and sees this as part of the process: "If you're working on a design, you get so sucked in. But someone who hasn't seen it just says: 'So what if I do that?'"

At MHW, design is "collaborative"—a term that is used repeatedly. It captures their understanding of the positive potential of working collectively. Rob is explicit about the benefits of this way of working:

> It's very collaborative and open. That does have a massive influence on the designs that come out of the office. I think they're very well-rounded and very well considered as a result of that. A lot of discussion about what's right, what's appropriate, what are the options. And projects do get a lot of brain time. It's obviously usually one person taking that design forward, but in the design discussions ten people thinking about it for half an hour is quite a lot of fresh minds thinking on it. It's a powerful engine.

The resulting "layering of perspectives" is understood to produce a "richness" and "nuance." Alongside these collectively articulated sentiments, there remains an anxiety that collective design engenders its own problems.

The ideal of collaborative and collective design is articulated alongside an apparently contradictory set of ideals that relate to the importance of "personal vision." Megan makes this ideal explicit, as she describes the characteristics of a good architect: "Some of the architects' work . . . that I admire, and I think, 'wow, this is amazing,' they're so focused, you know, it's like they're single-minded, absolute, this is it, and bringing all their varied knowledge from all the different aspects of their life or varied streams of investigation all into that one thing, and it all comes back to that." There is a phrase that sometimes gets used in the office: "Hold on tightly, let go lightly." It captures a central tension: stick to your ideas doggedly, but let them go if others' prove better.

Much of the design work in the office takes place through movements between the seemingly conflicting ideals of collaborative design and personal vision. Architects negotiate the relationship between their own and others' ideas through more and less formally choreographed moments where people in the practice come together. The office architecture facilitates these collaborations. Ten people at ten desks in one room; a phone call comes in and everybody hears. "It's important to know what's going on," Milo explains. Weekly office design reviews are a chance to present and debate projects. More informally, conversations take place in the regular to-ing and fro-ing between desks. Design problems arise, and the solution seems unclear. Over-absorbed in the detail, architects on occasion experience a "loss of perspective" that makes them unable to see what they have done. "Can I borrow your eyes?" they sometimes ask. The sight of others is enlisted to see more clearly what has become obscured by detail and over-absorption.

Design involves interacting and collaborating with others, but also extended periods working alone.[57] Good design is held to necessitate moments of concentration, a state enabled by detachment from others in the office. While other people can help, they can also distract. Some of the architects achieve this by using headphones with white noise or by listening to music. For others, detachment becomes a habit that is learned—as both the prerequisite for and effect of concentration: imaginatively inhabiting the building that is the object of their design, they block out the distractions of people and things more immediately to hand.[58]

In their relationships to others in the practice, architects must be able to project their own perspective but also to receive and respond to the perspectives of others. Rob sees the ability to balance these imperatives as a quality instilled in part through the architectural degree: "that's actually one of the trainings of a designer, an architect: to take the criticism and use it positively, and not take it personally as a personal attack." Through architectural "crits," students learn the ability to take and receive criticism.[59] As Rob makes explicit, this involves a capacity to separate criticism of a design from criticism of the designer who produced it.

"The word alone, crit, is a stab of negativity," writes the architectural theorist and practitioner Jeremy Till.[60] Looking back on their time as students, many of those in the practice recall the brutality of these sessions. Rosy recently completed her Part I and still remembers vividly how, for her, the crits "literally involved blood, sweat, and tears." Late nights struggling to put together a project, exhausted from sleeplessness and work, before the project—sometimes only partially completed—is subjected to the views of tutors and other students. Sometimes students are "ripped to shreds" through the verbal attacks of tutors and fellow students. Many in the practice express ambivalence toward a pro-

cess involving brutality, even cruelty, that can crush creativity and make people deeply unhappy.

Even as he is likewise ambivalent, Phil highlights how this training leads, more positively, to the development of personal resilience and toughness:

> It hardens you up a bit. . . . I remember some crits, some people who got quite upset. You've spent quite a bit of time designing something, and then you might go into a crit, and you might have a tutor that just completely rubbished everything that you'd done. And I know some people got quite upset, and yes, in some cases it was quite a hard process. But, as I say, it did harden you up to that. At least you got yourself more prepared, and ready to take those knocks if and when they happened.

Through crits, architects learn to stand up to others, but also to project ideas of their own. Phil continues:

> If you think you've got a good idea there, then you should be positive about it, and be prepared to defend why you've made those design decisions and explain them. This is the thing about architecture and art, it's all very subjective. Everybody's got a view, and I suppose, there's never a very strict right or wrong way; I think there's multiple solutions to a problem. If we're designing a house for a site, we've come up with this option, but there's numerous other types of options that could probably work, but it's explaining your thought processes and the way you've got to that stage.

Architects learn to project their perspectives as justifications for their own designs and as critical responses to the designs of others: "You can be very positive and encourage people, but being able to negatively critique somebody's work, I think, is good."

During design reviews architects must reconcile receptivity to other possibilities with a commitment to their own vision. Good design, as they see it, results from a process that steers the difficult path between two alternative hazards: of taking on too many perspectives, to the point where a design becomes "compromised," "incoherent," or "lacking in clarity"; and of failing to respond to others, lacking nuance, interest, and complexity. In order to do this, architects shift between different kinds of relations to others in the practice, and accordingly must shift their relationship to themselves: sometimes single-minded; at others collaborative; on occasion as passionate advocates of their own ideas; in other instances deferring to the visions of others; sometimes selflessly responding to client and site and forgoing ego; at others demonstrating belief in themselves, faith in their own ideas.

FRIENDS, COLLEAGUES, COMPETITORS

Among these architects, the relationship between self and other is inflected by contradictory professional norms: collectively shared ideas about the importance of collegiality, camaraderie, friendship, and collaboration exist alongside ideas about skill and creativity as individual qualities of specific people.

Megan describes how close working relationships develop through the practice of design:

> I think they're all quite strong characters in the office and people I'd like to be spending nine hours of my day with every day. They're all friends, apart from a couple, maybe, who are more colleagues. The thing that holds us all together is that thing that comes back to the making and the material, so that's the thing that's brought us all here, that's the thing that Tom and Tomas see as their passion. And that's the thing that attracted everyone, and the thing that's kind of holding us all together.

The practice directors see these relationships as important and put time into cultivating them. Social activities include the Friday lunch, and occasional but regular office day trips. On one occasion they go to visit the conservation masons working at Gloucester cathedral; on another they spend a day kayaking in the Black Mountains. After work on Fridays, staff often go to the pub, sometimes followed by pizza. The activities and managerial approach are obviously of the current era, but the underlying ideal has echoes of nineteenth-century arts-and-crafts thinkers, who celebrated the collective endeavor of gothic craftsmen. Foremost among these, William Morris celebrated the "collective genius" of individuals acting together in free association: "every pair of hands is moved by a mind which is in concert with other minds, but freely, and in such a way that no individual intelligence is crushed or wasted. And in such work not like ants or live machines, or slaves to a machine—but like men."[61]

Megan highlights how friendships are made through the physical process of making. Design literally brings people together.[62] As she sees it, a collective ethos, a belief in the importance of making as a creative stimulus to design, anchors these interactions. At the same time, design practice forges social relations that extend beyond the narrow confines of work. Whether as friends or as colleagues, close working relations among those in the office are seen as integral to processes of design and construction:

> It's interesting, because everyone has different interests and different collections of knowledge, which they've got through the different projects they've worked on. If you're not sure about something, you get to know who to go and speak to in the office, because someone invariably has done something similar before. I think the more there can be a friendship and a common shared interest and ambition, the more you're going to collaborate and the more you're going to ask people's opinions and advice and be willing to share your views on things. It's fundamental.

Close working relations are integral to the architectural negotiation of a complex ecology of knowledge. These relations are also acknowledged to be beneficial to good design, enabling critical disagreements. Rob explains:

> We have a lot of fun doing it, and we're not afraid to disagree with people. It's never going to be a conflicting element. It's not going to be seen as a personal attack. I like you as a person, but this is just a design idea that I don't like. I think that's something that's sometimes hard to separate, but that's actually the training of a designer or architect. So take the criticism; take it and use it positively and don't take it personally.

In some cases, personal relationships pre-date professional relationships: Milo knew Tomas as a child, as a friend of his older sister; Tomas is the son of David; Tom and Tomas met at architectural school, long before they began working together; Megan and Tomas went out with each other and subsequently remained good friends before Megan joined the practice. In other cases close personal relationships are produced through the process of working together. Phil was appointed to the practice through a formal interview process last year, and only knew of the practice by reputation before he joined:

I suppose, [my] being new to the practice, they are mainly colleagues, but they're starting to become friends the more time I spend with them. I think that friendship you develop over time. At my previous practice, I had more friends there than I'd class as colleagues. You build up that working relationship, and that becomes a friendship. I can see how close a lot of guys are that work here. That friendship has grown over time.

Phil contrasts the practice with the larger architectural company he formerly worked for:

A lot of practices have more of a hierarchy of staff, so your directors, maybe associates, senior architects, and then all the way down to the technicians and students. Whereas here we've got Tom and Tomas overseeing things, but it feels that everybody else is on a level playing field. There I am, an architect of ten plus years' experience, and then you've got the others, some of the others, that aren't [formally] qualified, but still I'm learning from them, because of that open collaborative working.

Whether as friends or as colleagues, close working relationships arise from and enable a process of collaborative design. Phil echoes others in the practice, connecting this to a lack of hierarchy that facilitates the acquisition of knowledge and the dissemination of ideas.[63]

Celebrations of collaborative design and of close working relationships are in tension with ideas about the competitive nature of the architectural profession. Roisin describes how these tensions play out through university education and in subsequent professional practice:

Within the architecture studio you have some friends, but they're also enemies, because you're all against each other. You're competing against each other. In architecture school you're not marked against an even plane; you're marked against your colleagues. So if somebody's doing something that you think is better than what you're doing, then you should be doing that, otherwise your grade will be lower than their grade. It's as simple as that. Where you have friends, you don't tell them everything. So if somebody comes over and asks you how are you doing the drawing that you're doing, you tell them a little bit but you don't necessarily tell them everything. When you're applying for a job, you're applying based on your graphics skills and the way that you represent things, and you want that to be unique, otherwise you don't really have a selling point. So there is camaraderie, but there is competition constantly.

Architectural friends are also competitors. Where individual distinctiveness and originality are valued, architects resist the kinds of relationships that can undermine this. As friends, architects may withhold some knowledge even as they give of themselves in other ways. Friendship may itself be resisted, and is sometimes undercut by the competitive logic through which architects and their buildings are compared and ranked. In the practice, as more generally, design takes shape through oscillating relations to others: a negotiated space between friends, colleagues, and competitors.

DEADLINES

In the practice, time is sometimes seen as an agent of change, as something that does things. Phil and Ronan, both qualified architects in their mid-thirties, make this explicit in a self-recorded discussion. They have chosen to reflect on the importance of time in their work:

> PHIL: If the time period is open-ended, then you aren't forced to make a decision because to some degree you can go through endless permutations, particularly at the early design phases where there's endless possibilities, and that actually a deadline and the time pressure just make you go "okay, we've explored it so far, this is what we're going to go with."
>
> RONAN: I think those time pressures can always be good. At uni, having those deadlines focuses the mind and really gets you focused on the job in hand.
>
> PHIL: Yeah, it makes you distill the decision.
>
> RONAN: If you know you've got lots of time, I think you're less likely to properly focus down on the issue. I've always found that. I've always worked well under that sort of pressure, knowing I've got a deadline, and that really focuses you to get the things done that need to be done.
>
> PHIL: Defining the scope of what you need to do and the relevant time you have to do, it really focuses what you can achieve. Because you could detail some gothic cathedral for years and years and years, but actually if it's just a defined thing, then you strip it back and you

know what you can achieve in that period, and that takes experience as well.

Deadlines are not just cutoff points; they make things happen.[64] Phil and Ronan echo others in highlighting how this can be positive: the knowledge of a deadline on the horizon brings about focus, forces resolution; fear trains them to concentrate on the task in hand, shutting out the routine distractions of other colleagues. William Connolly observes: "In an up-tempo world people readily become more . . . experimental and improvisational . . . alert to fugitive currents in themselves—flowing in new directions."[65] Up against deadlines, architects are caught in currents of activity, sometimes finding they are able to do more than they thought they could. The imperative of speed can be the antidote to the debilitation of perfectionism and self-consciousness. "Better done than perfect!" they sometimes say in the office, the joke conveying the serious truth, well expressed in the aphorism of wider currency: the perfect is the enemy of the good.

Milo is trying to work out a window detail on a proposed design for a client meeting first thing tomorrow. It's already late in the working day. He professes to feeling "stuck" and enlists Roisin's help. Milo is normally generous with his time and thoughts, but now my questions about the design are rebuffed. There's a lot to do and only minutes to do it. Every second is crucial. Milo explains to Roisin that the windows look "wrong" and "horrible." He's not sure why, but shares one hypothesis: "There's natural scale, and once you break it, it goes 'boing!'" He looks at the building he has designed, zooming in and out, rotating around on the screen, and sees unwanted connotations: "like a military lookout or a castle"—"it's too austere." Quickly he plays around with different window arrangements and different renderings: at the click of a mouse, stone is replaced by wood; the windows are enlarged and then reduced in size. Nothing seems to work. The sense of panic grows, palpable as a strained look on his face, quickened speech, his voice higher than usual. "My eyes have gone," he explains to himself and to us, the desperation obvious: "You stop seeing things." Over-absorbed and lacking perspective, he professes to feeling "frustrated" and "stuck." The closer the meeting comes, the more he is resigned to his fate: he will have to present what he has, knowing that it is not what he would like it to be.

The thought of too much to do in too little time can be debilitating, expressed as anxiety, stress, and panic. The overriding imperative of urgency displaces other more thoughtful activities. Things are done too quickly, with insufficient consideration.

In the office, there is a last-minute discussion about the presentation of a project that will take place at a client meeting at ten. It has been agreed they need to leave by nine. Nine o'clock comes and goes. Megan goes through the slides, making

some "final tweaks." Sensing the panic at the dawning realization of more to do than time to do it, Rosy comes across to help. There's a problem with the printer. Urgency and haste are all-pervasive, animating forces. Words are exchanged quickly, communication kept to the minimum of what is absolutely required. "Why wasn't this done sooner?" Tomas asks rhetorically, exasperated. "It was, but then you made me change it!" is Megan's testy response. Tempers are frayed, but anger is contained. There's no time for an argument. There's a final rush to get out the door. Printouts are bundled up, stapled, and packed. The projector, essential for the presentation, is forgotten. Tomas runs back for it as the others get in the car and start the engine. In the car, faces are alert, eyes wide with adrenaline. There's relief to be off, but still anxiety: "Will we get there on time?" "We have the presentation, but what about the pitch?" Ideas batted back and forth, quickly and with the obvious focus of the imminent deadline of the meeting. Notes are made hastily as the basis of an agenda.

The collective sense of a lack of time is obviously having an effect: words spoken at speed and in ways they would not be spoken normally; agreement arrived at more quickly; conversation spare, stripped back only to what is absolutely essential. The lack of time turns them into different kinds of people, lends them distinct capacities.

MAGIC MOMENTS

Tomas and Megan are reflecting together on a kind of time that Megan calls "magic": those moments in design when suddenly something exciting happens. In a moment, it can seem that a whole design is unlocked. Why, they wonder together, is it not possible for more of their time to have this quality?

> TOMAS: What's interesting is that answering an e-mail or a phone call, the boring stuff, is often the easiest stuff to engage with. The phone's ringing, you pick it up, and there's someone inquiring about something that you have to respond to, but it might not be the creative stuff. Whereas the creative stuff, you do need to give a bit of space to.
>
> MEGAN: You do, you have to make the space. Like the site model [she is referring to a wooden scale model she recently built] that suddenly just took over. I was putting it off, putting it off, putting it off, and then it was just a matter of saying "actually, no, it's a high priority and it's fun, so just do it," and then it doesn't matter, it doesn't negatively affect the other things somehow.
>
> TOMAS: Yeah, I've had an interesting thing where I've stopped looking at my e-mails, so they're kind of mounting up a little bit. But I used to get into work and just instantly start going through e-mails, and I might sometimes be lucky if at the end of the day I had a bit of spare time at the end of that. Whereas now I've been more looking at my e-mails at the end of the day, or not actually dealing with any of my e-mails for two or three days. If you think about it, that's how it

would have been in the past: you wouldn't have been expected to give immediate answers. I think you can end up spending a lot of time just batting things backwards and forwards.

There is something inexorable and unrelenting about the administrative and contractual demands of a project that, as Megan and Tomas describe it, has a habit of displacing other more creative activities. Routine demands from clients and contractors take priority over the less immediate, less easily quantifiable activities that can only emerge in time that possesses other kinds of quality. But what must be immediately attended to is not necessarily what is important in a longer-term view.[66] Avoiding e-mails is one way in which Tomas tries to carve out other kinds of time, as part of his working day. On another occasion he explains the logic: "There's something quite liberating about just not responding! People have my phone number, so if anything is really important, they can always get hold of me. Otherwise there's a danger that day after day goes by and all you've done is answer e-mails. There's never any time for the stuff that really matters."

A central paradox, for Megan as for Tomas, is that the kind of creativity that sustains good design often, of necessity, emerges in the kind of time that, without immediate demands and finite constraints, seems expansive and "free." The difficulty, as Tomas sees it, is how to create this quality of time in a working environment that, of practical necessity, lacks these qualities: "It's tricky because I spend a lot of that time in the evenings, that's when I'll sit down with a glass of wine and start, without any time pressure, because it just feels like bonus time. The problem for the practice is making time for that within a structured day." Some things can only be done, and some thoughts can only be had, without the pressures of time that directs and is directed. Things happen because there is no expectation that they will; ideas arrive unbidden in the knowledge they don't need to come at all. A process unfolds according to its own logic, without the constraint of a deadline. This is the kind of time that emerges out of the rhythm of the task itself. Megan reflects that it's not possible to create the magic moments of design that can only come unplanned and unanticipated, though it is possible to carve out time for ways of working that are likely to lead in this direction: "Making space for magic. It's not necessarily magic, because magic are those moments that happen along the way. It's about making space for those high-value things which aren't sometimes prioritized in terms of the office day."

LISTEN: CREATIVE TIME

Megan, Rob, Tomas, and Phil are reflecting on the difficulties of making time for the things they want to do.

> MEGAN: We've tried to free up time to be creative in a few different ways, haven't we? With 'hack time' [this is the name they give to a weekly hour set aside for interesting activities of no overtly instrumental purpose] and things like that. And it happens for a little bit, and then we don't do it.
>
> PHIL: Projects take over.
>
> TOMAS: Well, this is a dilemma with the collective and the individual. Me, as an individual, that's what I'm doing. But I'm not making it happen as a practice. I think the problem I've got at the moment is looking at the cash flow, and it just doesn't feel like we've quite got that luxury to spend time on things that aren't so obviously profitable. But it is where I'd really want to get to. My fantasy is to get a really controllable, straightforward process that the practice just does instinctively for day-to-day projects, which are still highly creative and fun to work on but we have a high degree of control. Then working on these other things around the periphery, which don't necessarily make financial sense but have greater ambition. I don't know, what do people think?

SAM: Yeah, that's the goal, isn't it? To do things efficiently so it takes you four days rather than five, and then you've got a whole day to do something that may come back and repay you infinitely in the long run.

MEGAN: The thing is that time just gets sucked into the next thing, "okay, that next five-day project."

ROB: Well, let's protect it as a practice.

MEGAN: We're not very good at protecting time, any of us, for different initiatives.

SAM: Architects aren't by their very training. You're expected to spend one hundred hours a week doing projects. No, you should spend forty hours a week doing projects, and sixty hours a week enjoying yourselves! Part of it's because you enjoy what you're doing. But that instinctively doesn't lend itself to being good at managing your time while in business, because you say "oh yeah, we'll just tweak that detail, it doesn't quite line up"—

ROB: Perfectionism doesn't make money.

MEGAN: Back to our Monday morning meeting?

TOMAS: Yeah!

REFLECTION: CREATIVITY AND ITS LIMITS

Where do ideas come from?

In architecture as in design and art more generally, ideas of creative individuality have had a powerful explanatory hold, at least from the Enlightenment onward. One striking twentieth-century depiction is Ayn Rand's character Howard Roark in the novel *The Fountainhead*. Put on trial for blowing up a building that inadequately expressed the creative vision of his design, the hero delivers a speech:

> Every creative job is achieved under the guidance of a single individual thought. An architect requires a great many men to erect his building. But he does not ask them to vote on his design. They work together by free agreement and each is free in his proper function. An architect uses steel, glass, concrete, produced by others. But the materials remain just as so much steel, glass and concrete until he touches them. What he does with them is his individual product and his individual property.... The first right on earth is the right of ego.[67]

The embodiment of the midcentury modernist architect, inflected by Rand's libertarian ideas, Roark is a dramatic portrayal of an artistic and creative ideal with resonances in more recent public depictions. A strong tradition of writing is celebratory of similar ideas, telling the history of architecture as stories of the individual genius of "great" (usually male) individuals.[68] Peter Eisenman, a renowned American architect of the late twentieth century, echoes these ideas when he states, "There's no one behind my work but me. I am not selfish or immoral—I just want to *be* more every day for me."[69]

Recent scholarship reveals dimensions to the creative processes, concealed by these ideals:[70] in particular, how creativity is an action as much as an idea, and how this emerges *with* rather than *about* the world as part of a broader "ecology" of design.[71] Ideas do not just come through the imagination of individual architects but through a complex choreography involving materials and forces of various kinds.

While inspired by these perspectives, I have sought, through the descriptions in this part of the book, to show how ideas of creative individuality remain central to architects' own understandings of these practices[72]—specifically, how they are given ideological, material, and bodily substance through a range of everyday design practices. While the ideal is not always—or even ever—fully realized, it nonetheless shapes the practices in which architects engage, and the terms in which they understand these practices. These understandings set actions in motion and are integral to architects' experience of work.

As architects at MHW explain the process, individuals are important: design requires sustained periods of concentration and focus that can come only through cutting off from others; the individual architect is central, as the origin of personal visions and convictions that drive the design process. Through training and then in practice, architects learn to develop and project their own perspectives and to demarcate these from the other people and things among whom they were formed.

If design implicates the ideal of the creative individual, it also complicates it. In the terms developed in part one of the book, design emerges in myriad ways in the *space between* the individual architect and a range of external contexts. Designs develop through physical interactions with places and buildings; they are explored and developed as models, diagrams, and sketches, sometimes with, sometimes in opposition to other people: clients, colleagues, and other building professionals. These architects set in motion things that they seek to channel but never entirely control.

In practice, thoughts and actions are individuated in multiple ways, shifting from moment to moment: at times creativity is seen to emerge from the mind; at other points creative action extends to incorporate the hand, the body, and even elements of the material world. Consciousness expands and recedes, as creative acts draw things together and apart in specific and shifting configurations. Individuality can be more but also less than the corporeal limits of the body. Design involves collaboration, sometimes to the point where the question of creative ownership is moot.[73] Individual input can be abstracted from this social context, but establishing how can be difficult, and authorship may be contested in distinct understandings of where ideas originate.[74] "Inspiration" and "influence" are different ways of articulating the paradox of individual creativity: of a person that thinks and acts at once as himself or herself and through others. These are actions that occur *within* an individual without being *of* the individual.[75]

Creativity, as these architects see it, involves an openness to forces, actions, and ideas that are other than themselves: to be creative is to be receptive to people, places, buildings, or the perspectives of others in the office.[76] They recognize how their imagination is moved by various processes that exceed the comprehension and control of any given person. At the same time, their creative acts involve acknowledging and maintaining limits. At key moments in the process, creativity is abstracted as an individual quality, located within a person as distinct from what is created. Architectural subject and architectural object are made to appear through the separation of each from the other, at different stages of design and then most definitively when plans are completed.[77] In this sense the individual is an outcome more than an origin of design. Architecture involves an imaginative proliferation of the self, and the recovery of that difference *as* itself. Creative acts always ultimately lead back to the self, as a kind of enhancement, an incorporation of otherness.

The next section marks a shift in focus: a way of thinking about the difference between the issues of imagination, creativity, and design threaded through part three, and the more ostensibly pragmatic concerns that are central to part four. It can be read as an afterword to the former and a prelude to the latter.

INTERLUDE: TWO KINDS OF UNCERTAINTY

In the car back to the office, Tomas is feeling, as he often remarks, "stressed." A lot has been going on in the practice. Over the last year there has been a process of expansion, with more and bigger projects than usual. New staff have been taken on. Systems have been changed, to try to make the process more efficient. Changes have been difficult to implement, alongside the usual pressures of building and design deadlines—"like changing the engine of a car while you're still driving," as he puts it.

If stress is amplified by these changes, and specifically for Tomas in his role as director, the broader uncertainties inherent in the process of designing and making buildings play no small part. Architects bring together a range of people, with different kinds of knowledge. Interactions between them are often unpredictable: clients change their minds and their budgets; large amounts of money are spent on designs that may or may not get planning permission; builders get behind schedule, construct things wrongly, or question the wisdom of what has been proposed; uncertainty is amplified when new technologies or new materials are used (builders may be unsure about how to build with them, and there may be issues of compatibility and questions about the veracity of manufacturer claims in relation to what is actually built). Then again, various uncertainties arise from the process of design. Good design may remain elusive or emerge in an instant. Architects are constantly making decisions, knowing these are based on partial knowledge of an infinitely complex system.

Tomas reflects that when he started out, he saw uncertainty as a problem and spent a lot of his time trying to control and manage it. Increasingly, however, he has come to think of uncertainty as something to be, as he puts it, "embraced" and "held." Months later, we return to the subject during an interview, where he reflects further on the architect's relationship to uncertainty, and the different forms this can take:

> There's managing uncertainty on the one hand, as someone managing the build of a supermarket does, and then there's dwelling in that uncertainty. There's a difference [between] managing the uncertainty and actually celebrating it. . . . You could just manage it and be professional. Our professional obligations mean that we need to manage that uncertainty, and our creative obligation is that we need to dwell in it.

Tomas sees this comfortableness in uncertainty as a distinguishing feature of the practice and one he is keen to cultivate. Mass construction manages uncertainty, reducing risk through the use of tried and tested design and construction methods, the repeated application of known procedures to ensure predictable outcomes. If these help to ensure budgets are low and tightly controlled, the management of certainty also imposes significant constraints on the creative possibilities of design. At MHW, an ideological commitment to good design entails ambivalence to profit as an overarching motive. The desire to dwell in rather than simply manage uncertainty relates to an understanding that good design involves dedication to a process that is inherently unpredictable.[78]

Tomas sees "comfort with uncertainty" as part of a commitment to good architecture but also acknowledges the extent to which this ideal can sit ambivalently in relation to their work as professional architects, enmeshed in broader regulatory frameworks and in the expectations of the various clients and building professionals with whom they interact. Profit is not a determining factor but neither is it an insignificant one. As private-sector architects, the practice depends on the financial viability of the projects it undertakes. This context imposes financial and professional obligations that must be managed and discharged. The imperative to dwell in uncertainty emerges alongside the imperative to manage it. Different orientations to uncertainty are given greater prominence at different times.

Early on, uncertainty is embraced as part of a process in which drawings, models, and precedents are thrown together. These activities are governed by a desire to go beyond the manifest or obvious, to imagine a building that is more or less subtly different from anything that has gone before.

Later, the management of uncertainty becomes more important: design, and then the process of planning, fix in place key elements of the form; budgets start to solidify through design and through interactions with clients; the building is given still greater fixity as details are specified through the tender package on which builders quote. The schedule of work fixes time, to tasks and to budgets,

and prescribes the role of different people in fulfilling these. Even before building work starts, the structure is stabilized through words and plans, supported by
tacit agreements, and given legal status by the contracts that support these plans.
As the form of the building is fixed, along with the price and time of its construction, uncertainties arise, as a series of problems to be dealt with, resolved, and
managed.

At the uncomfortable intersection between a plan and a building site, architects seek to cultivate a disposition that is a judicious mix of interventionism
and fatalism. They try to bend circumstances to their will while recognizing that
problems are inherent to the endeavor—that sometimes their will has to bend to
events beyond their control. This is another but distinct way of being comfortable with uncertainty: problems are "held" by the architect in the faith a solution
will be found, however unlikely this can sometimes seem. All these uncertainties
are framed by the constraining certainty of the contracted plan. The end is certain, though the means are not.

Different stages of design and construction can be broadly correlated with
different orientations to uncertainty. The practice of how these are encountered
and resolved is more complex. The vocational commitment to avoid the prema-
ture but quick certainty of a design that is "easy" but not "right" may override
the professional commitment to manage time strictly as a way of maximizing
profit. In theory, fee proposals fix and measure the time available for design, but
in practice this may be stretched to find the time to keep the process open. On
other occasions budget or time constraints may determine a less than optimal
design outcome.

Likewise, different orientations to uncertainty are embedded in practical interactions in the later stages of construction. Here again, the question of
whether uncertainty should be embraced as part of the process, or managed
out of it, is often moot. Among other considerations, the "professional" impulse
to regulate risk is often in tension with the more "vocational" commitment to
design integrity.

Even within an architectural practice where the creative imperative is ubiquitous,
it is not all-pervasive. Part four focuses on those elements of architectural practice defined, by contrast to the creative work of design, as "pragmatic." Mostly,
though not exclusively, these are descriptions of activities that come to prominence in the later phases of projects.

LISTEN: ANGST IN ARCHITECTURE

Rob and Megan are talking about angst in architecture: what is it, and where does it come from, they wonder together.

> ROB: There's a broad, general, underlying angst, and I think you get a day-to-day angst which is more like you've got a big list of things, you've got a lot of different projects to move forward, at different stages, and sometimes there's a design problem that you can't quite figure out how to do it. You sit there, but you just can't quite see it. I think in the past a lot of that angst has come from me not being confident, and so not knowing when to just go and ask someone, or when to pick up the phone or call a friend. Do you know what I mean? It's that feeling of "I don't quite know how to resolve this."
>
> MEGAN: Then not knowing where best to go to find that, to alleviate it.
>
> ROB: To some extent that's probably a learning process of any job, but I think architecture is a particular juggling act, or a particular set of very real problems.
>
> MEGAN: One thing I've found is that before I was doing music [Megan has recently begun to learn the piano] I didn't have that creative freedom outside work, so I was expecting so much from doing architecture on a day-to-day professional basis. Expecting so much from that, and expecting so much from

myself, and taking things to heart. If something wasn't feeling quite right, everything was so personal. But then having the music thing come in somehow opened that whole thing up to me. My expectation of what I was wanting to achieve in architecture changed. By just dropping that expectation, I've found a new, lighter level of angst. Before it was much heavier!

ROB: In the same sort of way doing my own extension thing [Rob is in the middle of building an extension to the terraced Victorian house he recently bought], building it myself, it opens your eyes to very real problems. I mean, it's a very superficial problem, but putting two bits of material together and the problems that come from that, and therefore appreciating the problems that builders are up against, and being able to kind of put the office angst into perspective. Having Amy [Rob's girlfriend], her job being very people-centric, the idea of someone who's ultimately quite privileged in the world having angst in "oh, my building's going over budget by £10,000" . . . It's obviously a massive problem for us, but . . ."

MEGAN: . . . Yeah, it's a very good angst to have.

ROB: Yeah, it's a pretty privileged angst.

MEGAN: Rather than "Where's my next meal coming from?" That's a totally different type of angst.

ROB: And I think having that perspective is really important. I mean, ultimately it doesn't help client relationships, but at least in your own personal head space it's probably quite important to remember.

MEGAN: What about in the context of your negotiating these final costs, running a contract of a project coming to completion?

ROB: Yeah, there's definitely lots of angst in that. Although it's interesting, because throughout the process the builder's been very accommodating and sensible about things, and the client's been understanding, and it's only when it comes to drawing to the close, to the crunch, that tensions start getting higher. Managing expectations, and having to be the mediator, is quite difficult in itself. Then being the architect who designed those, and was basically acting on the behalf of the client in the first place, that adds another level of angst and tension.

MEGAN: Because it becomes their personal thing, it starts becoming personal, doesn't it?

ROB: Potentially. You're trying to mediate a situation, whereas actually you are part of that situation in the first place. It's very difficult to just be a contract administrator, because you feel partially responsible or you are directly responsible for something that was omitted or added or changed.

MEGAN: It's kind of weird that we're professionally taking on that role, of being part of something and separate, and mediating it as well. It's very strange. But there's a fine line between angst and pressure, because a kind of pressure can be a positive thing, like having a deadline, you know, and you kind of create a pressure to really focus yourself. . . . It's like a positive form of tension, which is like a pressure that doesn't have anywhere to go.

ROB: It's not frustration, it's pressure.

MEGAN: It's like the same thing, isn't it, but in one it's being channeled into something positive and a way forward, and then in the other it's sort of imploding. It's just building up continuously, and it's like "oh my god."

ROB: There obviously is a threshold, beyond which you sort of accept that pressure.

MEGAN: That's difficult, that thing of not knowing what the answer is. That's one type of angst that I used to feel a lot more: not knowing what the answer is, and not knowing how to find it.

ROB: That's quite interesting; that's where Tomas's belief in process helps a lot, and relieves a lot of tension, because you're like, "Well, I'll just do this next little step and the following bit will be exposed to me, will become clear through just plodding away," but I think that is a very difficult thing to have faith in.

MEGAN: Yeah, but then there's an angst in feeling like you're not progressing.

ROB: I suppose that's difficult, these client frustrations—not relying on them for choices, but there are decisions and requirements that they need to fulfill as well, and having decisions made and then unmade two months down the line. I think we're probably bad at holding those things, because if the client changes their mind two months down the line, we should just say, "Well, hold on Mr. Client, it's okay to change your mind, but the implication is that we've wasted two months' work, or a proportion of two months' work, and therefore we have to redo it." But then I think it comes from making things happen. There's that real difficulty of investment: it's the investment in ourselves, of ourselves, or our ideas, in something.

MEGAN: Yeah, that's why it's hard not to take it personally and to let go.

ROB: And I think it would be a shame if we never took those steps, then maybe we would never create great spaces or something. I don't know, it's an interesting question.

Part 4
PRAGMATICS

PETRIFIED DRAWING

We arrive on-site in sunshine. Carpenters are busy, singing loudly along to the radio: an uninhibited celebration of tunelessness. They are erecting the wooden frame that, as Rob puts it, "is beginning to make the house seem real." "That's exciting!" Tomas remarks, eyes lighting up with obvious satisfaction. "The experience of seeing a design built is always strange and always exciting," he later remarks. "As an architect, you spend time coming up with ideas, playing around with sketches. Everything seems very abstract and conceptual. Then you arrive on-site and suddenly it's all very real. Walls are being erected, concrete set. You think, 'Someone's actually built it'—you're like, 'it was only an idea!'" He describes returning to a completed building, and the uncanny sense of literally inhabiting your own imagination: "I'm now inside my drawing!"

On another occasion, Tomas and Rob are reflecting together on the relationship between design and construction:

> Tomas: You've got design and construction, and something happens between those two processes. You guys [the project architects] now, with Elmsleigh [a project in the office nearing completion], in your head it's fully built.
>
> Rob: It's fully built, but you walk by up the site and it's like, "what? There's nothing there!"
>
> Tomas: And yet something happens between that process of design and construction that I don't think you can control.

As a design, the building seems paradoxically to exist before it is realized. When all goes—literally—to plan, it appears that nothing has been added beyond a shift in material and scale. However, implementation is never straightforwardly procedural,[1] involving an effort to control a range of factors that remain resistant to these efforts.

The architect and historian Robin Evans describes how, "through the miracle of the flat plane, lines transfer with alacrity from paper to stone and the wall becomes a petrified drawing."[2] If, in this process of translation, "what comes out is not always the same as what goes in . . . , architecture has nevertheless been thought of as an attempt at maximum preservation in which both meaning and likeness are transported from idea through drawing to building with minimum loss."[3] Correspondingly this "doctrine of essentialism" is associated with a blind spot between drawing and building: "We can never be quite certain how things will travel and what will happen to them on the way."[4]

What happens between a design and a building, between an idea and a structure? This section focuses on the various ways in which architects create and inhabit the space between these, predominantly through a kind of work they characterize as "pragmatic."

BETWEEN CONCEPT AND PLAN

How does a design concept become a detailed plan?

During the initial stages of design, sketching predominates. Architects draw, relating creative freedom to a representational technology that is understood to lack specific practical consequence.[5] This imaginative process aims to move away from existing realities toward a "design concept." In later stages of design, by contrast, architects aim to make their drawings consequential. The process of "detailing" is a way of anticipating the reality of the concept. It is oriented to give substance and specificity to what exists abstractly. At this stage, architects must understand and resolve a range of more practical considerations, including those of planning, construction, and cost.

Tomas is talking to Roisin, who has been struggling to a make a design work. The brief and issues are relatively common: how to extend a traditionally constructed Cotswold stone building to make the house larger and better adapted to the domestic life of the family who now live there. The basic problem is that what the client wants seems too big for the existing building. Roisin, the main designer on the project, is not happy with the way the proposed extension looks, and is not convinced the design would get planning permission. Tomas, the named project architect, suggests the solution might be to revisit some of the earlier decisions that have been made. He draws a diagram for Roisin to illustrate his point. It gives a broader insight into how he sees the design process: like a tree turned on its side, with a single line that bifurcates into ever more branches. At every stage, decisions are made that lead to further decisions. The movement is from the general "design concept" to the particular "details." Broad questions about building size and location give way to decisions about the configuration of specific rooms, the position of doors, compliance with building regulations, and so on. Each decision represents one possibility realized, at the expense of others. "Sometimes you go down one branch, getting into details before the bigger issues are fully resolved." When that happens, the trick is not to keep going but to retrace your steps—to "pull back," as Tomas puts it—and think, "Have we taken the wrong route?" Sometimes "big" decisions get made too early, creating problems that cannot be resolved at the level of detail. This is one way in which a design can get stuck: the scale of the problem is incommensurate with the scale at which the solution is sought.

While the process involves an overall movement from the general to the particular, the tension between these levels is inherent in all design. In practice, architects do not simply work from the whole to the detail, but backward and forward between these. In Schon's terms, "the whole is at stake in every partial move,"[6] so that the designer "must oscillate between the unit and the total."[7] A key concern and difficulty is to keep each in mind simultaneously. The early stages of design are oriented to the development of an overall concept but should anticipate the detailing that will later take place. Roisin explains:

> I think initially when you come out of university and you start drawing buildings for planning, you just start drawing them. You don't really think, "Okay, I need three hundred mil there for floor depth, and then I need a floor height." You kind of put in two-floor heights, and then when you check it with the directors, in detail design you've got a lot of issues because you haven't put in things in the right places.

Just as design of the whole building must anticipate later detailing, so, detailing is done bearing in mind the whole of an overall design concept. The difficulty is to retain the coherence of the overarching idea, even as architects must also work out the details that are necessary for a design to be successful. These include specifying the materials that build up the walls and resolving the kinds of conflicts that routinely result from various contradictory imperatives: cost, aesthetics, energy performance, structural integrity, waterproofing, and various practical considerations of "buildability." At the intersection of these considerations, design necessarily involves compromise and trade-offs. Detailing has to respond to these but should not be driven by them—designs become "compromised," in the pejorative sense, when details overwhelm the coherence of the whole. The skill of detailing is to resolve these contradictions in a way that is subservient to the initial design concept: to anticipate and reconcile a future process of construction to the overall concept already established.

Unusually among the architects in the office, Phil finds the later phase of detailing one of the most enjoyable. He has a precise and meticulous way of working that seems reflected in the deliberate and careful manner of his speech, as well as in his dress—informal but neat. He is one of the few who tucks his shirt in! Prior to working at MHW, he was employed for a large architectural practice, mostly undertaking big public projects. There, distinct stages of design were undertaken by different teams. His role related almost exclusively to the later detailing phase. He moved jobs partly hoping to develop his "creative side," but describes how detailing involves its own distinctive satisfaction. "The beauty is in the detail," he explains as I watch him at work, designing the build-up of a wall, magnified on the computer screen at almost actual size. The satisfaction comes from the process: "dealing with all the small problems" has a specific reward distinct from the outcome: "Everything starts to come together . . . the building starts to become real."

"Detail" and "abstraction" are relative terms. At any stage of design, it is possible to engage with designs in ways that privilege one or other perspective. Much of the difficulty of the process is in striking the necessary balance between these: being aware of pragmatic considerations and design details that can make a building, without losing sight of the bigger whole. There are dangers in details but also opportunities. Get too absorbed and the architect becomes buried in the detail, unable to see the bigger whole of the design concept.

"Detailing" also has a more precise, more restricted meaning. The formal stage of detailing starts once the planning drawings have been approved. In both a temporal and conceptual sense, details follow from and are therefore subservient to the design as a whole. In practice, the relationship is less linear than this general characterization implies. Phil describes how the process of detailing involves a two-way process, working back and forth between the plan and the detail: "Sorting the micro can sort the macro," as he puts it; "you resolve a detail and then go back to the plan to change it." The noncommensurability of the part and whole of design are the problem to which detailing routinely responds. The skill is in creating a reconciliation that does not, de facto, exist.

Detailing is an attempt to anticipate the practicalities of construction— in these architects' own terms, to give the building a "reality" before it has an "actuality". From the Enlightenment onward, the authority of the architect has depended on a capacity to prefigure the process, rendering construction a matter of implementing an already existing design.[8]

As self-acknowledged Jacks of all trades, these architects are also aware that they are masters of none. Their efforts to anticipate construction therefore involve assembling the knowledge of others more able to speak for these pragmatic concerns. How does this happen?

COMING INTO FOCUS

The meeting takes place at Glyme Farm, a barn conversion that is a former project of MHW. Mary, the client on that project, now lives there with her husband and two children. We have come here because she is now employed as a design consultant on the project we are here to discuss. Client, turned friend, turned colleague. Tomas is joined by Phil and Milo who are here as representatives of the design team. They have done most of the design work, though it is Tomas who speaks most as the representative of their collective perspective. The clients, Hugh and Jenny, bought a 1970s house, which they originally planned to renovate but which, following initial estimates for the cost of this work, they now intend to demolish and replace.

The architects have come up with some initial plans, but the clients are concerned about the cost of building these. Jack, the quantity surveyor, has been contracted to cost the plans. The meeting is to work out whether it is possible to build the house the clients want, for the money they have available. To be discussed are a range of issues relating to the practical feasibility of the design. There is also a more profound uncertainty about whether the project has a future at all. Hugh has a background in commercial property development. He is explicit that this project, a house for their retirement, "is not about [us] making money." Even so, the question of cost is a central consideration: "If the numbers don't make sense, then it's better just to walk away from it and find somewhere else."[9]

Unclear how or even whether to proceed, Tomas explains that the point of the meeting is "to work out a strategy for the way forward." Already, cost and design are in a relationship, but as yet key elements of this are unclear and uncertain.

From the start, architects design with a budget in mind. In general terms, this frames decisions about the scale of the building and the structural and material palette that form the overarching "tectonic." The quantity surveyor then prices this, making assumptions about design. Architect and quantity surveyor proceed, producing designs and costings in the knowledge that each has less than the full picture. These working assumptions are embedded in the documents laid out before us: an initial set of plans produced by the architects specify approximate sizes and dimensions but say little about materials and levels of finish. The budget produced by the quantity surveyor is correspondingly vague, based as it is on assumptions about construction techniques and materials. The quantity surveyor is explicit about this as he hands around the itemized list of projected costs: "It's very rough, probably completely wrong, but a starting point. . . . I've had to make a lot of assumptions about how things will be built and to what level of finish." Each has an imprecision that relates to uncertainty about the other: the details of the design depend on unknown costs of construction; these costs are contingent on the specification of design details.

What Hugh, the client, describes as a "gradual coming into focus" is a matter of relating these with greater precision. Through discussion, further details about the design translate into greater certainty about the cost. Greater understanding of the cost in turn clarifies the likely scope of the design. As the meeting proceeds, assumptions are turned into decisions of a more or less certain kind. At the intersection of budget and design lies a need for balance—as Hugh describes it, "between what's affordable and what we want." Though all are there to assist in the resolution of this relationship, they have different roles that involve distinct orientations to this shared objective. Architects and design consultant are there to highlight what is possible from a design perspective; the quantity surveyors are there to calculate what this is likely to cost; the question of whether this is affordable ultimately falls to the client. Nick, the quantity surveyor, has a wry sense of humor that both highlights and deflects the tension that his role entails. "I'm not always the most popular person in the room," he comments before the discussion commences in earnest: "You all want a perfect building, and I'm the one that tells you that you can't afford it!"

This sets the tone for the meeting, framed by the knowledge that the quantity surveyor's initial estimate exceeds the client's original budget by a considerable margin. Hugh—who throughout the meeting speaks for his wife—responds, observing, "We need to decide whether to expand the budget or contract the scheme." This translates, throughout the meeting, as a series of questions regarding how to cut costs and what to prioritize. Working through the calculated figures, the participants discuss elements of the design in descending order of cost. Meetings produce focus by isolating some issues from the many uncertainties and unknowns at play. The agenda is one way of achieving this: points up for discussion are isolated from the many potential issues that are not.

Jack has budgeted £15,000 pounds for a staircase: "It's a significant sum. I assumed you want something nice." "Yes, that is very, very important," Hugh responds. "It's something we picked out on the Pinterest board," he explains, referring to the digital collage they assembled as a way of conveying ideas. The cost seems to reflect the degree of importance attached by the client, who gives his general assent for the sum. Eyes are focused on the plan, depicting the staircase only as an outline that says little of its form and nothing of the materials that might be used to make it. Tomas, as architect, clarifies the design implications of this budgeted sum: "My feeling is that's enough to do something interesting," he comments, sketching a couple of possibilities and throwing out some thoughts on the kinds of materials that could be used. "We're proposing a building that's quite light and modern, so the structure should reflect that—something heavy, in hard wood, might not be appropriate. So we might save a bit of money there. On the other hand it always costs more to do something interesting and bespoke." Still, significant details remain to be resolved, but there is enough agreement that the meeting can proceed. The clients have clarified the brief; the architects have clarified what can be achieved; the quantity surveyor has greater confidence that his sum is realistic.

Meetings entail expectations that conversation will be central: the medium of talking is central to the message that is conveyed.[10] However, the negotiation of perspective is more than simply verbal. Possibilities are explored through sketches; these produce alternative design possibilities, and sometimes greater clarity about cost implications. Jack punches numbers into a calculator to arrive at initial assessments of feasibility; even as these remain necessarily vague, they are the basis for decisions that lead design in particular directions, discursively and visually explored through further discussion and drawing.

Jack places a tick beside the item and moves the discussion on to the cladding: "So next up is external walls—I'm assuming Cotswold stone for these?" He often costs projects for the practice, and is extrapolating based on knowledge of the general design principles that inform their approach. Hugh is unsure: "That figure jumped out. Do we need stone for planning? Are there other materials? Or could we use a combination of timber and stone?" Tomas describes the architectural rationale: stone and timber; "the play of solid and lighter forms." There is no absolute need for these materials in planning terms, though they are part of a "design language" that ties the building into the place. Whether or not that material palette is instrumentally necessary, he thinks it ties into a "story" that gives the building "a reason to be there." Hugh agrees, but wonders if the cost can be justified on aesthetic and design grounds: "I think render [a smooth-textured external cement surface] and glass is a lovely combination—it can be very, very modern." Jack offers his opinion in assent: "Nice and clean! You see, I could become an architect!" The joke acknowledges his lack of authority to pronounce on this. The view is a "personal" one and of little consequence.

Cost and aesthetics are implicated in a range of structural and technical considerations that are woven through these discussions. For the structure beneath the cladding, the structural surveyor suggests the possibility of using traditional masonry construction, solid blockwork, in place of the timber that has been specified. It might help save cost, but as Tomas points out will have implications for thermal performance: thinner wall cavities allow for less insulation, leading to a less efficient house that will be more expensive to heat. Reduced energy performance also has environmental implications.

Some of the items on the list are uncontroversial. Consensus settles easily that the finish of the master bedroom needs to be prioritized at the expense of the guest bedrooms, where savings can be made. Likewise, the sum allocated for bathrooms is agreed virtually without comment. For other items, the relationship between cost and outcome is more complex, for instance where uncertainties arise from the specification of nonstandard components and bespoke designs that are difficult to model. The clients have stated from the outset that they are keen for the building to be "green." Hugh reiterates this during the meeting: "We want to get the best energy performance we physically can—way beyond the minimum." Sometimes, the desire for greater energy performance conflicts with the pragmatic need to keep the project within budget. At others there are necessary trade-offs with other elements of the design: the clients want a design that will be "modern," "light and airy"; "We're mad keen on glass," Hugh explains. This can be accommodated, but, as Tomas points out, it will reduce the energy performance of the building. Jack mentions that micro-renewables (sustainable technologies that generate heat or power on a small scale), are listed under the "exclusions" and have not been costed in the existing budget. Hugh wonders aloud: "Should we be looking at that? Something a bit modern and a bit green?" There is some discussion about the payback times of solar thermal and solar voltaics. Hugh mulls this over: "It's a cost-benefit issue. But it would have to look okay." He is worried about the visual impact of solar panels. An environmental commitment seems likely to conflict with what is aesthetically optimal.

Some decisions are made, but in other cases uncertainties remain. To move discussion on, some of these unknowns are put aside for now, noted but bracketed for future consideration. The discussion of micro-renewables reaches no firm conclusion beyond the minuted point that a renewables expert will need to be consulted. Sometimes decisions are suspended: "Okay, let's move on, we can come back to this later." In others, the complexity of the issue requires further work, minuted as future actions: research to ascertain costs with greater certainty; more time to work on designs to respond to discussions in the meeting; the consultation of others with relevant forms of expertise—planners, structural engineers, mechanical and electrical engineers, and so on.

Summing up the discussion, Jack goes back through his list, tapping on a calculator, totting up the budget in light of what has been agreed. "So a very, very crude 'where are we at,' perhaps"—he qualifies that while there is greater certainty, there are still many unknowns—"about £39,000 added. When we've got more detail on the design, we can home in a bit on the cost." Tomas responds, bringing the discussion to a conclusion: "I think overall this is very realistic for what everyone's thinking." Then he recaps the various potential cost-saving options that have been discussed: the design specification could be reduced, obvious areas being the use of cheaper flooring material than the hardwood that is budgeted for; changes in construction techniques that would reduce thermal performance; and the simplification or even exclusion of the external landscaping scheme. Alternatively, the design specification could be higher if the size of the house were reduced. Hugh responds in turn: "We're going to have to go away and have a proper think." From an architectural perspective, further focus will be possible only once these decisions have been made. Mary, the design consultant, highlights the difficulty of doing so: "It's very, very difficult. You're not just building your house—you're building the next stage of your life."

At the end of the architects' desks are bookshelves containing project folders: large ring-binders, containing the documentation relating to each project. Some are contained within a single binder; more complex projects may need four or five. For someone flicking through these, the central role of one particular, ubiquitous but unremarkable social form is striking: among the initial sketches, detailed plans, expert reports of one kind or another—on lighting, green technologies, from planning consultants and so on—page after page records the minutes and action points resulting from various kinds of meetings.

Meetings are an elemental part of the practice. As they are regarded as less overtly remarkable than the more obviously creative elements of architectural work, it is perhaps unsurprising that meetings have not been given more attention.[11] In their explanations of the design and construction process, architects at MHW did not say much about them. Still, in practice, they are central to the process by which designs acquire more detail and greater focus, through a range of interlinked processes: disaggregating issues and focusing discussion on key decisions; relating perspectives as "agreements" on how to proceed; and factoring out or postponing issues that remain unresolvable.

LISTEN: COST AND DESIGN

How is cost linked to design? Megan, Phil, and Rob wonder together.

MEGAN: Often you're in a hurry. You've got six days to do that work, so you're getting your costs for your materials straightaway, and you're like, "oh, that's ridiculous, it's not going to work!" [her voice rises in exasperation] and then you just go back to the drawing board before you go any further. Cost is part of your design straightaway. I mean, yes, we might have a quantity surveyor [QS] involved, but the QS is another abstract entity. So you sort of do your detailing up to a certain point, then you go to a QS, and then it comes back and they will say, "Well, it's over budget." We say, "Well, we've done our work." Are we going to redo it? And then there's an ambiguity there.

PHIL: In the ideal situation you have the QS all the way through the project. They start right at the start, so right at the start you've got your client's budget, your client's ambitions and their brief, and initially you test that: the QS does a cost assessment, and you say, "Well, it doesn't work," or "It does," and then you make that decision. And then the QS is involved at key stages all the way through.

ROB: The QS costing is based on a kind of a plug-and-play, kit-of-parts world of architecture, and we're doing a bit of that but also a bit of totally bespoke, which is based on the skill of the builder and the speed at which they work.

MEGAN: But there's a huge unknown in all the finishes, isn't there. It's easy if it's just the fabric of the building, because we've got an in-depth knowledge of that and you can do it based on the size, like "Okay, it's stone here, it's a double stud timber frame, and then it's timber cladding over there," and that's easy to price depending on the size. But there's such a huge unknown with the finishes because they vary so much.

PHIL: Yeah, internal fixed furniture is the main thing for me. It's like a massive entity, which is quite difficult to cost, but in my experience the QS hasn't necessarily looked at that in any huge detail. They say, "Well, a provisional sum is about two grand [£2,000]."

ROB: But then you need to gauge the aspiration from the client at the off—so if they want to go for gold taps, or if they're going to go for budget fittings—and then base the cost plan on that.

MEGAN: But often they know what they want, but they don't know how much it costs, so they think "Yeah, I want this," but then it's actually only when you go out and get a price for that then they say, "Ooh, we can't have that, we have to choose something else."

PHIL: It's more of a dialogue.

ROB: Yeah, it has to be a much more regular back and forth, checking every sketch by them.

WHERE KNOWLEDGE MEETS

Mill House is a Cotswold stone structure, with a grade 2 "listing"—an acknowledgment of the building's historical significance that affords formal protection through the planning system. Originally a working mill, it was bought by its current owners about a year ago. Mark and Cathy are accountants, in the process of moving from London—for her to retire and for him to commute. Tomas and Megan are here for a project meeting. Already, the broad outlines of the design have been agreed: Mark and Cathy were drawn to the character of the building and want to retain as much of the history as possible; but as they see it, the building has too many small rooms, insufficient light, and a poor connection to the garden. A number of schemes were initially considered. The most radical of these was the one they ultimately decided on; the essence of the plan is simple and was arrived at quickly: a small external courtyard—formed on three sides by the existing house and a barn to the rear—will be enclosed by a glass roof, creating an internal space that other rooms will open onto. As the project moves from concept development to detailing, there are many issues still to resolve. On this occasion considerations of cost are less central than those relating to planning approval and the technical feasibility of the proposed design concept.

Tomas and Megan have had less time to prepare than ideally they would have liked. Mark and Cathy leave us to make teas. "The mechanical and engineering consultant and the quantity surveyor are coming later, and before that we need to go through the plans—there's lots to get through," Megan tells Tomas in a half whisper, hurriedly talking as she notes down the points that will form an informal agenda. Cathy and Mark return with teas. Interactions remain informal, but take on a seriousness that seems to reflect the importance of what is at stake: large amounts of money and decisions about details that will contribute to the success or otherwise of what ultimately gets built.

Tomas kicks things off. "I'm aware that time is marching on, and that there are a lot of decisions to make and details to resolve." He apologizes that the project is developing more slowly than he would have liked. The planners took longer than hoped to arrange an initial consultation meeting. In the office "things have been hectic." Cathy is also keen to get things moving, but acknowledges, "That's actually been quite good for us. We had a lot on, but now things have quietened down, and we're all fired up again!" Tomas outlines what the meeting needs to achieve. Various issues are up for discussion: some of these relate to the need for input and feedback on details that are currently unspecified or uncertain in the proposed design; others relate to the technical questions of how the design will work, and how much it might cost ("the mechanical engineer and the quantity surveyor will be joining us later on"). At the start of a meeting it is uncertain how these will be resolved, though the meeting carries with it an expectation of resolution. Plans are laid out on the table—more detailed developments of the agreed proposal. Cathy looks at these quizzically, then her eyes alight on some images Megan has brought along: "Good, I like a picture, because I can't visualize anything!"

One of the key issues is to consider how the opinions of the conservation officer, expressed in an earlier meeting, relate to the proposed design. Although she was comfortable with the overall scheme, the original plan contained a number of alterations to the form and fabric of the listed mill that she highlighted as likely areas for a planning objection. There is some discussion about whether, and how much, they should compromise, and what strategic approach to take. Megan explains: "Our approach is generally to negotiate informally before the final plans are submitted—then you know what you are up against, and can work with that. They like to feel involved." From the outset, designs are created in anticipation of planning objections. Cathy is in agreement: "Yes, we're saying we want to preserve all the history; it's about working together." Her sentiments about the history of the house seem genuine, although, as later becomes obvious, a common commitment to the building's preservation does not mean that her views will coincide with those of the conservation officer.

As architects and clients talk, they are hunched toward the plans in the center of the table, eyes trained on details highlighted by pointing fingers. One issue relates to an internal wall that has original skirting boarding, and which the conservation officer is keen to see preserved. The proposed design has retained this, but with negative aesthetic implications: "That's a bit weird," Cathy comments. "It's not weird; let's just go with it," Mark contradicts. Meaningful glances are exchanged. Without a word, the point is conceded—the skirting will stay. Megan makes a note, and discussion moves on. More or less starkly opposed opinions are resolved through subtle, even ineffable, shifts in conversation. Decisions are made without the requirement that perspectives fully coincide. It is only necessary that the perspectives of those assembled coincide *enough*, about *enough* things, for the process to move on.[12]

Similar problems have been created by the retention of a door that the conservation officer indicated as a significant element of the planned form: "It's a bit of a weird detail, this could be a bit strange," Tomas remarks as he points to it, highlighting how this creates a corner with no light. "It's dark, it's so dark," Cathy agrees. "Let's negotiate with the conservation officer," Tomas concludes. Megan notes the point, and discussion moves on.

Next up are a series of questions about replacement of existing windows and the possible placement of new openings. We get up from the table, walking around the house as we consider these various points. On the third floor, the attic room they plan to use as their bedroom has exposed beams and high dormers on one side. Frustratingly, for Cathy, there's little light and no view: "I really want to push for windows here." In this instance Tomas is sure an application will be unsuccessful. New windows would have a significant aesthetic impact on the key front elevation and would result in some destruction of original fabric. He agrees to pursue this application if Cathy wants, but his inclination is not to: "We need to choose our battles." The minutes may record an uncomplicated narrative of agreed points, but in practice it is rarely this straightforward. Much more is discussed than is ever recorded.

Often meetings take place on-site. Tours of sites isolate objects of shared attention. People move together, eyes focused in the same direction in response to pointing and gesticulating. Even then, the reality of a physical building may be too complex to sustain focus. Sketches and plans are used to direct attention in specific ways.[13]

Downstairs, we congregate around one of the stone mullioned windows. The other side of the valley is visible in the distance through the leaded fenestration and irregular glass of an eighteenth-century mullioned window. In this instance the assessment of client and architect align easily with the assumed view of the conservation officer: "Great, aren't they!" Tomas pronounces on the windows, to assenting smiles and nods. The only question is what to do with the existing secondary glazing, the aluminum frames presumed to be from the 1970s. "They're a bit ugly," Cathy comments. "What could we do?" Tomas says they could be replaced in wood or metal, and agrees to look out for some samples. Mark sounds a note of minor discord: "I think they're fine, let's keep them." Without consensus, it's agreed the issue will be deferred until samples arrive and costs are known.

Bob, the quantity surveyor, arrives, and then, shortly afterward, Patrick the mechanical and electrical engineer consultant. The group assembles in a loose circle. Introductions are made and welcomes extended through the shaking of hands and the offer of tea. I'm struck by the contrasting attire of those present: Tomas, en route to an awards ceremony, is wearing a baby blue jacket over a salmon pink T-shirt; Megan, in jeans and a T-shirt, has a crew cut—as she has earlier explained to Cathy, her response to a significant relationship that recently foundered ("A fresh start!"). Wittingly or not, they are communicating unspoken elements of their identity: of architectural individuality and creativity; of nonconformity and informality;[14] perhaps even of the status that comes of not having to demonstrate status. Bob and Patrick work for different companies but are similarly dressed: smart trousers and collared shirts; neatly parted short hair. Their appearance speaks of professionalism, objectivity, reliability.

We have slipped, momentarily and unremarked, out of the meeting: jokes, smiles, and pleasantries exchanged, notepads and documents down. Megan brings us back to it: "Okay, there are lots of details to iron out and lots to discuss. Let's go around together so we can all *see* it." She stresses the word, highlighting a dimension of these interactions that often goes without comment: in different ways, each holds knowledge that makes sense only through the understanding that comes from seeing the specifics of a problem. The physical properties of the building are integral to the relations that are then negotiated between those present: these are not so much discussions *about* as *with* the building. "Then you"—Megan is talking to Bob and Patrick—"can hear each other's thoughts."[15] The knowledge of each has to be made to fit the context of the knowledge the other provides; they see separately but also together. Patrick's is a building of heating, lighting, electricity, energy. These various kinds of circuits and flows are depicted in the diagrams he draws and consults, and are central to the understanding that is evident from what he says. Bob's is a building of costs and budgets. He has to understand the design, the heating, the lighting, structural issues—in fact everything—but only in relation to this very narrow concern: how much will it all add up to?

Trained ways of seeing have their counterpart in tools and materials that make the nascent building a profoundly different kind of object for the clients and experts involved. The building is constituted as a different kind of object through these different kinds of practice.[16] The QS calculates the cost of building using a calculator and spreadsheet; architects realize designs through sketches and various plans; plans are also produced by structural engineers, whose knowledge of loads and materials depends on and produces models of a qualitatively different kind.

Materials, documents, models, and tools also facilitate the process by which these professional visions are brought together, however momentarily and partially. The structural surveyor and the architect may arrive with a different set of documents, but each is modified in relation to the other: budgets are recalculated and recorded in scribbled annotations; plans are drawn over; sketches are produced in response to the implications of cost constraints.

The meeting shifts from questions of conservation to the unresolved relationship between technical performance and cost. Megan is taking notes, asking questions, standing back from the group. It seems to literalize her role, detached from a set of practical considerations she must nevertheless coordinate and control. As we stand and walk, she is recording in a notepad the skeleton of what is said and agreed. From time to time she consults her plans for information. Key decisions are noted, as are the uncertainties that will call for further research.

Outside, we congregate on the worn flags in the courtyard. Currently, the plan is to cover this space. Heating is briefly considered. Patrick suggests that underfloor would be best, providing radiant heat that would be more efficient in a space of this size. Megan mentions the added benefit that the floor would feel warm. She professes to like the worn and weathered surface of the existing stone, and wonders if this can be kept. "Possibly, but it's probably too thick" Patrick replies. Bob continues, "They look pretty irregular, so it would probably cost a lot of money in labor." Technical performance and cost are momentarily aligned, but both seem at odds with the aesthetic look and feel that Megan, as architect, values. The clients, Cathy and Mark, are consulted but profess to have no strong opinion. Cathy says she likes the stones as they are, but it will probably come down to money in the greater scheme of priorities. "We can give you a detail for the floor build-up," Patrick tells Bob. This technical specification will form the basis of the initial budget Patrick draws up. "We can get some rough costs for that very easily."

Still in the courtyard, eyes are directed skyward, necks craning upward to the walls that will take the glass ceiling to form the internal space. Megan has the plans, which she points to as she describes the proposal: "It's basically just a big area of glass!" she jokes, aware of the technical understatement of what she is saying. Even to get to the point of proposing this, she has had to do her own technical research: "It's going to be a big component of the cost. There are a lot of details to work out." Patrick doesn't immediately know what the solution will be, though he knows the approach to get to it: "It's pretty much going to be a greenhouse, so it will tend to overheat in the summer and could be quite cold in the winter. We'll need to build a model." Glass will be specified on the basis of a CAD package that models solar gains and thermal losses. Gains can be reduced by tinting and reflection; losses through insulation. Building regulations will require that the glass can take the weight of a person for the purposes of cleaning, another factor that will dictate the specifications and cost of the glass.

The meeting ends as the tour of the building is completed. Some details have been resolved; new issues have been raised; still others remain unresolved. Patrick speaks for everyone when he concludes, "We're just getting our bearings." He will come back to do a full survey; designs will be developed, and an initial budget drafted. Other people will need to be brought in: Megan flicks through the condition survey undertaken by a surveyor: "It highlighted a number of potential structural issues. We'll need to get a structural surveyor on board." Even as much remains provisional, unknown and undecided, Tomas and Megan reflect in the car back to the office that the meeting has been a good one. Enough has been learned and agreed on to chart the next stages and define, as meetings routinely do, "the way forward." It is through conversations such as these that buildings begin to be realized, as myriad practicalities are anticipated and resolved long before projects start on-site.

The space between a design concept and a detailed plan is one in which multiple interests and perspectives collide. During this process, the power of the architects but also their fragility are functions of their role: not simply as one perspective among others, but as choreographer of these differences.[17] At the apex between a range of people, they must reconcile and relate, if not entirely resolve, these differences. They have to anticipate the various practical considerations and concerns involved in the construction, planning, and finance of a project, while seeking to retain the coherence and integrity of the initial concept. The aim is to transmute practical problems into architectural ones, to anticipate and to frame a process of construction in advance of building. The constant hazard is of being deflected by the concerns and interests of others in a way that can compromise the design. In practice there is always a tension: between the architect's efforts to bend these practicalities to the logic of a plan, and the ways in which those practicalities will tend to take the plan in other directions.[18]

The history of architecture is sometimes told as a story about the triumph of the architect over others involved in construction: during the middle of the sixteenth century, the invention of orthographic projection (a means of representing three dimensions in two, through the use of parallel projection), allied to the widespread use of detailed plans, was associated with a new division of labor. Where previously many of the detailed design decisions were made on-site, the "creative" work of design was increasingly detached from construction, prefiguring the process of building as "mere" implementation of an already existing plan.[19] Renaissance ideas of the architect as gentleman "mind worker" reflected this new understanding of the architect as a detached but authoritative presence, an idea that continues to have resonance even today. Yet in practice, architectural authority is often fragile, a matter of convincing others of the merits of a spe-

cific plan and, more generally, of the importance of design relative to other concerns and interests. Architectural authority is expanded and diminished through countless everyday negotiations, framed by a broader set of assumptions, institutional arrangements, and legislative contexts.

Operating in this space, the ability of the architect to be persuasive involves many things: getting along with people; building the trust outside a meeting that equates to authority within it; triangulating the views of the various actors so that agreement is produced as a consensus; framing issues in such a way that one or another option seems more favorable; "sheer bloody-mindedness," sticking to a point unwaveringly, with more determination, or for longer than others; acquiring the rhetorical skills to present a case with conviction. It is through these negotiations, as much as through the practice of design, that plans and then buildings actually take form.

PROBLEM SOLVING

In the office, Tomas and Megan sit paging through sheets of detailed computer-generated plans, neatly and precisely laid out. "Like an instruction manual for the building," Tomas remarks; "in theory, this is all the builders should need." These documents will form the basis on which contractors will tender, and will later form the basis of the contract that is drawn up between client and builder. Megan became a fully qualified architect last year and is, by her own admission, still relatively inexperienced at this stage of the design. Their discussion focuses on the apparently minor details that can cause the kinds of ambiguity that lead to problems on-site. Tomas has acquired an eye for these troublesome details through over a decade in practice, often learning the hard way. He points out possible problems that need more work to resolve and clarify. Other details will remain unresolved and will need to stay that way. "They'll make that bit up on-site," Tomas explains to Megan. Pointing to a junction where various materials intersect, he highlights the need to be clear about this: "You need to TBC it," he cautions her.

TBC: to be confirmed. As the basis for a contract, it is important that plans are clear, and that they are clear about their own limits. The plans anticipate their own and others' later improvisations. Of necessity, construction goes beyond what is formally specified, even as the space in which this happens is carefully framed by design. How does this happen on site?

"Building is a business fraught with problems of a very diverse nature," Edward tells me. He's in his late fifties, dressed in site-soiled jeans and a T-shirt. Part administrator, part builder, he divides his working day between office and site. I've seen him at the fortnightly site meetings, jokily performing his role through bantering relationships with architect and client: the put-upon builder, battling on in the face of all the various problems that come his way—delays, bad weather, the vagaries of other contractors, dealing with architects, and so on. The performance acknowledges the tensions it is intended to diffuse. This is the first time we've spoken at any length. I stay on-site after the meeting, sheltering from torrential rain under the newly erected first floor of the building. The project is already a couple of months into a schedule with a planned completion date in a further four months. Wormwood House, a large domestic building, is being constructed for the clients, a middle-aged couple, who live in the area. A "dream house," they tell me on another occasion, it is being built on a site that slopes dramatically away to views of a wooded valley and the town at the bottom.

Around us, carpenters pull on jackets but continue putting up stud-work. Nail guns and power tools can only just be heard over the sound of rain on tarpaulin. Even though we're shouting, it's hard to follow the conversation. I'm aware that the noise is not the only obstacle to communication: "I'm not an academic," Edward tells me on a couple of occasions. His statement of the obvious seems part apology, part celebration of a kind of knowledge that responds to a different kind of logic. In his own words, "a simple, practical man," he sees these as valued qualities on a building site.

Edward tells me how he came to be a builder. After a career as an army officer, he wanted to do "something more creative and rewarding." The military supported his training as a carpenter. Then he found work as a local builder. Over time the business grew, partly through a desire to increase profitability, partly from a sense of responsibility: "You build a team around you and then they need feeding." Edward tells me about the satisfactions of the job: a way of fulfilling a "desire to build and create things"; the sense of achievement solving problems; and the gratification of "doing a good job." These were also some of the things that spurred him on to a business that at one point employed over sixty people. As the scale of the business increased, so did the problems. I'm talking to him on what he hopes will be his last project. "I'm retiring early because I've burned myself out. Thirty-six solid years of constant phone calls and problems. Extremely pressured. You can't describe it. You have to be laid back, or you'd end up jumping off a bridge. There's so much to go wrong. You go into business because you like adversity, but I've had enough. Absolutely everything is your problem—they run out of nails, it's your problem." His voice trails off. His look is distant. "It hit me about a year ago that I'm actually very weary." He looks at me, tired eyes confirming the truth of what he has been telling me. Then a resigned smile, perhaps intended to deflect attention from the profound seriousness of what he has just said. He has a plot of land in Devon, where he plans to build a house and retire to a simpler and easier life in the country.

Edward describes the problems that characterize the working life of a builder: "Every day you wake up and think, 'bloody hell.'" His day starts at six in the morning and ends at nine in the evening. Anxieties carry through to sleepless nights. He has almost no holidays. Office work is in the mornings and evenings—jobs to price, e-mails from clients, suppliers, and architects—or squeezed between the sites he manages during most of the working day: overseeing tradesmen, coordinating contractors, checking plans, sourcing supplies, finding solutions when things go wrong, chasing tradesmen who fail to turn up, sometimes even working on-site. "Everything about building is hard. Eventually everything will be beautifully finished, but to get to that finish you have to go through an absolute mess. Getting there is torture." Edward's account highlights the specific managerial problems that result when a situation of decentralized production and a culture of working autonomy persist in the face of declining skills and working conditions. Low levels of motivation and pride result from these professional circumstances and compound the problems of construction.[20]

Problems abound. There are problems to do with personnel, "working with people not of the highest order" as he puts it, half joking. "Most builders end up on the site because they haven't done well at school. If they're lucky, they latch on to a good tradesman. Most eventually fall by the wayside. They don't like the winters. The cold is absolutely wicked: numb fingers, aching limbs, day in, day out." Wages are low. The job is repetitive and physically demanding. "Most don't care. They turn up late and do what they have to do to a minimum standard." Over the years he has built a small team he trusts, but even so, relationships have to be continually nurtured. Low pay and lack of motivation are associated with absenteeism, poor workmanship, and worse: "stealing has probably happened since the dawn of time." There was a point, a while ago, where he realized "I couldn't trust any of them. They were all on the take." He sacked the team and started from scratch. Lack of apprenticeships and training opportunities, combined with increasing availability of easier and better-paid jobs in other sectors, has resulted in "the declining skills and standards of UK tradesmen." A lot of his job is about man management: "constantly trying men with other men to see if they get on. I like to think if you treat men fairly and with respect, you get a bit of respect back."

Even as skills in the construction industry have declined, the process of construction has become more complex. Edward describes building regulations that are specified in ever greater detail; complex health and safety regulations; more and more building technologies and materials; improved energy efficiency that reduces acceptable levels of tolerance. "Every seal has to be absolutely right. You need men you can rely on." On top of all this, problems relating to the supply of materials are compounded as the country comes out of economic recession: "The construction industry is picking up, but manufacturers take time to get back to original capacity. . . . Everyone is understaffed and under-resourced."

The stress that Edward describes is a product of his role: trying to make things cohere; bringing people and materials together; organizing and ordering in a world of chaos and complexity. "Under contract and driven hard, it can become a huge burden." His striking phrase conveys a sense of the contract as an ever-present force in his working life, pushed on and pressured by the demands it sets up, with specific tasks that must be undertaken to a fixed schedule and budget. The contract specifies what must be done and when, but crucially not how.

His position is a difficult one, occupying the space between the precision of a contract, a building already specified before it is built, and the imprecisions and uncertainties of a world that shares none of those qualities. If all goes well, the building is a realization of the plan as contractually specified. In practice there are many ways in which reality and contract can diverge. Improvisation, skill, and patience are needed to make a fickle and unpredictable world bend to a design that is already fixed. In construction, "mess is the law," writes the architect and theorist Jeremy Till.[21] Edward would agree, but that is not the end of the story. His job is to create order out of the mess.

Construction is complex, entangling people, materials, technologies, and places through interactions that are never completely predictable.[22] In various ways, the work of builders involves an effort to achieve order against the constant pressure of all those unknowable and unpredictable forces that threaten chaos.[23]

During construction, architects are implicated in these problems at a remove. David explains:

> It's the presence of the actual builders and how they actually build the building, which is quite interesting. It's nice to watch sometimes, just look at them and see how they work out things and how they read the drawings that you've produced and then how that actually becomes translated into a building. I find it interesting that buildings aren't really the product of architects, they're the product of the builders. What we actually produce is the drawings and the models and whatever else, and then the final product we don't have a huge amount of control over. We administer a contract that says it should be this way or that way, but we don't actually lay any of the blocks. There's a certain amount of removal there.

His thoughts echo those of architect and theorist Leon Krier: "I do not build because I am an architect: I am an architect, therefore I do not build."[24] While

architects remain detached from the practice of building, they are centrally involved in dealing with the problems thrown up by the process. Martin explains:

> One common rule is that toward the end of a building project, it invariably becomes a bit more fraught, because money runs out, time runs over, design changes mean more problems for us. It's quite rare to have a harmonious thing all the way through. And I think it always bubbles up and then often surfaces toward the end because the builder says, "Yeah, it's fine, it's fine, we'll meet the deadline, yeah it's fine," and then sometimes it's, "Hang on, actually, no we won't because the glass is late and there's this reason why the floor's not in." So there are often a few little things, but I think we always say to clients that it's going to take longer than you think and cost more than you think, because it always does.

Disagreements are often acrimonious because building sites are places of high stakes. For the builder the line between profit and loss can be tiny; fortunes are made and lost through their ability to know the unknowable, to look at a set of plans and commit to build them for a set amount of time and money. They must do so aware of the many factors unknown and beyond their control: the weather; supply problems that might emerge; problems that could lie under the ground. Known but complex, the plan on which they tender might contain an overlooked detail or misinterpreted sentence. Contractors must quote low in order to get the contract, but quote too low and the risks of losses and even bankruptcy are ever-present dangers.

Clients who take on projects of this kind are normally risking a lifetime of savings. Building houses, they are also building the futures of their lives, pursuing dreams and ideals. Even if they are wealthy by relative standards, as they must be to take on this kind of project, they are often building at or beyond their financial limits. During construction, the realization of these anticipated futures is inextricably bound up with the unknown and unknowable risks that surround the endeavor. Even a well-planned project can founder: bats are discovered in roofs, and work has to stop in order to protect them; archaeological remains are uncovered during groundwork, and excavation has to be paid for; a contractor goes bankrupt, so time and money are lost.

As contract administrators, architects find themselves at the intersection of various relationships, in a situation of unrelenting practical problems. In some respects the role is one of objective and dispassionate intermediary, though the risks and rewards are also high for them, and their commitments to the buildings are often very personal: designs carry forward a huge investment of time, each the culmination of anxieties, stress, sleepless nights. Good buildings make careers. Badly managed projects can ruin reputations and cost the practice money.

FORMALITY AND INFORMALITY

In different ways, builders and architects encounter the space between a plan and a physical building as a series of problems and issues. It is possible to resolve these through more or less formal ways of working.

The history of MHW is, in general terms, one of increasing formalization. As the scope and scale of the practice's projects have expanded, so have the budgets, the number of people involved, and the associated risks. With more to go wrong, contracts provide a way of managing risk. In the practice, architects describe what is gained by working with a contract: greater certainty that the building will be constructed as designed; an ability to control costs; and clarity about the roles of the different people involved in a project—who will do what, when, and how. They are also aware of what can be lost by working in this way.

Before she came to the practice, Megan spent a year working on a project in India, where there were no contracts. Designs were frequently worked out and changed on-site. She compares this experience favorably with working practices that prevail in the UK, as experienced at MHW:

> I've seen these different ways of working, and I think here it is very much about how you cover your back. It's a lot to do with making sure you know where your responsibility and liability ends and where the next person's begins—making that clear and covering all your steps. It's more about confrontational relationships, rather than about how to build collaborative relationships where everyone's best interests are at heart and where that starts to actually facilitate really great projects that

everyone's involved in. I feel quite constrained by commercial architecture as it's practiced here [in the UK]. It's hard for me to see the
possibilities within that confinement. Whereas in India, on that project,
the possibilities were endless. You could go wherever the process took
you. So it was very different. I find it continuously difficult to work
contractually.

In the office, they work in ways that are professional and contractual, aware of
the benefits and even necessity of doing so. Sometimes they lament what can be
lost by working in this way. Greater certainty is experienced by Megan as a loss
of the possibility and freedom that come from a more open-ended process. With
a contract in place, unanticipated eventualities cannot be seen as creative opportunities; they are only ever problems. Contracts separate roles and responsibilities, distinguishing the inputs and expectations of different parties concerned,
controlling but also fragmenting the process. Criticisms of contractual working practices reflect broader ambivalences to forms of modern bureaucracy that
architects are both complicit in and critical of.

Bigger projects tend to involve higher levels of contractualism, but every project is different. Megan explains: "On some projects we work in more formal ways,
on others it is not so formal. I think that it comes down to the characters of the
people, the budget and what's available in terms of resources, the scale of the
project, the nature of the project, and the nature of the clients. That level of formality's determined by lots of different things."

Smaller builders, in particular, often echo architects' ambivalences to highly
formalized ways of working. "I think of myself as a builder, not a contractor—
it's not just about costs and balance sheets and filling out forms." Edward, the
builder, is explaining to me the ethos that informs his work, drawing on a contrast
between builders and contractors with wider currency in the industry. He inflects
this distinction with a series of related contrasts. As a builder, he is primarily
interested in "actually doing and making things," rather than "filling out forms."
The industry is dominated by "the big boys who just want the hard cash, who live
and die by the sword of the contract." He claims his motivation for doing this is
less about making money than the "job satisfaction" that comes from doing a job
well. Where contractors make their money through rigid adherence to the terms
of the contract, he sees the process as one of "give and take": as a builder, he tries
to accommodate changes to the contract in the hope and expectation that others will be similarly flexible. "You build up relationships with architects and get
to know how they work. Over time trust builds up; it comes down to trust and
respect. If an architect makes a mistake, you think 'I'd rather they hadn't,' but try
to find a way around it."

Edward's claim to be a "builder" conveys an ideological orientation and sense of identity that only loosely relates to the scale and nature of his business. From a formal perspective, "contractor" is the generic term for whichever party undertakes to do the contracted building works.

Edward echoes Megan in his general ambivalence to excessively formalized, contractual ways of working. Proximately they both highlight what is thereby lost: trust, flexibility, creativity, and time spent on "bureaucracy." More fundamentally they express ambivalences to the kinds of standardization, commodification, and conformity they associate with modern working life. As a reflection of their specific disenchantments with the mainstream construction industry, they share a sense that bureaucracy crushes individual freedom and that money can displace other forms of value. In practice, such ambivalences to contracts are refracted as a series of specific negotiations that happen around sites. As we will see, contracts are not opposed to informality: informal interactions are required to make contracts work.

AT THE LIMITS OF THE CONTRACT

On a site meeting at Wormwood House, the groundworks are completed and the stud walls are in construction. Edward, the builder, is unfazed by a minor amendment to the plan, resulting from a client change of mind: they want to move a window. "It might cause a small delay, but we will try to make it up." Edward sees this as part of the "give and take" of building. Rob pushes for clarity: "It's a design variation, so in the worst-case scenario what would it cost?" he asks. Later, in the car on the way back, he describes the balance inherent in managing interactions on-site—between what's "contractual" and what's "sensible and friendly." For a project to run smoothly, it is important to cultivate good working relationships: the architect tries to accommodate and be flexible if things are built other than to the plan. In return, the builder might accommodate small changes without additional costs. "Often it works best to be friendly and a bit jokey—to keep a positive dynamic," he tells me, recognizing the instrumental importance of *appearing* not only to have instrumental motives at heart. However, problems can result from a lack of formal communication: "Often the builder doesn't mention additions and modifications as they come up and then wants an extension in time and more money at the end. As an architect you can see that this relates to issues earlier discussed, but the client can't see why there is suddenly an additional cost." Keeping relationships "contractual" and "professional" is a way of retaining control—of time, money, and what is built.

From an architectural perspective, seeing where a building diverges from the plan is an important skill. Returning from a site visit to Wormwood House, Tomas and Rob discuss the construction of a damp-proof course, built in a way that doesn't correspond to the plan. "A good spot," Rob jokes, annoyed that he missed it himself. Tomas puts it down to experience: "You develop eyes for these details—that's what you get from ten years of worrying and sleepless nights!" As they discuss the issue, they are sketching, trying to work out whether it is a problem and, if so, what the solution might be. The impermeable membrane has been laid under, rather than on top of, a wall footing: "Does it matter if the rain can come in on the top?" Tomas wonders aloud. Issues of design are inextricable from questions of liability and risk. Architects' words and drawings occupy the space between these. They are trying to make assessments in relation to factors they cannot entirely know about. How likely is water penetration? How much of a problem would this be? They discuss various scenarios and reach a tentative agreement: the "deviation" is unlikely to affect the structural performance of the building, a decision that is later checked in the office and confirmed in writing.

Builders and contractors are attuned to identify gaps between the contracted plan and the built reality, in a focus that mirrors that of the architects. Where architects are concerned to highlight problems in the building, contractors are concerned to find shortcomings and inconsistencies in the plan. These can be exploited to maximize profits. Now in his mid-thirties, Phil spent much of the last decade working on large, publicly funded projects. He identifies this approach as a definitive characteristic of larger contractors:

> You get some builders where it's a business, and they're there to make as much money out of it as possible. They will look for all the loopholes in the tender documents and add on the extra costs where they can and do the tricky things when they're tendering. They'll look for all the things that are missing, and put in the lowest cost, and then hit you for it later.

Money is made by exploiting the gap between what is specified and what will be needed. Some contractors will cost for the former, knowing that they can amend the contract to account for the latter without competitive tender, and therefore end up being in a stronger position to dictate the price. On one MHW project, the architects fail to adequately detail where the electric supply will be taken from. Lacking this information, the contractor legitimately costs for the minimal length of cable to reach the edge of the site, knowing they will be able to charge for the additional work without formal tender and hence on more favorable terms.[25]

Whether or not the contractor's motivation is purely to maximize profit, the identification of deviations is understood as a necessary part of the process of managing costs and time. Edward makes this explicit: "Architects can try to roll you over if you don't put everything in writing. But if you do, it can get out of hand; you do nothing but write letters." All plans require builders to improvise in order to make them work.. What is crucial, from the builder's perspective, is that these expected accommodations are distinguished from additional work, set in train by factors outside those specified through the contract. In practice the question of where the contract begins and ends can often be moot.

On another occasion Rob is discussing progress with Edward the builder and Toby the mechanical and electrical engineer. Wooden stud walls are now finished on the ground floor. As they discuss developments with the construction, it becomes apparent that there's a problem. The ventilation system was meant to go in the joists, but some metalwork is in the way. Contractually speaking, it is initially unclear where the blame lies. Efforts to resolve the problem take the form of good-natured banter between architect and contractor, though possible cost and time implications give these negotiations a more serious undercurrent. Edward suggests the problem arises from an incorrectly detailed plan. Rob wonders whether the issue has developed from inaccuracies setting out the foundations, though he concedes to uncertainty: "Engineers always like to stick in steels without telling me!" he quips, as he rifles through the ring binder containing the detailed contracted plans. "Well, they know how to build—unlike architects!" Edward retorts, a joking parody of the profession that seems intended to plant a further seed of doubt.

The issue of blame still unresolved, various options are discussed: the steel could be cut, but would need to be sent away, with the possibility of extra cost and delay; the ventilation pipe could be rerouted around the beam but would need to be boxed in, with a negative visual impact that neither client nor architect want. Builder and architect continue to talk as Rob sketches some possible ways of resolving the issue. Perhaps the steel could be drilled, to allow the pipe to go through it? The structural engineer is called, and he says that the necessary modification would not compromise structural integrity. Both agree to proceed in this way. Rob jots down a "minute" to this effect. A sentence is the only formal documentation of complex negotiations that have taken over thirty minutes.

Edward, the contractor, is sanguine and sees it as part of the process: "There are no certainties in building. Or to put it another way, nothing ever goes to plan!" On building sites things rarely go to plan but must be *made* to do so. In a range of practical interactions, most significantly regular site meetings, the relationship between plan and site is a central focus. Architects and contractors, among others, bring distinct assessments of how and whether these diverge, who is to blame, and with what consequences. As one relatively minor issue among countless others, the issue of the wrongly located steel beam shows how architect and builder collaborate to improvise solutions to bring site and plan together.

Contracts have a clarity that is impossible to fully sustain in the face of the relationships and negotiations required to realize the transaction a particular contract establishes.[26] A building can only be constructed through a set of practices, negotiations, and relationships that necessarily exceed the formal terms of the contract.[27] Architects aim to maintain a distinction between elements of these interactions that do and do not bear on the formal terms of the contract. The day-to-day work of architects routinely reproduces this in countless minor, mostly unremarkable, decisions: which elements of a discussion are significant enough to require documentation as a formal "minute"? When does an action arising from a site note warrant an architectural instruction to be issued? Of all the many interactions and minor accommodations between site and plan, which do and do not affect the overall terms of the contract? Often, but not always, there is agreement as to where this distinction is to be drawn. Minor amendments, seen at the time as part of the necessary give and take, can add up so that one or the other side later retrospectively interprets that they have given more than they have taken. Worrying about shrinking profits or even losses, builders may seek to recover what they feel they are losing, attempting to frame earlier work as contractual deviations with cost implications.

DISENTANGLEMENT

Construction entangles various people and things that must be disentangled for the building to exist as "property."[28] As contract administrators, architects oversee these transactions, acting as independent adjudicators to regulate the flow: the contractor must build to the specifications that are contractually outlined in the schedule of works according to the outlined timeline; the client must in turn disburse a given amount of funds at a time agreed in advance.

As a project progresses, labor and materials are assembled as structures that the client owns, as money is progressively made over. Regular site meetings (normally every two weeks) are key moments in this exchange: the architect inspects the work and, if satisfied, will issue the certificate that obliges the client to pay. Martin explains:

> The builders will do weekly evaluations, or maybe fortnightly or monthly on big projects. They'll say to us, "Okay, we've done 100 percent of the groundworks, we've done 60 percent of below damp, we've done 20 percent of the windows, we've done 10 percent of this, therefore you owe us this amount of money, minus what is a retention, normally a 5 percent retention." So, for example, they'd say, "Okay, you owe us £23,100." We'll often then check through that, go to site and say "Yeah, I can see you've done all that, that's fine." And we'll release an interim certificate of payment to the client for the client to pay the builder. So there's this kind of iteration, of the builder saying, "We've done this, we want to be paid," and us saying, "Yeah, that's all fine"; or, if not, we can

turn up on-site and say, "No, hang on, that wall there is not to the spec of the design," or "It's wonky," or "There's something wrong with it, take it down, rebuild it at your time and expense." So there is that legal thing of contractually administering a contract on-site. The builder asks us for money; we check progress and then release payment through the client to them.

Contracts assume and require the existence of independent agents—autonomous individuals whose actions and interests are distinct—but the process of construction can proceed only through actions and relations that enmesh them. Those involved—architects, builders, engineers, clients—must be dependent in some moments, and independent in others. Where those involved make these movements in tandem, the process proceeds without problem or comment. Issues arise where relationships cannot be easily disaggregated into the specified roles of the contract: whether or not parties have acted contractually may become a point of contention.

On one occasion Tomas expresses exasperation at a project that is taking up time they at the practice do not have; their project fee was used up weeks ago. A design to which they feel personally attached now seems unlikely to be built as planned, if it is even finished at all. Nobody is blaming the architects, but even so they feel empathy for both parties: an honest and likable builder, with whom they have previously worked, is being pushed to the verge of bankruptcy; the future of a couple's "dream home" is threatened by the complications of a building project that have also put a strain on the couple's relationship.

Prompted by a frustrated call from the builder, the practice directors Tomas and Tom, together with the project architect Martin, are discussing how to proceed. It is one of a string of conversations about a building that, although almost completed, has become mired in problems. Animosity has built up between builder and client to the point where the parties are no longer talking. For weeks, the only communications have been via angry calls to the architect, each side laying the blame firmly with the other. Misunderstandings have been compounded by the lack of communication that is both cause and result of the breakdown of the relationship. It is hard to disentangle cause and consequence, though this is what they now need to do, and is partly what the conversation in the office is now about. The bare facts of the case are simple: the client feels the contractor has not acted, in contractual terms, "duly and diligently." The work, the client says, has not been completed on time or to standard. He is withholding payment on these grounds. The builder will not finish the work until he is paid, and the client will not pay until the work is finished. At issue is the question of how to proceed from here.

One way would be to try to rebuild the trust that has been lost in the relationship at the heart of the problem. Such mediation is one element of the practice's duty as contract administrator: "Our job is to build relationships as much as buildings," Tomas explains to me on another occasion. Cajoling, persuading, facilitating communication and understanding between the people involved, or sometimes simply "being nice to people": these are all part of the complex role of building and maintaining good relations. This has been an element of negotiations to date, but the office discussion solidifies the consensus position: the situation has developed to a point where restoring trust is no longer possible. Tomas summarizes: "Working relationships have broken down completely. The only way forward is to resolve it contractually."

This is a difficult end to achieve. It involves the retrospective work of disentangling a situation characterized by the blurring of lines that should contractually have remained clear. Tomas explains the irony that an initially good working relationship seems to have generated some of these contractual uncertainties: at one point, when builder and client were "almost friends," decisions were made between them that started, as Tomas puts it, "to take them away from the contract." In disregard of advice from the architects, changes were made on an ad hoc basis and went undocumented. Extra work was agreed to, without formal notification of deviation from the contract. Roles became further blurred when the client started to do work the builder was contracted to do. The architects' role of contract administrator was bypassed, in a series of minor decisions that were never recorded and are now in doubt. Only later did it become apparent that the two sides did not share an understanding of the nature of the work and the cost incurred.

"Our job is to bring them back into the contract," Tomas says. What does this involve? Disputed understandings of what happened and what was agreed have been compounded by inadequate documentation; bringing both sides back to a contract requires an effort to retrospectively establish a degree of clarity. Claim and counterclaim are disregarded, the only considerations being what the contract specified and what has demonstrably happened (money paid, work done) as evidenced by existing documentation and the building itself.

Relationships are reduced, as Tomas puts it, to a "purely contractual form": what has been done, and what has been paid. The architects draw up a balance sheet of transactions: money on one side; the more or less completed stages of a building on the other. Bringing both parties "back into the contract" requires the fleshy and practical affairs of everyday interactions to be transmuted into a relationship that exists in documented form: a set of carefully constructed words and numbers. Not voluntarily inclined to interact in this way, both parties have to be coaxed and cajoled into "acting contractually."

David describes another project where roles had become blurred:

> There was an issue with one client where things were looking like they
> were heading in a litigious direction, and I volunteered to kind of
> go in and try to smooth things over a little bit. It was a very difficult
> situation, partly because of a very difficult client, who was making
> enormous numbers of requests for changes to the contract, involv-
> ing extensions of time and modifications to the price, hundreds of
> minor little changes of mind and everything, and the contractor tear-
> ing his hair out and getting defensive. I went in and really took a lot
> of pleasure in getting all the paperwork together and going through
> it meticulously, and balancing all these elements—like an accounting
> exercise. There's something of the geeky computer person in me there,
> which relished that and loved it.

There is a procedural satisfaction to achieving clarity. Distinct from this is the
more personal pleasure of what it accomplishes—helping others. "It's to do with
a sense of assurance and allaying people's fears. It's all to do with saying 'don't
worry, it's all right, we've got it all sorted out.'"

David dropped out of the architectural profession before doing the practically
oriented Part III—the final stage of an architect's training, in which the work of
running contracts is central. Various personal and ideological factors played a
part, but an antipathy to the contractual system of mainstream architecture was a
significant factor. "The attitude was, 'there's going to be a revolution, so we don't
need to bother with that! That will all kind of be sorted out in a different way,'" he
tells me. His tone conveys amusement at the vagueness of his own youthful idealism, though he retains a lingering sympathy for the radicalism that propelled it.
Influenced by broader antiestablishment thinking of the time, he was skeptical
of a system that seemed unnecessarily bureaucratic, which was tied into capitalist
forms of production, and which seemed the antithesis of the creative and even
anarchic tendencies that initially drew him to architecture.

It was to his own surprise that, returning to the profession over thirty years
later, he found that contracts held a strange appeal: "I then went back to do my
Part III at Bath, which I loved. I loved learning about contract law. Nothing to do
with buildings, but all to do with contracts, building regulations, the breach of
law." I ask him what the attraction was.

> It's formal, it's mathematical, almost. And the notion it's enforceable,
> the notion that words—a carefully constructed system of words—can
> constrain people's behavior and be enforceable; and at the same time,
> in an ideal situation, the contract serves as a safety net. If you know the

contract, then you can do all sorts of acrobatics above it and interact with clients and builders in really creative and informal ways, but there's always that contract that sits below you in case anything goes wrong.

For David, the revelation was that contractual constraint and creativity need not be at odds, as he had previously imagined. The image of the contract as safety net makes this vividly evident: as the safety net allows the acrobat to perform breathtaking maneuvers of otherwise impossible risk, so, in his view, the contract enables the architect to innovate and experiment. Sitting below the informal interactions through which building work proceeds, ideally untouched, it allows risks to be taken in the knowledge that lines of responsibility can be disentangled if things go wrong. In one sense "outside" the contract, informal and creative interactions with builders and clients are in another sense enabled by it.

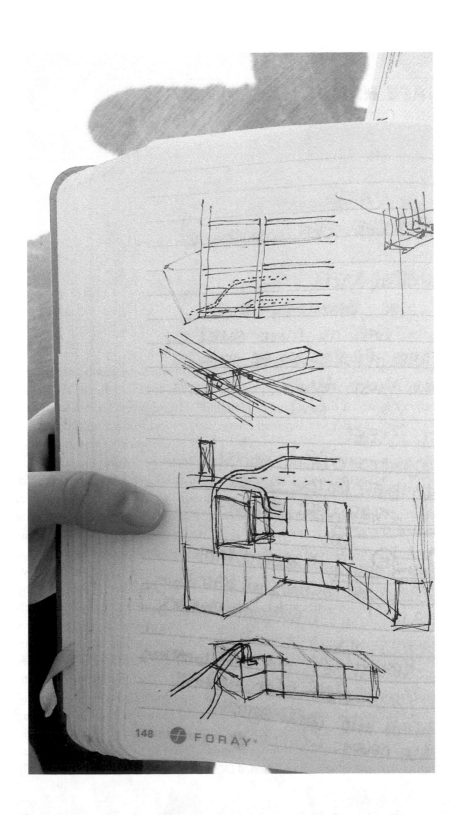

FORAY

SAFE HANDS

As we arrive on-site for a meeting at Wormwood House, the clients, Robert and Judith, are already there and are chatting with Edward the builder. "We've just been talking about the meaning of life itself!" Edward jokes. Their relationship has a contractual element, but their interactions on and around the building also encompass other interests and concerns. Later in the week Robert and Judith reflect on the relationship at the heart of the build, over a drink in their local pub. From the start of the project, they knew they had a limited budget to work within, but also that it was crucial to "get the right person." Considerations of character, ethos, and approach were an important element of the selection process, once the tender quotes came back. Robert explains: "We wanted to get a feel for them as people, really. You know, it's a major project, we needed to choose somebody that we felt we could work with, and we wanted to feel like they engaged with what we were looking for. . . . We wanted the builder to be enthused by the site and really latch on to what we were trying to create. That was important, wasn't it?" Judith agrees: "Edward seemed calm, confident—you felt you were in safe hands." As a client, there is no contractual reason for her to be involved in site meetings, but she normally goes along anyway. She lives locally and occasionally looks in at other times: "Just to see how things are progressing. . . . I'm interested in getting to know the builders a little bit, and there's different people that come on-site, and it's nice to have a bit more of a relationship with them—to know what's going on, and chat to them a little bit." Robert's work takes him away during the week, and he visits less frequently, though he agrees, "It's nice to know who's building your house." Judith continues, "Well, it is, and, you know, they're working really hard, in searing temperatures at one point. . . . I like them to think that we're appreciating what they're doing—really, it's great. I know they're getting paid and everything, but . . ." She leaves the thought unfinished, though her point is already made: building a house involves relationships that, in sometimes profound ways, develop beyond their straightforwardly pragmatic and contractual dimensions. Like Edward, Judith and Robert stress the importance of the informal dimensions of these relationships: the appointment of a contractor with shared values, the nurturing of trust and the give and take that go with it, can facilitate the work at the heart of the contract. Yet their accounts also involve a moral distinction that goes beyond this instrumental logic: as an embodiment of values they hold dear, the house retains a relation to those involved in its construction that is not, as they see it, entirely discharged by the transactional logic in which the house as "property" is exchanged for money. The significance of the building is partly established through the process of its construction: it matters to them who built it and how.

PROFESSIONALISM

Tom, the codirector of the practice, describes the personal attributes required to oversee a contract: "Running a project on-site, as a contracted administrator, requires very little of what I would call the deeply creative stuff but lots of being very process driven, logical, practical, and interpersonal." These are elements of "professionalism." What does this mean in practice?

A set of designs have been handed over to a client, who has sent these out to tender. It is a small project, so MHW's formal involvement is over. However, the client is unsure how to interpret the contractors' quotes. In the office they are unclear whether the quotes have all been priced to the tendered schedule, and therefore whether they can be compared as equivalent. The client has e-mailed, requesting further advice. A meeting was agreed to, "wanting to be helpful," as Tomas puts it: partly through a sense of duty to a client they have come to know and like; partly to a commitment to the design itself. Rob, the project architect, thinks they can offer useful advice that will help the client understand the tender process and which could prevent major problems when the building commences. Tomas is concerned the result may be to "blur lines." He is worrying about appearing to give reassurance in relation to factors beyond their control and outside their responsibility: "It would be more honest to say we don't actually know what might have been missed out. Problems have occurred in the past where we overstep our responsibilities to try to be helpful, and end up making the situation worse by providing reassurances we can't actually guarantee." He reflects on one project in particular, where the client was a friend before he became a client: "We were trying to be helpful, doing things that weren't really our responsibility."

On another project, there is a disagreement relating to the contractual relationship between client and builder. The issue is whether work already undertaken involves a contractual deviation, with implications for time and cost. The builder is claiming it does, in an e-mail that is read aloud and then the focus of a brief discussion in the office. Tomas, as director, reminds Rob of the need to be "detached": "It's not your opinion—you're quoting case law, so you can distance yourself from it." Professionalism is in this sense the act of disconnecting who they are from what they know, through the careful adherence to established principles and forms of conduct. Tomas continues: "As contract administrator it's up to you to give your judgment, not to negotiate." The issue is not just *how* to interact, but also *how much*. Professionalism involves resistance to being drawn into forms of interaction with the potential to compromise their role as "detached" mediators.

Often the architects work with people they know well: friends become clients; building work creates relationships that develop beyond what is required from a narrowly contractual perspective. Acting in accordance with professional procedural norms—"being professional"—does not mean that other more personal relationships cannot be sustained alongside this; it simply means that these different kinds of relationship are treated as distinct.[29]

Professionalism is the imperative to align actions and words with the collectively established principles and procedures of the discipline. It relates to a kind of authority established through the extrication of the individual, subjective self— those many thoughts, emotions, and characteristics that are personally specific to them. This involves playing a role. Words are delivered in a precise and measured manner, with even pace and steady tone. Facial expressions are minimized in a way that similarly downplays the individual characteristics of the speaker.

Professional knowledge is the explicit focus of the training that architects receive during their Part III. Undertaken while architecturally employed, instruction on the legislative and contractual elements of architecture is combined with reflection on the routine issues that arise during the management of projects. Over time, these are embodied as a largely tacit set of understandings relating to the legal and contractual elements of the profession. As architects gain more experience of professional practice, much of this knowledge becomes routine. Even so, the specific question of how to be professional remains. On the one hand, the legislative and legal basis on which they act is of an order of complexity that can never be fully mastered. On the other, the question of how this is applied to particular projects always involves some element of interpretation and elaboration. "Professionalism"[30] is an ideal, relating to the virtues of acting procedurally, but achieving this ideal depends on the extension of this logic to specific cases.[31]

LISTEN: CONTROL AND CREATIVITY

Tomas, Milo, and Rob are in discussion.

TOMAS: A lot of the issues we deal with are about control. While I feel we ultimately are in control of the projects we are working on, sometimes in the thick of a situation there can be a feeling of a loss of control. The more we can do to counter this, the better. You will never be in control of everything, but there can be an ambition toward that. I can imagine processes that we become really in control of, and I feel really confident that we know how to do them. Actually, I think we're very, very close to it, where it's things that we're doing again and again, like a new-build house. These things are difficult, but learning from the previous projects, we can really learn to control them—control clients' expectations, control contractors on-site. I'd really like to get to the position that we just feel in control on all of those things, which I think we're close to. But there are some things we don't, and that's including our own time on a project. I think some of my recent frustrations have been when I feel we're slightly out of control, and that's where I just get frustrated, because I feel like we should be there. There's another question, though, on top of that. So, say we achieve this position where we're now totally in control of the project. I then want to question it, like "Is that where we want to be?" I want to get there first.

MILO: Yeah, there's a place where it's just like, "well, you want that detail, plonk that detail in." It's almost like being more a kit of parts, and you can be totally in control of a plug-and-play symbol library with a cost attached. We could put ourselves in that position quite quickly, quite easily. Do you want to be in that place? I don't know. It's just like Lego blocks.

ROB: Well, I don't want to try and be in that much control; I want people to pay me for my creative design time.

MILO: Yeah, fascinating territory. Is it two design consultants and a factory beneath? That's not a very good model. I'm not saying it should be, but it could be.

TOMAS: Yes, it could be. I think it's a really interesting question.

ROB: But I think that kit of parts, and knowing the cost of those, is quite a closed loop. I sort of think the joy of having engineers and quantity surveyors and designers, it's a team, you know, it's a team process, and yeah, we're the ones that have to coordinate that and be in control of the process. So it doesn't stifle the creativity, or it shouldn't stifle creativity, but the process needs to be controlled.

TIME FRAME

Contracts specify what must happen but also when. Architects must coordinate things in time as well as in space, making sure buildings are constructed "as planned" and "on time."[32] Each project is made up of a series of phases. The completion of phases is linked to the payment of fees. Intervals are prescribed in advance, limited by a fee proposal through which costs are fixed. Projects anticipate a series of known future outcomes that are worked toward: the definition of a brief; the development of a design; the detailed development of plans for planning permission and then for tendering; and the construction of the building. The time of the project is linear and sequential: each phase follows the next, one after the other. Keeping things "on time" is an important but difficult accomplishment.

"I suppose the architect's age-old problem is running out of time and meeting the client's deadlines. It runs all through projects, doesn't it?" Phil is talking with Ronan about a pervasive architectural experience: a lack of time. Where does this come from? they wonder together.

> RONAN: It's the little changes and things, which add up frequently until you think, "Oh, I'll just provide that piece of information or tweak that little thing," and those sorts of things can add up incredibly quickly, can't they?
>
> PHIL: Yes, I suppose the unexpected. You can program for what you're aware of, but I think projects have a sort of life of their own, and I suppose there's a number of factors that affect that, whether it's

the client, the contractor, site issues, planning, building regs: it can completely skew the time frame.

RONAN: Generally we make little to no profit on the construction and admin side of things, or significantly less than on the early stages.

PHIL: Yes, with traditional contracts it's a lot more onerous. You're the ones being chased by the contractors for construction information, clients changing their minds—obviously that's something for us to be very aware of when those things do come up.

RONAN: Do you think there is a tension, as well, between just running the contract as an administrative exercise, but at the same time there's the desire on the part of the architects to ensure a sort of aesthetic ambition, so as architects we tend to bend over a bit too far?

PHIL: Yes, we as architects want the best building we can create, and I guess that we will put the extra time in to make sure we get it right. Contract admin, that's set, and that can be done pretty efficiently and quickly. But if it's design tweaks or seeing something on-site that isn't quite working, and us wanting to get it right, I think we are always going to be extra mindful of that and want to get it right. That probably makes the time pressure worse. It's not just on-site; it's getting the tender information, detailed design, and wanting to get that just right. You end up spending more time than probably you should do getting that done.

Ronan and Phil describe a number of linked ways in which the process of design and then construction expand beyond the time that is allocated. To claim, as they sometimes do, that "projects have a life of their own" is to highlight the difficulty of controlling the many people and things that design and building bring together. On another occasion one of the architects remarks that buildings and design "create their own time," an acknowledgment of the diversity of these relationships and hence of time itself. Tasks expand to take more time, because processes develop in ways that cannot be controlled as anticipated and hoped. Tasks are expanded by the "aesthetic ambition" associated with a perfectionist impulse. This often leads architects to invest time in pursuit of buildings that exceed what is minimally acceptable.

If time and task have a habit of diverging, considerable effort is exerted in trying to bring these together. Marianne, the office manager, is responsible for invoices, sending these out at the end of phases, as outlined in the fee proposal that clients are sent at the start of a project. "How much should we invoice for this project?" she asks Tomas, on one occasion among hundreds. "Look at the dashboard," Tomas tells her, directing her to the place that project time is logged. But how much time has been used often relates imprecisely to how much progress has been made. "How far through are we?" Tomas asks the project architect, wondering how far the design has come. Nobody is exactly sure, principally because there is no precise way to gage the "completion" of a design: improvement is always possible, in principle. From a brief discussion of progress on the project, consensus emerges that there is more to do than time to do it—time and task have, as often, diverged. Their reconciliation will require various kinds of accommodation: "speeding up" and "focusing" work to accelerate "progress." Alongside this is the recognition that more time will have to be spent than has been budgeted for in the fee proposal. Overruns can be a source of concern within the office. Time costs money; delays can lead to frictions with clients and contractors.

"Managing time" is in practice a matter of *making* time. Events are ordered so that they conform to the time that is allocated and budgeted in contracts with clients. Architects must recognize where these diverge and take action to make them converge. The linear, phased, time of the project is not an all-pervasive determining principle of design and construction. Practices and events frequently elude or challenge this. At the same time, this understanding of time significantly orients how processes of design and construction take place. Architects act with these ideas more or less centrally in mind, even as they recognize the gap between what *should* happen and what *actually* happened.

Different projects order and measure time in the same basic ways, assuming sequential progression from one phase to the next. These apparently singular representations of time are associated with a range of qualitatively different experiences. Work is sometimes boring, and time can "drag"; as deadlines approach it can "fly." The project sets its own time, but events may not follow this: time can be "lost" and needs to be "made up"; it is possible to "fall behind" or "catch up." Sometimes, there are "blockages." A task seems impossible to complete, but all the while project time and money are progressing. The disconnection between what should have been done and what has been achieved is associated with various experiences: anxieties relate to doubts about personal inadequacy or inefficiency. There is concern, particularly among the directors, that as time is lost, so is money.[33]

Project time is not an invariant or given. It is created, produced, and managed through the interactions of architects.[34] Mundane documents and bureaucratic procedures are central to how this is done. Contracts specify how long various phases of design and construction will take. Architects fill out time sheets to log the amount of time they spend on specific projects. Meetings mark the beginning and ending of phases, making visible what has been done and setting up future

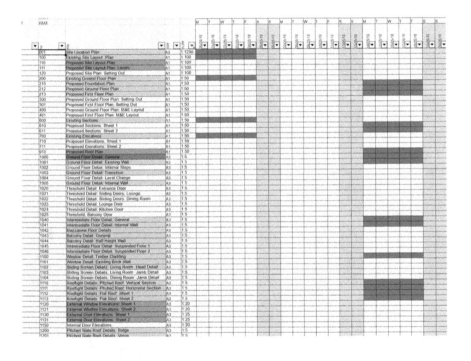

001	Site Location Plan	A3	1:1250
100	Existing Site Layout Plan	A1	1:100
110	Proposed Site Layout Plan	A1	1:100
111	Proposed Site Layout Plan: Levels	A1	1:100
120	Proposed Site Plan: Setting Out	A1	1:100
200	Existing Ground Floor Plan	A1	1:50
210	Proposed Foundation Plan	A1	1:50
212	Proposed Ground Floor Plan	A1	1:50
213	Proposed First Floor Plan	A1	1:50
300	Proposed Ground Floor Plan: Setting Out	A1	1:50
301	Proposed First Floor Plan: Setting Out	A1	1:50
400	Proposed Ground Floor Plan: M&E Layout	A1	1:50
401	Proposed First Floor Plan: M&E Layout	A1	1:50
600	Existing Sections	A1	1:50
610	Proposed Sections: Sheet 1	A1	1:50
611	Proposed Sections: Sheet 2	A1	1:50
700	Existing Elevations	A1	1:50
710	Proposed Elevations: Sheet 1	A1	1:50
711	Proposed Elevations: Sheet 2	A1	1:50
910	Proposed Roof Plan	A1	1:50
1000	Ground Floor Detail: General	A3	1:5
1001	Ground Floor Detail: Existing Wall	A3	1:5
1002	Ground Floor Detail: Internal Steps	A3	1:5
1003	Ground Floor Detail: Transition	A3	1:5
1004	Ground Floor Detail: Level Change	A3	1:5
1005	Ground Floor Detail: Internal Wall	A3	1:5
1020	Threshold Detail: Entrance Door	A3	1:5
1021	Threshold Detail: Sliding Doors, Lounge	A3	1:5
1022	Threshold Detail: Sliding Doors, Dining Room	A3	1:5
1023	Threshold Detail: Lounge Door	A3	1:5
1024	Threshold Detail: Kitchen Door	A3	1:5
1025	Threshold Detail: Balcony Door	A3	1:5
1040	Intermediate Floor Detail: General	A3	1:5
1041	Intermediate Floor Detail: Internal Wall	A3	1:5
1042	Mezzanine Floor Details	A3	1:5
1043	Balcony Detail: General	A3	1:5
1044	Balcony Detail: Half Height Wall	A3	1:5
1045	Intermediate Floor Detail: Suspended Floor 1	A3	1:5
1046	Intermediate Floor Detail: Suspended Floor 2	A3	1:5
1100	Window Detail: Timber Cladding	A3	1:5
1101	Window Detail: Existing Brick Wall	A3	1:5
1102	Sliding Screen Details: Living Room, Head Detail	A3	1:5
1103	Sliding Screen Details: Living Room, Jamb Detail	A3	1:5
1104	Sliding Screen Details: Dining Room, Jamb Detail	A3	1:5
1110	Rooflight Details: Pitched Roof, Vertical Section	A3	1:5
1111	Rooflight Details: Pitched Roof, Horizontal Section	A3	1:5
1112	Rooflight Details: Flat Roof, Sheet 1	A3	1:5
1113	Rooflight Details: Flat Roof, Sheet 2	A3	1:5
1120	External Window Elevations: Sheet 1	A3	1:20
1121	External Window Elevations: Sheet 2	A3	1:20
1130	External Door Elevations: Sheet 1	A3	1:25
1131	External Door Elevations: Sheet 2	A3	1:25
1150	Internal Door Elevations	A3	1:20
1200	Pitched Slate Roof Details: Ridge	A3	1:5
1201	Pitched Slate Roof Details: Verge	A3	1:5

"actions." They do not simply take place "in" time but are moments in which time is ordered, organized, segmented, and divided into phases.[35]

"Managing time" is, in this respect, a matter of trying to contain the complex and unpredictable process of design within the finite periods that projects assume and require. This involves efforts to make the latter conform to the former: doing things more quickly; prompting responses from intransigent planners or builders; enforcing deadlines within the office even where this may mean lowering expectations of what can be achieved; focusing a process that has been open-ended.[36]

RHYTHMS OF WORK

During one of our discussions Tomas reflects on the problems of setting a collective pace for their work, contrasting the activities in the office with those of a more obviously manual character.: "In the office I find people are going at their own paces, whereas on a building site, if one of you is fitting a set of cabinets and the other's fitting a bench seat, at lunch time, when you look at each other's work, it's really obvious how far along you've got with it." Seated at computers, the processes and products of the working life of a designer lack these obvious qualities of visibility. Consequently, the pace and tempo of these tasks can be difficult for others to discern. Designs are tucked away in digital folders, or glimpsed only in the fleeting movements and partial perspectives of the flickering screens of others. Watch what they do and it is equally difficult to tell anything about the pace of their work: mouse clicks; eyes absorbed; bodily movements are minimal. In any case, there is little if any visible relationship between the speed at which the task is performed and the rate at which the design progresses.

Coordination is required: to keep a project on time, and to manage the competing demands of different projects.

The "9:35" meeting involves everyone in the office. It is intended, as Tom explains to me, as "a quick 'what's everyone doing?'" The aim is to brief everyone on what everyone else is working on. "Very quick and snappy." There is no agenda. Minimal notes are taken. Without documentation, talk is less consequential, and so freer. To encourage the virtues of brevity, the meeting takes place in a loosely assembled circle of standing bodies, in the center of the room, away from desks. People speak in turn, describing what they are working on, highlighting any significant issues that are likely to impinge on the work of others. More than a couple of sentences and Martin moves discussion on: "Next!"—shouted with a good-humored abruptness. In the same room, the architects inhabit the parallel worlds of their different projects. The 9:35 meeting is one of the meetings that bring these worlds together. Deliberately bracketing detailed considerations of design and construction, it is intended as a way of coordinating and allocating work. Who is working to schedule, and who needs to catch up? Who needs what help, and who can provide it?

An online calendar shared across the office makes it possible to coordinate the competing demands of different projects in time and in space: a typical week looks like this: Monday: Sam, Rob, and Milo away; 9:30–11, weekly project meeting; 1800, backup server. Tuesday: 2, Rob to Back Lane (TBC); 2–3, John and Steve to the office. Wednesday: Tom and Tomas, prospects; Thursday: 10–11, practice development; 2, Franacker, on-site. At once a description and a prescription, this mostly unremarked-upon tool creates the order it presupposes, coordinating people in place and in time.

Until recently, time management across projects mostly happened, as Tomas puts it, "intuitively." The directors looked at projects and allocated them on the basis of their understanding of who was over- or under-worked. Weekly meetings were one way in which this was regulated. Tomas describes a change in approach:

> We've been looking at our time prediction, which is the first time that we've done this. So this is looking at all our future jobs and how much work we think is going to be needed on each one and then putting all of that into one big database so we can get the picture of the whole office at any one time. We're starting to do that a bit more scientifically, in a kind of measured way. That seems to have been met with quite a lot of appreciation from everyone else, who maybe at times have suffered from having multiple projects with overlapping timescales and expectations.

The change of approach is partly driven by a desire to improve "efficiency": fitting more things into less time is more profitable, but is also associated with a qualitative difference in how time is experienced. Megan describes the change: "It's also a shift from being on the back foot to being on the front foot, because I think when you're on the back foot it's like 'fuck!'"

She is chatting with Tomas, who agrees: "It's really not fun, either." Megan adds in turn, "It's like it doesn't matter, you're just keeping things as they are; you're not really directing anything." The desire to control time relates to the fear of being controlled by it.

"Stress," a word commonly used in the office, describes a pervasive, if variably experienced, feeling: of more things to do than time to do them. As I observed the activities of the office, projects seemed well resourced and run, but the competing demands of projects can set up expectations that cause individual anxiety, compounded by the perfectionist imperative: that a design can always potentially be improved. Tom and Tomas regulate the amount of work MHW has, being selective about what the practice takes on, but often it is difficult to do this with precision. Lead-in times cannot always be judged; projects run over; staff take vacations and can leave at short notice. What appears from an organizational perspective as a problem of coordination is personally experienced as a sense of disjunction: between the amount that needs doing and the capacity of a person to do it.

In the office the directors, Tom and Tomas, are the fulcrum for a lot of the interactions—when big decisions need making or problems arise, they are deferred to them. "When am I going to do any work!" Tomas exclaims on one occasion, in only half joking desperation. "There are different kinds of work!" Tom replies. But earlier he had himself voiced a similar sentiment. "Are you particularly busy at the moment?" I wondered, picking up on a series of comments about lack of time, lapsed deadlines, and stress: "We are always particularly busy!" he jokes.

The term "stress" is invoked for different reasons: as an explanation of things not done, or an implicit request not to do them; a call for assistance or sympathy. What does stress feel like? Architects register this emotionally and physically in various ways: as a tightness across the forehead, a pain between the shoulders, the mental discombobulation of feeling "pulled apart," or the dizzying disorientation of being taken "in different directions"; conversely the feeling of external forces pushing in: being "squished" and "squashed."

LISTEN: BLOCKED

Tomas is talking to himself. He is reflecting on the day on his way home from work, a semi-regular audio-diary he agrees to keep for me after I have finished the main period of my research. "What am I going to talk about?" he wonders aloud. There's a pause, and then he settles on his theme for the day: "I think I might talk a bit about working and project management and time management." His daily commute takes about ten minutes—over Minchinhampton, then down through winding, wooded lanes into Stroud valley. The monologue is punctuated by the sounds of a now familiar journey: gears shifting up and down; the engine strains then idles; frequently indicated turns:

> We've just been having a conversation in the office about how people get blockages about things. So you'll do some things really quickly and easily, and something that should take ages you do very quickly, and then something that should be very quick, like writing a short letter, you can get a blockage about. I think we all in the office have different things that we find difficult, or get a blockage about on a project. Seeing that in someone else can be quite frustrating, but then it's very understandable when you consider your own blockages. And I think it's a well-known thing that there are some things that you just never get round to doing. . . . But I suppose as an architect you don't tend to get trained in that stuff, you're just expected to have those abilities already, or pick them up, but you're

kind of learning from people who've taught themselves as well. It's easy to not talk about that stuff. So you can be in the office and you can talk about design, and when something needs to go out, or what work needs to be done. But you might be less inclined to talk about generally how a project gets done and the typical things that might get in the way of it being done as quickly as possible, or as well as possible. And people seem to appreciate it when you talk about it, and realize that they're not the only person sitting there with something that they're not doing. So what's interesting about that with architecture? I suppose it's a creative process, isn't it, and so it's not something that has a strict procedure. If you work in a McDonald's there are just some strict processes that you have to do, and an amount of time that a burger needs to be done for and how many customers you're expected to do per hour. Maybe in our line of work individual architects are given quite a lot of freedom for their own time management, and that's right because it requires judgment on how much something should take, and on different projects that might be different amounts. So on one project you might arrive at a design very quickly, and on another project it might take much longer. So there's quite a high degree of personal responsibility for that process amongst all the designers in the office. But that also opens up the potential for lots of different ways that people handle that process, some of which may be very efficient and some of which may be highly inefficient. That's not something we talk about an awful lot, but people seem to appreciate it when we do.

The end of his train of thought coincides with the end of his journey home.

REFLECTION: MAKING THINGS AS THEY ARE

Architects are constantly moving toward something that does not as yet exist.[37] The reality of the building comes after the fact of a plan. At one level the plan and the reality are obviously unalike; yet at another level the relationship between these must be a literal one. In the process of building, some elements are kept constant, while others transform out of all recognition. Radical shifts in scale and material substance take place, as proportions and forms are exactly preserved.[38]

The contract is a way of specifying this process of realization, through a carefully constructed system of words and drawings. Much of the work of the architect is to ensure correlation, in the face of the various transformations that construction work involves. Plan and reality—drawing and building—are not encountered as a single gap but in the multiple shifts that take place as a design is realized as a set of plans, and then throughout the subsequent phases of construction. Alongside these shifts in material and scale are shifts in the orientation of architects, between their own plans for buildings and worlds as they want them to be and the uncertainties of people, places, and events that respond to other logics. Poised between these distinct and often competing imperatives, architects attempt to reconcile forces that do not in and of themselves cohere.

In this process, architects participate in a complex web of relations that enmeshes people, places, materials, tools, and documents in shifting and unstable alliances. In their formal role of contract administrators, their task is to oversee construction at a remove from the daily negotiations that happen on site. The job of contract administrators is to coordinate people, materials, and money in time and in space. Their activities, like those of contractors and builders, are oriented toward the completion of the building, but the tools by which they achieve this have a less obvious materiality. Their modus operandi includes meetings, documents, contracts, plans, minutes—more or less formal interactions through which the building is made.

"Ninety percent of what we do is administration, coordination, and negotiation," Megan explains on one occasion, with obvious frustration. It is probably an overstatement but conveys a basic truth: much of their working life is taken up with administrative tasks relating to the processes through which designs are developed and then built: these include meetings (on-site and with planners), the management of contracts, and project administration—various everyday practices through which they coordinate the work of others and between themselves.

These aspects of architectural work are not without personal reward. Most take pleasure in the process of overseeing the realization of a building. Within the office, Phil is unusual in his knowledge and enthusiasm for overseeing contracts, and relates this to a specific kind of pleasure: "The bit I really enjoy is actually seeing that building emerge and be built, and come to a reality. After drawing it and designing it for months, there it is coming together and being built, and you get to physically walk through it. It sort of takes shape." Many stress the satisfaction of seeing a project that is well managed: the professional pride in a job done well, a kind of procedural satisfaction distinct from the outcome of seeing clients' lives improved.

Even so, a professional valorization of creativity tends to be associated with ambivalence if not antipathy to these aspects of their work. These orientations are inherent in the structure of architectural training: whereas the first three years focus on the "creative" elements of design, Part II and then Part III are more about what Martin describes as the "boring practicalities" of contracts, budgets, and legislation. Megan explains the shock when she first started to work in a professional practice: "I felt like that degree didn't really prepare me very well at all for actually working in practice, and I was shocked to see what a small percentage of the job design actually is, and all the other things that come into play—all the administrative side of it, coordinating of all the different characters and professionals involved in the projects."

For Tomas, the role of practice director has involved a further shift away from those aspects of design that first drew him to the profession. After a difficult week, he reflects: "Sometimes it feels like I'm just constantly dealing with the crap!"

Elizabeth Hallam and Tim Ingold highlight the work involved in implementation: "The gap between these non-specific guidelines and the specific conditions

of a world that is never the same from one moment to the next not only opens up a space for improvisation, but also demands it, if people are to respond to these conditions with judgment and precision."[39] Questioning the polarity between invention and convention, they argue, "Improvisation and creativity . . . are intrinsic to the very processes of social and cultural life."[40] My account follows theirs in emphasizing the skill and difficulty of implementation, but suggests this expansive definition glosses an important distinction: between creativity, as a way of making things other than as they usually are, and implementation, as the application of existing principles or plans to specific cases.

The spaces between a design concept, a detailed plan, and ultimately a building are ones of irresolution that must be reconciled, according to terms already established: through an existing plan or logic. Through these descriptions we glimpse the effort required to realize what already appears to abstractly exist: to give substance to form; to elaborate principles and guidelines to meet the demands of circumstances. The building is constructed in conformity with the design; activities are made to fit within the schedule of the project. If creativity is seen as a way of opening up possibilities, pragmatics are a way of closing them down, resolving them to existing codes, rules, norms, designs; focusing them sufficiently in order to make intervention possible. Divergences are not opportunities but problems: indeterminacies must be reconciled rather than amplified, closed down or "dealt with" rather than explored. Temporally this implies a difference: between creativity as a way of opening up the present to an unknown future, and pragmatics as a way of making present circumstances converge toward a future that is planned.

It is a paradoxical kind of work that makes itself invisible if done well.[41] Perhaps that is another reason why these practices have tended to be overlooked and undervalued—both by architects and those who write about them. Yet there is nothing "mere" about these processes of implementation. The realization of a design requires skills, of interpretation, negotiation, improvisation—a multitude of ways in which these architects practice the art of elaborating abstractly existing plans or principles in relation to specific cases.[42] Where design implicates the self as a locus of creativity, these pragmatic tasks extricate the self through the logic of "professionalism": embodying forms of conduct, though which they act procedurally and objectively: detaching who they are from what they know.

Part 5

PRACTICAL
COMPLETION

KNOWLEDGE AT ITS LIMITS

In architectural terms "practical completion" describes the moment where the building is declared formally complete and the client takes legal ownership. It is the point at which architects formally let go of the building, releasing it for clients and others to inhabit. Often they find unanticipated uses and problems. It is in this spirit that I offer these final thoughts.

Megan is reflecting on the changing nature of architectural knowledge: "It used to be that an architect was the master builder, and he had that whole process under his wing. So from the design to the construction to the engineering, he'd oversee the whole thing. That started getting split up into different specializations, and that's necessary with enormous developments where it just becomes impossible to contain it all in one mind." Oversight was possible in a way it no longer is:

> These days an architect is someone who knows where to find out information, who knows how to navigate the parameters of the project and the constraints of reality. So being able to bring all these different things together—to kind of hold something and bring all that information together back to that vision . . . It's about this kind of collecting and holding, and finding the way to bring it all together.

Architectural knowledge, as Megan sees it, is always configured against an infinitely expanding horizon of the unknown. Whether or not her characterization of the historic shift is accurate, her account makes evident an important quality of architectural knowledge as conceived within the office. Rather than its being a set body of knowledge that can be mastered, it is learned and acquired in an active relationship between the known and unknown. Knowing what they do not know makes architects aware of the provisional nature of what they think they know, and the possibility that this may be challenged or changed.[1] Knowledge, in these terms, is practical rather than propositional: a matter of collecting, holding, finding, exploring, and assembling. Insights and understandings are built up through encountering new kinds of problem. But even as knowledge is gained, new understanding brings awareness of fresh areas of ignorance. The more they know, the more they recognize they don't know. "I find it continuously hard. It's not easy. The whole process, I feel like I'm continuously learning, and, you know, that kind of tacit knowledge that builds up, as soon as I feel like it's beginning to grow I feel like I'm automatically into something new. It's a difficult process." The difficulty, but also the interest, of their working life is that they are always learning in a world that always ultimately exceeds their ability to know and control it.

Architects' understanding of the limits of their own knowledge results from a perception of disjunction: between their own finite capacities and a world that perpetually seems to exceed and surpass these. From one perspective this disjuncture is a possibility: creativity develops in this space, as architects use the world to explore and challenge themselves (see part three). From another perspective it is a problem: processes of implementation are ways of trying to close the gap, of seeking to make the world conform to their plans for it (see part four). The imperative to creativity that underlies the former does not always sit easily with the imperative to professionalism that frames the latter. Much of their work concerns the never entirely resolved question of the relationship between these two orientations. The issue is not simply how to act professionally but whether and when that ideal should prevail, in relation to other ideals of a less procedural kind.

ARCHITECTURAL EXPERTISE

The architectural historian and practitioner Robin Evans was interested in things "opposed but not necessarily incompatible."[2]

The descriptions in this book are about many things but most centrally can be read as an ethnographic elaboration of this idea: how, in terms set out at the start (part one), architects create and inhabit "spaces between": through their daily working lives, fabricating specific compatibilities between things that seem abstractly opposed, contradictory or in tension. These spaces are of many kinds. They include those routine yet mysterious spaces that are integral to the representational process in which architects engage: between a site for possible development and a design concept; a concept and a plan; a plan and a physical building. Alongside these are spaces between the different, sometimes irreconcilable, forms of knowledge of those involved – between planners, builders, engineers, clients and other building professionals. Within the practice, among the architects, there are spaces between competing conceptual approaches to design, compounded by different understandings of how conceptual design should be.

If these "spaces between" take many concrete forms, as the descriptions in this book show, the ways in which architects occupy them are correspondingly many. In practice these ways emerge variously as possibility, problem, and constraint. My descriptions highlight how architects occupy these spaces in ways that reproduce even as they question these oppositions. They show how architects move between them, negotiating, straddling, struggling with, sometimes collapsing them, at others reproducing them, sometimes questioning at others taking them for granted. The structural tensions are widespread, but the reconciliations must always be specific.

What is made in these gaps can be different kinds of things: the self-knowledge gained from the attempt to fathom how a professional and working life relate; the imaginative design stimulus of trying to relate what can't be resolved; the professional knowledge that extends from known principles to new contexts, or between approaches of apparently contradictory kinds There is pleasure, enjoyment, excitement, and fulfillment in these spaces, as new things are found, learned, and made through the imaginative work of design and the more pragmatic work of implementation. There is also frustration, anxiety, and even despair when the tensions seem intractable, the solutions unobtainable, interests irreconcilable, or binaries unhelpfully opposed. These spaces can be ones in which designs become "compromised" in the pejorative sense and fail in the eyes of the architect or client. In the movement from "plan" to "reality," contractors may be forced out of business, clients can run out of funds, and legal action is sometimes taken where problems lead to stalemate. Not all projects reach fruition.

Architects are particular kinds of experts. Their claims to know things imply authority. What is the basis of this authority, and (how) is it justified?

The heyday of architectural modernism in the middle of the last century coincided with a more general enthusiasm for expertise.[3] It seemed axiomatic that the route to a different, better future lay in the knowledge of specialists, specifically in the technical and scientific solutions they offered to a range of social problems.[4] As experts in design and more generally the built environment, architects embodied authority from two essential sources: from the "genius" of the creative individual; and through the professional mastery of principles of aesthetics and design. Both of these are related to an idea of architectural knowledge as transcendental and universally applicable.

In the latter part of the twentieth century, the profound questioning of these architectural truths coincided with a wider public skepticism toward the authoritative claims of experts. This is perhaps most obviously expressed in the "post-truth" discourses and anti-expert populism of the last few years, but is prefigured by developments from about the 1970s onward. In complex and specific ways, postmodernism, postcolonialism, and postindustrialism are associated with fundamental and pervasive challenges to the universal claims of modern expertise. Even before that the civil rights, feminist, and environmental movements (among others) began to converge in an image of experts as a powerful establishment, perpetuating social injustice. No longer the privileged source of powerful and benign truths, expert knowledge has increasingly been viewed as both a manifestation and justification of elite interest.[5] Over the past three decades, critics have highlighted how the architectural profession works as a form of elite "distinction"[6]: both architects and their clients perpetuate a position of social and economic privilege through claimed intellectual and aesthetic superiority. External critiques have been echoed from within the profession, through an increasingly skeptical orientation to their own professional knowledge and, relatedly, efforts to integrate a broader range of perspectives in a more "inclusive" and "participatory" vision of design.

My account, self-evidently very specific in focus, is not inconsistent with the possibility that aspects of this characterization may sometimes be well founded. Indeed, elements of these critiques are echoed within the office of MHW, as we have seen. Yet the move to treat expertise as "relational," as merely a social attribution of limited consequence and utility, elides appreciation of the practical substance of this knowing. In a wide-ranging comparative discussion of scientific expertise, Harry Collins and Robert Evans propose that having successfully "leveled" the epistemological field to displace the position of experts as quasi-divine infallibility, it is important to ask: "What makes it that, though there are no tall mountains left, there is also not just liquid mud?"[7] As an answer to that question from the perspective of architecture, my descriptions point to expertise as a way of knowing that is situational but substantial, which emerges through particular interactions while having effects and indeed utility beyond them.

These ways of knowing cannot be readily summarized or codified insofar as they inhere in myriad responses to particular circumstances. Nonetheless they have a specific kind of rigor. In Donald Schon's terms, this is the rigor of "practical competence and technical artistry,"[8] of improvising new relationships between known and unknown circumstance, putting knowledge to work in more or less routine ways, of tacit and explicit understandings derived from but never exactly congruent with previous situations. By contrast to other more circumscribed forms of expertise, architecture is not really a specialism, a clearly bounded method or domain of knowledge in relation to which authority can be confidently claimed through well-established principles. As I witnessed it, architecture involves knowing a little about a lot, awareness of what is necessarily not known, and the ability to use that awareness as a stimulus to new knowledge. The rigor is not only about the elaboration of (known) principles to the partly known complexities of practice but, centrally, also the navigation of a highly diverse and contradictory set of principles.

This knowledge is not infallible, but even so it can be useful in a myriad of situations: in those that require understanding of a problem with elements that are complex and unclear; where clients know they want a kind of building they cannot quite imagine; if thoughtful choices and careful syntheses are deemed to be preferable to any singular interest or imperative; where problems exist to which no straightforwardly procedural answer can be given; or in circumstances where more complexity is involved than anyone can ultimately understand. Even in these circumstances architects rarely, if ever, produce the perfect intervention.

The more modest ambition of these architects is that they routinely result in good outcomes, to their own and others' satisfaction: balancing different imperatives, interests, and "truths" in a way that is broadly beneficial to those who will use and inhabit the buildings they design. In these respects, they are not so much uncertain experts, as experts *in* uncertainty.

EVERYDAY POSSIBILITIES

I have attempted to describe what happens in an architectural practice as faithfully as possible. Focusing on the transformations that take place from an idea, to a design, to a set of plans, and then to a building, my aim has been to show the complexity, difficulty, and interest of this endeavor. I hope these descriptions suggest parallels and differences: with other people, other places, other processes. I do not offer any ultimate answer to the question of how designs, ideas, inspiration, buildings, or for that matter architects are produced. There is no proposal for how architecture might be done better or differently. I want instead to highlight that even as these architects' themselves acknowledge the problems inherent in the professional contexts they face, there are also possibilities. Focusing on these everyday practical entanglements makes this evident in ways that are less obvious in generalized accounts of the profession and discipline.[9]

Mainstream architecture and mainstream construction powerfully constrain the kinds of buildings that can be imagined and built. But even as these circumstances structure how architects think and act, they do not entirely determine the thoughts and actions through which buildings are constructed. In the face of the problems of a profession and the world as it is, there are indeterminacies, choices, and possibilities—for buildings and worlds never entirely encompassed by any single systemic imperative. These architects are aware of their own complicity, even as they are critical of what they are complicit in. Often that means they are critical of themselves.

In this light, it would be wrong to overplay the emancipatory possibilities that dwell within these practical entanglements. Yet I want to highlight a set of dynamics often overlooked in overarching theories and programmatic descriptions, that in their various and contradictory forms reveal visions of what architecture should and could be. Architects share a broader modern obsession with novelty, arguably in a particularly acute form.[10] Perhaps, in this context, it is important to recognize and remember the productive potential of tendencies and ways of working that already exist—in the striking phrase of Anand Pandian and Stuart Maclean, "possible worlds" that are overlooked, lodged as they are in the "apparent banality of the actual."[11]

I hope the descriptions in this book point to the less overtly radical but perhaps more subtly profound alternatives that exist *within* the everyday circumstances of mainstream architecture. Poised, as they are, between different kinds of truth, the lives of architects can seem constrained, contradictory, difficult and compromised. The lack of resolution can often feel unsatisfactory. But in these tensions there are also choices, and in these constraints lie opportunities—creative possibilities, points of resistance, ways of reworking the circumstances that shape their professional existence. My portraits of architectural practice are intended as a testament to the everyday problems that architects face but also to the opportunities that reside there. Through amplifying and echoing the voices of these architects, I hope to have conveyed something of their own sense of what is at stake in occupying "spaces between."

CODA: AN ARGUMENT FOR DESCRIPTION

Les Back has written, "Our culture is one that speaks rather than listens. From reality TV to political rallies, there is a clamour to be heard, to narrate, and to receive attention. It reduces 'reality' to revelation and voyeurism."[1] The move to privilege a particular form of theorized argument can be seen as part of this broader tendency. Back explicitly makes this connection, and cautions that the conditions that pull academics in this direction are the very ones that make it important to resist that pull. As a form of writing oriented more to listening than to speaking, ethnography acquires a broader value precisely in the face of changes that make it increasingly difficult to research, write, and publish in this way (discussed above in "A Note on Structure and Approach"). Because these truths are complex and difficult, they take time for the author and then the reader to understand—not just because quantitatively speaking there is a lot of detail, but more profoundly because others' lives are shaped by ideas and practices other than our own, and the effort to grasp these is difficult and time consuming—for the researcher as for the reader. The world that marginalizes and devalues these slower, more complex, kinds of writing is arguably the world that gives them new and specific relevance. When all around there is a clamor to speak and be heard, ethnographic description is a way of recovering the less loudly proclaimed— even the silent, unsaid, and unstated—elements of the lives of those we describe. Descriptions allow us to pause and reflect, to dwell in details, to see the actual that exists beyond the manifest and obvious. Ethnographic description, in this predicament, is a kind of "recovery" of the everyday, those elements of life that get overlooked from the perspective of sound bites, meta-narratives, and polarized argument.

Ethnography stands as a counterpoint to the celebration of novelty, reminding us of the possibilities and insights that lurk in the conditions of actual lives as already lived. The understanding and description of complexity become more important and more interesting in the face of didactic arguments and boldly proclaimed simplifications. As part of an academic world that aspires to research that is "world leading," it reminds us that there are many worlds, variously understood and inhabited, and already many directions in which it is led. Anthropologists have important things to say, but only insofar as that is premised on the careful, thoughtful, slow, and sometimes difficult process of listening to others, and then of carefully describing what has been heard.

To recognize that a particular mode of theorized argumentation has become pervasive is not to suggest that all or even most accounts now take this form. I am not suggesting that anthropologists need new models of writing, but rather to urge greater recognition of those elements, approaches, and orientations that seem consequently less pervasive and less valued.[2] In these broad terms, I hope my account adds impetus to a small but significant number of other voices urging what could be termed a "descriptive turn," or perhaps more accurately, since many of the best examples come from the past, a "descriptive return."

Acknowledgments

This book could not have been written without the help, support, friendship, kindness, and insight of very many people. More have contributed than I am able to name here, in ways that are more important than I am able to fully acknowledge.

Most importantly, I owe a huge debt and much gratitude to those at Millar Howard Workshop: David, Marianne, Martin, Megan, Milo, Rob, Roisin, Ronan, Rosy, Tom, and Tomas. After the main phase of research, others joined the practice and helped carry on the conversation, including through feedback, self-recorded dialogues, and assistance with images. Thanks to Laura, Martina, Rachel, Ros, and Sam. I hope it is already evident how much the insights of the book are directly derived from the architects among whom the research was undertaken. In addition to underlining that debt, it is important to state profound gratitude: for the warmth, friendship, openness, trust, and time that was shared; for the welcome that was offered; and then for the freedom I was given, to tell their story as I saw it, including some aspects that I know have been uncomfortable to see in writing. I hope that readers see these candid reflections as a sign of an underlying integrity and honesty, and any contingent acknowledgments of "failure" as a fundamental product of the intractable difficulties of a profession composed of conflicting interests and approaches. Additionally, I am grateful to the many clients, builders, planners, and associated professionals who shared their time and knowledge, mostly with great generosity, often with a little perplexity. My uncle, Edward Dodd (not the "Edward" in the book), a builder, was not a formal part of my study but helped me understand what is involved in the work of construction and to better appreciate what some of my informants were telling me. During the final stages of writing my own home was renovated by Ralph Gurrey and his team, Ben, Marcin, and Pete, whose thoughtful reflections on building also helped my analysis.

An initial draft was read and improved immensely through the comments of others, both supportive and critical. In addition to transcribing many of the interviews, David Yarrow gave extremely detailed and helpful comments prior to review. At Cornell University Press, I am immensely grateful to Dominic Boyer and Jim Lance, for seeing the potential in an unconventional manuscript, and for encouraging its development in this experimental form. Ange Romeo-Hall went above and beyond the call of duty with editorial guidance that helped me see where I had said too much and not enough. I am thankful to Glenn Novak for thorough and sympathetic copyediting. Thomas Dodd showed me in forensic detail how what I had said was often not exactly what I meant and how some simple and important points had become buried in unnecessary complexities. I am also grateful for his help rethinking the title. Three reviewers provided careful and constructive criticism, and numerous specific suggestions that made the manuscript better than it would otherwise have been. Adam Reed, Catherine Alexander, and Matt Candea provided incisive feedback and helped me to keep faith in the path I had chosen, even when the terrain sometimes seemed inhospitable and the destination uncertain. Comments from Michael Carrithers, and the conversations that followed, allowed me to realize what I was trying to do, as did the inspiration of his written work. Along the way research and writing was helped by more people than I can properly acknowledge, including Simone Abram, Les Back, Prue Chiles, Taras Fedirko, Sian Jones, Oliver Lowenstein, Dawn Lyon, Simon Marvin, Lesley Mcfadyen, Keith Murphy, Morten Nielsen, Anand Pandian, Bob Simpson, Marilyn Strathern, Dimitrios Theodossopoulos, Diana Vonnak, and Albena Yaneva. At Durham, the anthropology department has been a congenial environment in which to think, research, and write. I am grateful to my colleagues for making it so, as well as to my graduate students who have shared and shaped some of these interests.

During fieldwork, the endeavor was given personal and practical support during a very enjoyable stay with my brother and his family in Cirencester. Thanks to Hugh, Jess, Eddie, Martha, and Iris for some fun and happy times. The book could not have been written without the love and companionship of my wife, Chantal, and my son, Joe. Their profound lack of interest was a helpful form of perspective! Thanks to Tony, Judith, and Rachel Yarrow for encouragement with the book and in numerous other ways.

My grandfather Gresham Dodd died over twelve years ago but leaves a legacy that continues to inspire. As a practicing architect, he helped develop my interests in this area, and encouraged a general curiosity in life. If he has helped shape this account in these and other ways, I also like to think that through writing this book I have come to know him a little better.

The book developed through a research project, *Building on the Past*, generously funded by the Arts and Humanities Research Council (AH/L000032/1).

Notes

BEFORE THE BEGINNING

1. Back, "Journeying through Words," 769.
2. Schon, *Reflective Practitioner*, 19.
3. Rapport, "Consequences of Anthropological Writing."
4. Boyer, Faubion, and Marcus, "Theory Can Be More Than It Used to Be."
5. Boyer, Faubion, and Marcus, "Theory Can Be More Than It Used to Be."
6. Rapport, "Consequences of Anthropological Writing," 681.
7. This point was made some time ago and with particular clarity by sociologist W. G. Runciman. In *A Treatise on Social Theory* he notes, "The concepts of a descriptive theory . . . reconceptualise 'their' account of what they think, say and do but with the difference that instead of reordering 'their' ideas about their own experience in terms of presumptive causal connections they reorder them in terms of a presumptive relation to a latent Weltanschauung [worldview]" (229). See also Candea, *Impossible Method*.
8. See particularly Strathern, *Gender of the Gift*; Strathern, *Partial Connections*.
9. The argument is not in relation to any specific kind of theory but is rather a point about the methodological and descriptive ways in which "our" concepts are related to "others." Various debates center on the question of how and whether "our" theories become ways of understanding or overlooking the ideologies and practices at the heart of those that anthropologists and others study. In "On Recalling Actor-Network Theory," Latour highlighted over a decade ago how the approach closely associated with his work had already acquired a conceptual coherence that was a barrier to understanding the specificities of practices that respond to diverse and other logics. Recently the "ontological turn" in anthropology represented a desire to put the concepts and ideas of others more centrally at the heart of analysis, but has been criticized for having the diametrically opposite effect (see, for example, Killick, "Whose Truth Is It Anyway?").
10. Lienhardt's approach to ethnography has some resonances with recent accounts, in their insistence on starting from understandings of the ontological basis of others' categorical distinctions (I am thinking particularly of Viveiros de Castro's "Perspectival Anthropology and the Method of Controlled Equivocation" and Holbraad's *Truth in Motion*). My own account draws inspiration from these approaches: in their insistence that "theory" and "description" occupy a single plane of explanaton, and in the methodological orientation that engenders commitment to the effort to understand others' lives, as the necessary corollary to a skepticism toward anthropology's own concepts and theories. Description of the particularities of others' lives requires that we—professional anthropologists—reconfigure our categories in the act of bending them to circumstances for which no encompassing explanation exists. By the same token, ethnographic description is the means by which new concepts are generated, as old ones are extended or found to be wanting. The rationale is compelling (Englund and Yarrow, "Place of Theory"), and many of the resulting descriptions are insightful. However, asymmetries are reintroduced, where the point of this equivocation is less the production of faithful descriptions than the novel conceptual points that derive from these. Despite a number of notable examples to the contrary, proponents of this approach seem more often oriented by the aim of unfolding theory (ethnographically derived concepts) from description (the circumstances of

other people's lives), than to the production of accounts in which description *is* the point. In this respect Lienhardt exemplifies a distinct approach, from which I draw inspiration.

11. Carrithers, "Anthropology as Irony and Philosophy."

12. Iser, "Interaction between Text and Reader," 111.

13. Stevens, *Favored Circle*, 17.

14. 1996; first published in 1991.

15. Yaneva, *Making of a Building*, 4.

16. See also particularly *Made by the Office of Metropolitan Architecture*.

17. See particularly Harkness, *Thinking, Building, Dwelling*; Houdart and Minato, *Kuma Kengo*; Murphy, "Imagination as Joint Activity" and "Building Stories"; Loukissas, *Co-designers*.

18. Particularly Gunn and Donovan, *Design and Anthropology*; Smith et al., *Design Anthropological Futures*; Murphy, *Swedish Design*; Pink et al., *Making Homes*; Chumley, *Creativity Class*.

19. See, for instance, Yaneva, *Making of a Building*, on models; Rose, Degen, and Melhuish, "Networks, Interfaces, and Computer-Generated Images," on renderings; Nadaï and Labussière, "Playing with the Line," on maps.

20. Chumley, *Creativity Class*.

21. Pandian, *Reel World*.

22. Wilf, *School for Cool*.

23. Denzin's *Interpretive Biography* has been particularly influential.

24. Boyer, "Thinking through the Anthropology of Experts," 45.

25. Boyer, 45.

26. Particularly Miyazaki, *Arbitraging Japan*; Harvey and Knox, *Roads*.

27. Particularly Laidlaw, "For an Anthropology of Ethics."

28. Compare Murphy, *Swedish Design*.

29. Compare Schon, *Reflective Practitioner*; Cuff, *Architecture*.

30. Boellstorff, "The Digital That Will Be."

31. Particularly Schon, *Reflective Practitioner*; Collins and Evans, *Rethinking Expertise*.

32. Particularly Dingwall, *Essays on Professions*; Abbott, *System of Professions*.

33. Particularly DuGay, *In Praise of Bureaucracy*; Brown et al., *Meetings*.

34. Thiel, "Class in Construction"; Applebaum, *Construction Workers, U.S.A.*; Lyon, "Labour of Refurbishment"; and see Pink et al., "Ethnographic Methodologies for Construction Research," for an overview of recent work.

PART ONE: THE OFFICE

1. On David Goldblatt's account in "The Dislocation of the Architectural Self," the renowned architect Peter Eisenman espouses a form of postmodern architecture in which the state of "betweenness" is embraced: "The idea behind an arbitrary text in the context of the dislocation of the self is to remove the hands from the hands of the architect, to eliminate the major motivation from a highly motivated self in order to place the self in a new position regarding its own work" (166). Betweenness, for Eisenman, is a proposition about how architecture could and should be done, as distinct from the more conventional, more mainstream forms this routinely takes. I wish, by contrast, to highlight the more quotidian forms of betweenness and to suggest that these are already present in architectural practice, including of a more overtly conventional kind.

2. See, for example, Crinson and Lubbock, *Architecture*; Lowenstein, *Architecture of Elsewhere*.

3. See Vesely, *Architecture in the Age of Divided Representation*.

4. I take inspiration from recent work on the anthropology of ethics, highlighting in various ways how social life is not determined by preexisting social structures, but through

people's efforts to negotiate contradictory ideological imperatives in situationally specific ways. James Laidlaw's "For an Anthropology of Ethics and Freedom" is foundational to much of the subsequent "ethical turn" in anthropology. He asserts: "Wherever and in so far as people's conduct is shaped by attempts to make of themselves a certain kind of person, because it is as such a person that, on reflection, they think they ought to live, to that extent their conduct is ethical and free. And to the extent that they do so with reference to ideals, values, models, practices, relationships and institutions that are amenable to ethnographic study, to that extent their conduct becomes the subject matter for an anthropology of ethics" (327).

5. Schon, *Reflective Practitioner*, 78.

6. Quoted in Gutman, *Architectural Practice*, frontispiece.

7. Anthropologists and other scholars routinely adopt critical orientations that engender antipathy to modern forms of rationality, and by the same token celebrate practices that elude and challenge these. The universal is challenged through the particular; systems are deconstructed from the perspective of the inchoate and indeterminate; the global is challenged through the lens of the local. These broader tendencies are prevalent in work on architecture and design. By contrast, I have tried to show how the negotiation of these oppositions is itself an integral part of architectural practice. Sidestepping the implicit or explicit normativity of these approaches, my own account has attempted to describe how these oppositions enter architects' own understandings of the work in which they are engaged. At times their positions are animated by romantic sensibilities, but, enmeshed in modern construction systems, their rejection can only ever be partial and situated.

8. For an extended discussion of these see Andrew Saint's *The Image of the Architect*. Through detailed historical and literary analysis, the book describes various architectural ideals, including of the individual hero and genius; of collaboration; of the businessman; and of the architect as professional, among others.

9. These tensions are discussed extensively by Crinson and Lubbock in *Architecture*, an extended account of the development of the profession in England. In *Swedish Design*, Murphy discusses similar tensions in relation to product designers.

10. For critical accounts of this see Sennett, *Craftsman*; Ingold, *Making*; Vesely, *Architecture in an Age of Divided Representation*.

11. In "The Social Production of Built Form," Cuff describes a similar set of tensions: "I observed nearly every building to be socially constructed by the invisible hands of planners, policymakers, occupants, developers, architects, bankers, engineers, and clients. In this complex arena, practice was seen to consist of a series of contradictions, which, once resolved, presented new dilemmas" (435).

12. This focus is particularly inspired by Boyer, "Thinking through the Anthropology of Experts."

13. Barry Dornfield likewise notes: "The ethnography of office work, in which subjects' primary activities are speaking on the phone and typing on computer keypads, leaves little room for productive observation without conspicuously disturbing their work" (1998, 23), quoted in Boyer, "Corporeality of Expertise," 257.

14. Ingold is critical of conceptualizations of fieldwork as "data," highlighting in his book *Making* how anthropologists "go to study *with* people and learn *from* them" (2). He suggests, drawing on the work of fellow anthropologist Gregory Bateson, that "this kind of learning aims not so much to provide us with facts about the world as to enable us to be taught by it" (2).

15. Cuff describes a similar gap between actions and words in her book *Architecture*, an ethnographic study of architectural practice in the US.

16. My understanding of the central role of talking as a way of doing things through design is influenced by Murphy's *Swedish Design* (particularly 128–133).

17. R. MacFarlane, "Introduction," xv.

18. This approach takes inspiration from a number of recent and less recent accounts in and beyond anthropology. Geographical restriction involves intensification insofar as there is always as much meaning as one can find. In *The Body Multiple*, an ethnographic account of medical practice, science studies scholar Annmarie Mol observes that if you blow up the details of any one site it immediately turns into many (51). If a relatively narrow geographic focus helps to produce a sense of depth, this is partly because it forces attention on the specific practical ways in which abstractions are located. The view from an office does not "exemplify" a social or structural totality beyond this, just as the architects who practice there do not exemplify the practice "as a whole." In terms set out by Bandak and Højer in their excellent "Introduction: the Power of Example," this situated perspective is "less than everything but more than itself" (14). Elsewhere they note: "The example excels in exploring the tension between, and the instability of, the specific and the general . . . , the concrete and the abstract, motion and structure, ethnography and theory, and it does so by never fully becoming one or the other" (6).

19. RIBA, *Business Benchmarking 2016*. According to their data, the average national practice size is 13.7 in the U.K. About half of all staff are employed in the one hundred largest practices, mostly concentrated in London; the other half are in more than two thousand smaller practices.

20. According to RIBA statistics (*Business Benchmarking 2016*), a mean salary of £32,500 for architects employed up to five years from qualification compares with £38,000 for those qualified over five years and £43,600 for partners and directors. Architectural salaries are high relative to the national mean of £28,000, but relatively low as compared to other professions, particularly given the length of formal training.

21. In *Architectural Practice* Gutman describes the "dequalification" of labor, from the 1970s onward, as specialization within the profession is associated with increasing confinement of creative elements of the work to fewer, usually senior, employees. Cuff highlights how these tendencies result in a situation in which the ideal of architecture as creative practice is increasingly in tension with the institutional realities in which most architects now work. MHW's working practices take place conscious of these tendencies and as a deliberate attempt to resist them.

22. For example see Ghirado, "Architecture of Deceit."

23. For example see Till, *Architecture Depends*.

24. For example see Stevens, *Favored Circle*.

25. In making this point I draw inspiration from Anand Pandian, who makes a parallel argument in relation to film in his book *Reel World*, 2.

PART TWO: LIVES

1. In *Architecture*, Crinson and Lubbock outline the typical route taken by UK architects through education: "An introductory first year course is followed by two years in which projects are set for students to design for periods of four to twelve weeks. In addition there are lectures on the history of architecture, structures, construction and other subjects. Students spend a year out in an architectural practice after finishing their degree (three years in England, four years in most Scottish schools). This year of practical experience is a relic of the old pupillage system. . . . Finally there is a two year diploma course . . . in which students continue the pattern of the second and third years" (162). As Cuff similarly notes in the US context, in her book *Architecture*, architectural training emphasizes design as formal problem-solving, emphasizing creativity and downplaying technical knowledge and administration (44–45).

2. Till, *Architecture Depends*, 9.

3. See Cuff, "Through the Looking Glass," 94–98.

4. Cuff, 95.

5. Jackson, *Between One and One Another*, 20.

6. Cuff, "Through the Looking Glass," 94.

7. Cuff, 94.

8. Cuff, "Through the Looking Glass."

9. U. A. Fanthorpe, "Atlas."

10. Denzin argues in *Interpretive Biography* that "lives are biographical properties. They belong not just to the persons, but also to larger social collectivities, including societies, corporations and, for some, the world system" (29). Later he suggests, "The point . . . is not whether or not biographical coherence is an illusion or a reality. Rather, what must be established is how individuals give coherence to their lives when they write or talk self-autobiographies" (62).

11. In "The Marital History of 'a Thumb-Impression Man,'" Jonathan Parry likewise describes how his interlocutor's self-narratives "appear to fly on automatic pilot and to reproduce not the memory itself but the memory of how he has told the story before" (285).

12. In *Interpretive Biography*, Denzin notes the frequency with which family and childhood experiences are the "zero point of origin" (16) in biographical narratives across a range of Western contexts.

13. Greenhouse, *Moment's Notice*.

14. In *Creativity Class*, Chumley describes how Chinese art students learn through "critique classes" to "publicise the personal" (147) and to "personalise the public" (147), in the sense of taking things from other artists and making these "their own" (147).

15. In *Exchanging Skin*, Crook develops the concept of "the textual person" to describe the mutually eliciting qualities of person and text in anthropological knowledge production. From this perspective he foregrounds the person-like qualities of texts, and the text-like qualities of people.

16. See Cuff, *Architecture*, chap. 4.

17. See Murphy, *Swedish Design*, chap. 3, for a discussion of the similar logic by which product designers routinely work with those they met during their education, while rejecting the "conservativism" of that education.

18. On epiphany as a biographical narrative form see Denzin, *Interpretive Biography*.

19. Quoted in Forty, *Words and Buildings*, 13.

20. In Chumley's terms, these are ways in which architects "enregister" themselves (*Creativity Class*, 147).

21. In *Modern Architecture*, Frampton's acclaimed critical history, he points to the paradox of our time: "While techno-science in the form of digitally driven environmental and structural engineering takes the art of building to an entirely new level of cultural sophistication, this seemingly positive potential tends to be vitiated by our lack of any overarching vision beyond the perpetuation of a consumerist waste economy upon which our continual accumulation of maldistributed wealth fatally depends" (7). In "An Architecture of Elsewhere," Lowenstein describes a "new architectural mood" in response and reaction to what he terms "the ostentation and overkill of postmodernism; the rise to planetary dominance of a few hundred star architects selling particular brands of iconic signature buildings around the planet; and the big corporate yet terrifyingly soulless architecture which pervades the building culture dimension of Globalisation" (10). Practically and professionally complicit with these tendencies, yet often critical of them, architectural responses have taken various forms, as more and less self-consciously "romantic" reflexes to the modernity of the digital, neoliberal era. These include attempts to uncover the human element contained within architecture's modernist tradition, as described in

St John Wilson's influential *The Other Tradition of Modern Architecture* and as pioneered in practice by architects including Peter Zumthor. As part of a "broad cultural zeitgeist," Lowenstein suggests that "the dialects may be different yet a shared language is spoken" (11). This, broadly speaking, is the language of MHW. It takes many and contradictory forms, even within this single practice.

22. In *Swedish Design*, Murphy well describes how this tension is central to a range of interactions. Designs "endure the effects of forces that both fold them into utilitarian everyday objects and refashion them as something more akin to a work of art, as objects open to specific kinds of expert evaluation" (124).

23. See Andrews, *Lifetimes of Commitment*, a study of socialist political activists in the UK. In this context she highlights how middle-class activists, in their biographical accounts, more commonly highlight active choices, by contrast to her working-class interlocutors, who tended to stress the importance of chance. She sees this as reflecting and constituting the more general tendency for middle-class professionals to imagine their lives as controllable, and to stress their capacities to make these conform to plans of their choosing.

24. See Sennett, *Craftsman* (43–45), for a discussion of this context.

25. For instance, Ingold's *The Perception of the Environment* (particularly "Tools, Minds and Machines") and Sennet's *The Craftsman*; see Yarrow and Jones "'Stone Is Stone'" for an extended critical discussion of these romantic tendencies.

26. Berger, *Fortunate Man*, 147.

27. Vesely, *Architecture in the Age of Divided Representation*, 8.

28. In *Objectivity*, Daston and Galison describe the historical emergence of this scientific ideal during the nineteenth century. "To be objective is to aspire to knowledge that bears no trace of the knower—knowledge unmarked by prejudice or skill, fantasy or judgment, wishing or striving. Objectivity is blind sight, seeing without inference, interpretation or intelligence" (17).

29. See Rabinow and Stavrianakis, *Designs on the Contemporary*, for an extended discussion of similar concerns in relation to the vocational ideals invoked by author Salman Rushdie and artist Gerhard Richter.

PART THREE: DESIGNS

1. In *The Making of a Building*, Yaneva describes a process that is more typical in larger practices (chap. 3, esp. 138–139). At Rem Koolhaas's internationally renowned practice, the Office for Metropolitan Architecture (OMA), sites come to architects in the highly mediated form of briefs constructed by consultants employed by clients. Even in this form, the site is conceived as a set of constraints that are a stimulus to creativity, though the nature of these interactions is qualitatively different from those site-based interactions in the smaller practice of MHW.

2. Forty, *Words and Buildings*, 132–135.

3. The reification of vision has been widely criticized in architecture, as this is associated with the subordination of other senses and with the perpetuation of architectural expertise. These points are well taken, but as Grasseni points out in *Skilled Visions*, critiques of the visual have tended to be associated with a lack of attention to the specific practices through which professional visions emerge. Her own account highlights that ways of seeing are practically incorporated in ways of thinking and acting distributed through communities of practice. "Cattle breeders, archaeologists, laser surgeons, even police consultants . . . do each have a different world in front of their eyes, because they were each trained to see it differently" (3). By the same token, she highlights the importance of artifacts as powerful mediators and generators of sense, not simply as "objects"

of perception but as active participants in specific "ecologies of attention." Significantly for her (as for Willerslev in his contribution to the volume, "To Have the World at a Distance"), vision is not synonymous with the detached gaze (as, for example, in Lefebvre's influential arguments in *The Production of Space*). Rather, practitioners "strive to manage the required compromise between distance and proximity" (8).

4. Schon, *Reflective Practitioner*, 51–56.

5. I take this point from Ingold and Vergunst's discussion of walking, set out in the introduction to their edited collection, *Ways of Walking*.

6. In Keith Murphy's terms (after J. L. Austin), this language is not narrowly descriptive but "performative"; the point of words in many design interactions is not narrowly what they "mean" but what actions they set in train (*Swedish Design*, chap. 4).

7. After Murphy, *Swedish Design*, 147–148).

8. Murphy, *Swedish Design*, 145.

9. In "Playing with the Line, Channeling Multiplicity," an account of the wind-power planning process in France, Nadaï and Labussière describe a similar dynamic and interplay: "dialogue and . . . constant relay between . . . representation through the plan . . . and representation through the situation" (134). "Thanks to its graphic design (loose line, floating, or impoverishment of the form), the plan always posits an incomplete order that is relayed by the situation. Conversely, the order thus set allows the situation to be deployed as a principle and to act as a relay without being entirely indexed to its site of origin" (134).

10. In Murphy's terms (after Charles Sanders Pierce) in *Swedish Design*, this is an instance of "abduction": the features of one object are made contingently parallel with another in order to better understand its qualities. He describes how designers place emergent designs "within a framework of viable forms" (168), drawing comparisons with given design styles.

11. Ellis and Cuff, introduction to *Architects' People*, 6.

12. Quoted in Forty, *Words and Buildings*, 134.

13. See, for instance, the RIBA Plan of Work 2013, https://www.ribaplanofwork.com/.

14. Compare Yaneva, *Making of a Building*.

15. In *The Reflective Practitioner* Donald Schon argues of expert knowledge more generally that a focus on technical problem solving has often elided understanding of problem setting. Problems do not present themselves to practitioners as givens: "They must be constructed from the materials of problematic situations which are puzzling, troubling and uncertain. . . . Problem setting is a process in which, interactively, we name the things to which we will attend and frame the context in which we will attend to them" (40).

16. In *Conservation in the Age of Consensus*, Pendlebury describes how the tension between conservation and development has been central to UK planning from the nineteenth century onward. See particularly chap. 2.

17. See Forty, *Words and Buildings*, 120–131, for a historical account of the architectural development and use of the term. In "Retaining Character" I describe the ethnographic forms and affects associated with concepts of "character" in relation to building conservation.

18. Jones and Yarrow, "Crafting Authenticity."

19. Writing in his 1917 essay "Tradition and the Individual Talent," cited in Forty, *Words and Buildings*, 132.

20. See Thurley, *Men from the Ministry*, chap. 7, for a discussion of this historical context.

21. See Pendlebury, *Conservation in the Age of Consensus*, chap. 2.

22. Murphy, "Imagination as Joint Activity," 269.

23. I borrow the term from Sneath, Holbraad, and Pedersen, who in "Technologies of the Imagination" highlight how efforts to imagine are not straightforwardly "mental," being materially and technologically enabled. See also Barber, "Improvisation and the Art of Making Things Stick," who highlights how imagination, being never only "mental," involves a process of making ideas durable.

24. Murphy, "Imagination as Joint Activity," 269. In Barber's terms, these orientations are ways of creating "loop holes" in existing conventions and prevailing norms ("Improvisation and the Art of Making Things Stick"). Like Nielsen and Pedersen, my description of architectural practice makes clear that the relationship involved is not only from "the inside-out," from "mind" to "world": "imagination does not always operate and move from the subject outwards but also from the world inwards" ("Infrastructural Imaginaries," 239). For architects, as I describe, reality is imagined, as imagination is realized, in a process of oscillation between these states. Through this process, they give form and substance to their ideas, and use these forms as an imaginative stimulus.

25. Boyer suggests in "The Corporeality of Expertise" that intellectual activity is premised on and reproduces an opposition between active mind and passive body that inflects the phenomenological experience of a range of experts: "The obligation of subjective experience to mental activity concomitantly encourages the absenting or denial of corporeality. 'The body' comes to be objectified as something distinct from 'the mind' and to be understood, even to understand itself, as an entity opposed to the agentive self, a corporeal appendage or energizing medium, rather than as an aspect of the agentive self" (248–249). While highlighting the corporeality that architecture from this perspective denies, in ideas about the "mental" origins of design, I wish also to highlight how this oppositional understanding (active mind governing passive body) is experientially understood and performatively realized. It follows that while I join with recent commentators who highlight the analytic limits of dualistic mind/body oppositions, I am resistant to those formulations where the continuity of mind-body is rendered as analytic truth or empirical fact. This position, which has become increasingly foundational in discussions of imagination and creativity (for example in Ingold's influential *The Perception of the Environment*), seems often to presuppose the terms of ethnographic inquiry—specifically, whether and how ideas about the relation of mind and body are understood by those involved.

26. See Saint, *Image of the Architect*, for a critical, historical account of the development of these professional ideals.

27. Particularly Chumley, *Creativity Class*. She notes how creative education in China "overtly individuates students by forcing them to focus on their 'personalities' and 'selves'" (139).

28. In "The Corporeality of Expertise," Boyer highlights how this kind of framing is more generally pervasive in the experiences and understandings of experts: "Intellectual professionalism . . . is itself responsible for cultivating a phenomenological awareness of mental distinction into an 'ontological' divide between mind and body. Once defined in opposition to mind, the body of the professional intellectual is treated as an efficient yet passive mechanism for energizing mental activity. Its normative ideal is a state of 'productive calm'" (244).

29. Yaneva, *Making of a Building*, 138.

30. Chumley describes a similar oscillation among Chinese art students, in "critique classes," where "the . . . role of the artwork . . . was continuously shifting, from a principle with its own thought, to an animator of the artist's thought, to a reified message of a bit of speech" (137).

31. See Picon, *Digital Culture in Architecture*, esp. chap. 1, for a general discussion of the increasingly pervasive use of digital design tools and the architectural consequences of this.

32. These orientations resonate with those described by Yaneva in her discussion of models at the OMA in *The Making of a Building*. She suggests that models exist alongside one another, none logically prior: "The tie that binds them is that of a common time and space; their form is a collection, an additive entity rather than a system. In other words they offer a plurality, 'a large range of starting points of view,' which reveals the building through a cumulative process of adjoining, setting and re-adjusting, staging and re-staging, displacing, bringing together and accumulating models and other visuals" (188).

33. Sennet, *Craftsman*, 151.

34. In *Life on the Screen*, Turkle highlights a fundamental shift in the use of digital technologies, associated with the erosion of hitherto assumed distinctions between humans and computers, "real life" and "virtual life." Similar arguments are extended to architecture, notably in Picon's *Digital Culture in Architecture*.

35. The thrust of much recent scholarship on digital culture in architecture (e.g., Picon, *Digital Culture in Architecture*), design (e.g., Pink, Ardevol, and Lanzeni, "Digital Materiality"), and beyond (e.g., Boellstorff, "Digital That Will Be," Miller et al., *How the World Changed Social Media*) has been to undermine the conceptual opposition between real and virtual, showing how "reality" of all kinds is inherently virtual, and how digital technologies are embedded in the material and fleshy reality of life. While broadly sympathetic to these approaches, I aim to highlight an element they have tended to elide: how this very distinction remains salient for various practitioners (see Knox, "Is There an Ontology to the Digital?"). My account takes inspiration from Loukissas's account of computer simulation (*Co-designers*), specifically the crucial point that deconstructions of the digital-analog divide fail to account for the specific ways in which this is meaningfully elaborated in practice. He notes: "Although we might try to conceptually undo this duality, we should be attentive to the way architecture is still framed by its practitioners in terms of this choice, for the selection of representations has implications for who is in control" (15).

36. These ideas resonate with arguments have been made by architectural and social theorists (see, for example, contributors to Ingold's 2011 edited volume *Redrawing Anthropology* and discussions by Sennett in *The Craftsman* and Till in *Architecture Depends*). Here I am not concerned to develop a theory of (architectural) drawing but rather with how these ideas are ethnographically understood and elaborated as part of situated understandings of the design process.

37. See Picon's *Digital Culture in Architecture* for an extended discussion of the historical context of this, and Loukissas's *Co-designers* for a more extended ethnographic analysis of these ambivalences.

38. Compare Loukissas, *Co-designers*, 28.

39. Bredekamp, "Frank Gehry and the Art of Drawing", 23.

40. Massumi echoes these ideas in "Line Parable for the Virtual," an argument that digital technologies engender systematization, associated with the diminishment of virtual possibility.

41. Loukissas, *Co-designers*, 4.

42. In *Translations from Drawing to Building*, Evans describes a principle of "reverse directionality" (165). Unlike artistic forms of representation that aim to depict what already exists, architectural drawing is oriented to make real what is not. (See also Robbins, *Why Architects Draw*.)

43. Boellstorff makes this as a more general point in "The Digital That Will Be": "At the core of current debates regarding digital ontology are questions of the real, often confused by conflation with the physical. This masks how the digital (or the analogue, for that matter) can be real (or not) in various ways, and how the physical can also be real (or not) in various ways. . . . Just as worrisome as the dismissal of the digital as unreal is the concomitant assumption that everything physical is real."

44. This point is inspired by Massumi's discussion of digital and analog design in "Line Parable for the Virtual": he highlights the virtual capacities of analog media and the diminishment of virtual possibility inherent in digital media. The virtual appears "in the twists and folds of content, as it moves from one sampled structure to another," as "expanding contradictions and contracting expanses" (306). He suggests, by contrast, that digital technologies "have a remarkably weak connection to the virtual, by virtue of their enormous power of their systematization of the possible" (309).

45. See Rose, Degen, and Melhuish, "Networks, Interfaces, and Computer-Generated Images," for an ethnographic account of how these compatibilities are fabricated in practice.

46. Loukissas, in *Co-designers*, makes this point in a subtle discussion of the social negotiations around these technologies.

47. See Picon, *Digital Culture in Architecture* (47–50), for an account of a development of these ideas in architecture, for instance via the *Whole Earth Catalogue*, and in the work of Buckminster Fuller, both explicitly influences upon David.

48. These discourses have broader resonances. In *Design and Anthropology*, Gunn and Donovan argue that "central to engaging with others is finding ways of imagining oneself into another person's world" (1). Ideals of architect as creative individual have existed in relation to various more collective understandings of the creative process, including approaches to "participatory" and community-based design from the 1970s onward. See Frampton's *Modern Architecture* for a detailed historical discussion of the emergence of these linked approaches.

49. See introduction to Ellis and Cuff's *Architects' People* for an extended account of the intellectual context in which these ideas took shape, broadly as a response to the perceived excesses of modernism and its lack of attention to social context.

50. In *A Fortunate Man*, Berger writes of a similar dynamic. In relation to the practice of Sassell, a general practitioner of medicine, he describes how "within his outwardly circumscribed life . . . he is continually speculating about, extending and amending his awareness of what is possible. Partly this is the result of his theoretical reading of medicine, science and history; partly it is the result of his own clinical observations . . . but above all it is the result of the cumulative effect of his imaginative 'proliferation' of himself in 'becoming' one patient after another" (144). The professional practice of architects is significantly distinct but, I suggest, involves a similar kind of "imaginative proliferation" of self, in which an effort to understand the lives of clients goes hand in hand with an unresolved relationship to their own life and what it means.

51. Ellis and Cuff, introduction to *Architects' People*.

52. For instance, Saint relates an anecdote told jokingly but approvingly by Frank Lloyd Wright of architect Louis Sullivan: A lady comes in and asks for a colonial house: "'Madam' said he, 'you will take what we give you'" (*Image of the Architect*, 16).

53. The interweaving of conversation and drawing is highlighted by Schon, in the context of architecture. He notes, "Drawing and talking are parallel ways of designing, and together make up what I will call the *language of designing*" (80). My account also draws inspiration from Murphy's discussions of product design, where he emphasizes the actions that words set in train: "The way designers talk as they design" is a "primary force that structures how forms are worked on, out and through, and how they are given to objects" (*Swedish Design*, 130).

54. Murphy likewise describes how conversation proliferates and focuses possibility: "Every time a designer utters 'it could be . . . or 'let's try . . .' the horizon of possibilities expands; every time he shakes his head at a suggestion or draws a line through a sketch and turns the notebook page, the horizon of possibilities contracts" (*Swedish Design*, 147).

55. See Yaneva, *Making of a Building* (6), and Murphy, *Swedish Design* (introduction), for critiques of the concept of "inspiration" as all-at-once moments. Against this they both

stress how design unfolds as a more gradual process of accretion, though conversations, models, images, as myriad assessments.

56. See Robbins, *Why Architects Draw*, 36–37.

57. In *Why Architects Draw*, Robbins likewise describes "the push and pull between the drawing as monologic and dialogic function" (135).

58. Work on creativity has often stressed how ideas are generated through engagement with other people and with various materials and technologies. While these dynamics are also central in architectural practice at MHW, this discussion foregrounds an element of the creative process that has had less attention. The description reveals how, in various ways, detachment and engagement are mutually implicated dimensions of creative practice (see Yarrow and Jones, "'Stone Is Stone,'" and Candea et al., *Detachment*).

59. In *Creativity Class*, Chumley's account of the crits of Chinese design students highlights these as a process through which the self is discursively drawn out from students (142): "Practicing creativity means not just learning how to 'make things' but also to think, feel, talk, dress, and stand in particular individuated ways, and to make these various forms of practice work together semiotically" (150).

60. Till, *Architecture Depends*, 8.

61. Morris, *Unpublished Lectures of William Morris*, quoted in Saint, *Image of the Architect*, 39. As Saint elucidates, these writers and thinkers celebrated creativity in an almost mystical understanding of "the spontaneous effect of life upon life": "An object of communal growth and accretion . . . is supposed like nature itself to speak inevitably to the human spirit in a way that a work of individualistic art never can" (41).

62. Berger likewise describes how friendships are made through processes of practical making, in a description of hobbies in working-class Britain: "The easiest . . . form of conversation is that which describes action. . . . It is then not the experience of the speakers which is discussed but the nature of an entirely exterior mechanism or event—a motorcar, a football match, a draining system or the work of some committee. Such subjects, which preclude anything directly personal, supply the content of most conversations being carried on by men over twenty five at any given moment in England today [in the 1960s]. . . . Yet there is warmth in such conversation and friendship can be sustained by it. The very intricacy of the subjects seems to bring the speakers closer together" (*Fortunate Man*, 107).

63. Other anthropologists have noted how ideologies of friendship are connected to notions of freedom and the autonomous self (see contributions to Bell and Coleman's *Anthropology of Friendship*, particularly Paine, "Friendship"; Bell and Coleman, "Anthropology of Friendship," and Carrier, "People Who Can Be Friends"; see also Yarrow, *Development beyond Politics*, chap. 3): unlike with our kin relations and colleagues, we are free to choose our friends and do so on the basis of what is shared, ideologically, emotionally, and even practically, as opposed to strategically. Such broad ideals have specific resonance in the context of this architectural practice. Here friendship is not seen as subsidiary to or independent from the relationships that connect them as colleagues, but as a central dynamic of their creative endeavors. Celebration of friendship relates to an ideology of work as a form of expression that extends from rather than curtails the individuality of those involved: at least, ideally, it is understood here as a form of self-realization.

64. In "[Deadlines]," Riles similarly highlights how deadlines elicit specific forms of action in the very different context of the negotiation of UN documents.

65. Quoted in Pandian, *Reel World*, 230.

66. Academic work engenders a similar tension, as recently described by anthropologist Michael Taussig in *The Corn Wolf*. He relates the development of what he terms "agribusiness writing" (6) to the speeding up of the tempo of academic work. "Speed-up" and "overload" (139) displace the "Go Slow feeling . . . when time did not matter" (140): "Thinking [of] . . . the child with the sea water sluicing around as the epitome of Going

Slow, it seems to me that the basic contrast with work is that of living within things versus manipulating them from outside. The former implies a mimetic desire for empathy and a capacity for becoming Other, while the latter implies the opposite, a wrenching apart of the world so as to manipulate it. The former implies a yielding relation to the world, a mastery of non-mastery, while the latter colonizes that in order to master the world" (141). Later he clarifies that the contrast is not straightforwardly between fast and slow, but between forms of interaction that emerge more or less directly from interactions with the material to hand. What he terms the Go Slow party, is, as he puts it, "not all slow": "It is like a butterfly on a hot summer's day. It speeds up and slows right down to alight on something interesting or beautiful, making it more beautiful"; its own forms of speed are "carefully knitted into its being."

67. Ayn Rand, *The Fountainhead*, quoted in Saint, *Image of the Architect*, 2. Saint's book provides an excellent extended discussion of the ideal of the architect as creative individual, and of the image of the architect more generally.

68. See Stevens, *Favored Circle*; Ballantyne, "Nest and the Pillar of Fire."

69. Quoted in Cuff, "Through the Looking Glass," 66.

70. On creativity see, for instance, Hallam and Ingold, "Creativity and Cultural Improvisation"; Sennett, *Craftsman*. As applied to design see particularly Gunn, *Design and Anthropology*. In relation to architecture see particularly Yaneva, *Making of a Building*; Murphy, "Imagination as Joint Activity"; Houdart and Chihiro, *Kuma Kengo*.

71. The term is borrowed from Pandian's *Reel World*, in which he conceptualizes film production as an "ecology of creation."

72. Distributed and relational understandings of creativity are helpful as methodological starting points but are less satisfactory as theoretical propositions about the "actual" nature of creative action. Foreclosed from this perspective are more specific questions about the way in which different people locate the origins of their own creative endeavors.

73. Leach, in "Creativity, Subjectivity and the Dynamic of Possessive Individualism," similarly highlights how the ideal of creative individuality often leads to contested understandings of authorship.

74. Nigel Rapport argues that anthropologists should give more emphasis to the individual: "My experience leads me to distinguish at every moment between the symbolic forms of my public exchanges and the meanings with which I animate them—to imagine other human beings to do the same. At every moment I make myself aware of the articulate interior consciousness that proceeds alongside but that is absolutely distinct from the exterior life beyond the surface of the self" ("'Imagination Is in the Barest Reality,'" 5). Taking inspiration from phenomenological thinkers, notably Sartre, he is critical of anthropologists' tendency to reduce imagination to its material and worldly external manifestations. While his account highlights elements of experience that are often overlooked, his analytic commitments presuppose too much of what individuality is and where its limits lie. Traced as an ethnographic category, a less stable, more complex picture emerges.

75. Compare Reed, *Literature and Agency*. His account highlights the role of inspiration in author Henry Williamson's own understandings of his writing, and in the amateur writers in turn inspired by his example.

76. In "The Dislocation of the Architectural Self," a discussion of the work of renowned postmodern architect Peter Eisenman, David Goldblatt suggests Eisenman's embrace of the arbitrary is a way of dislocating the architectural self from the professional norms and assumptions into which architects are schooled: "If the quotidian architectural self is suspect, it follows that it will not do to *express* that self" (159). For Eisenman, the institutional and professional norms of architecture can be overcome only through removal of the self, achieved through an embrace of the arbitrariness of signification: "Forced metaphor provides a greater 'hang time' (to borrow from sporting life) than ordinary metaphor where

familiarity and propriety lubricate the closure of the activity . . . initiated by metaphoric introduction" (167). At MHW, architects do not embrace the arbitrariness of signification and indeed are often explicitly critical of postmodern approaches to design. Even so, I suggest their design practices are routinely oriented to what Goldblatt terms the "dislocation of self," seeking to question their own "common sense" through the attunement to people, places, and ideas that respond to alternative logics.

77. In a discussion of Western understandings of creative individualism, James Leach likewise suggests that "the relation that defines the self as a person is a subjective intervention within the world, which makes a difference to that world. This recreates the self in the same movement by which it objectifies something beyond that self. Each time a novel object is realised, as an element external from the person, the distinction between the self and the world is recreated" ("Creativity, Subjectivity and the Dynamic of Possessive Individualism," 108).

78. My account takes inspiration from Samimian-Darash and Rabinow's edited volume *Modes of Uncertainty*. Rather than focus on the quality of dangers "in the world," they propose a focus on how uncertainty is experienced, managed, produced, and controlled through specific practices: "uncertainty, as a concept, reflects a way of observing the future and how it facilitates forms of governing, as manifestations in policies and experiences in diverse fields of research" (introduction, 7). Of particular relevance to my description is Wilf's "The 'Cool' Organization Man," an account of the rise of jazz-related metaphors in recent approaches in organizational studies. For Wilf, this has been associated with efforts to harness rather than manage potential uncertainty, as a way of embracing institutional "creativity," an increasingly valued quality of the knowledge economy. Tomas's account entails a similar embrace of the creative potential of uncertainty. At the same time he acknowledges how he, and others in the practice, must at times engage in practices oriented toward its management. There are, then, indeterminacies relating to the very question of what their orientation to uncertainty should be.

PART FOUR: PRAGMATICS

1. See Hallam and Ingold, "Creativity and Cultural Improvisation."

2. Evans, *Translations from Drawings to Building*, 169.

3. Evans, 181.

4. Evans, 182.

5. Robbins suggests that the historical development of drawing as distinct from construction allowed the architects a freedom and a power, "freed from the time-consuming and costly realities of design—while building" (*Why Architects Draw*, 30).

6. Schon, *Reflective Practitioner*, 101. He further elaborates: "Once a whole idea has been created, a bad placement of the administration can ruin it. Hence the designer must oscillate between the unit and the total" (101–102). Quist (the master) articulates this as oscillation between "involvement and detachment" (102).

7. Schon, *Reflective Practitioner*, 102.

8. In *Why Architects Draw*, Robbins describes how "development drawings . . . delineate not only the building to be realized but the occupational and functional divide between the architect and those responsible for the materialization of the building. They do so by reinforcing the conceptual role of the architect, emphasizing, as they do, making as a virtual rather than a material practice and architecture, fundamentally, as a mental rather than a hands-on activity" (35). As such, the working drawing operates as "a disembodied but authoritative architectural presence" (36).

9. Accounts of architectural practice have tended to focus on design. Correspondingly these more "pragmatic" considerations have received less attention. Yaneva's *The Making*

of a Building is an exception, though even here the main focus is elsewhere. She notes that "amid the many interesting design questions, the issue of how plans are mobilized in discussion and negotiations among engineers, cost evaluators, designers and client, and how they are used for calculation and data extraction, remains insufficiently explored in design theory" (151).

10. Compare Yarrow, "Where Knowledge Meets."

11. In *Architecture*, Cuff describes some of the dynamics that happen "within" these, but mostly takes the meeting as a self-evident context, and, in common with other accounts of architectural practice, gives little consideration to meetings as social forms in their own right. Here and elsewhere my understanding of the forms and effects of meetings borrows centrally from Brown, Reed, and Yarrow, "Introduction," and other contributors to the *JRAI* special issue on meetings; Sandler and Thedvall's *Meeting Ethnography*; and Schwartzman's earlier work, particularly *The Meeting*.

12. Mol, in *The Body Multiple*, makes a parallel point about the construction of bodies through medical practice. Different medical practitioners see literally different kinds of bodies through looking in different ways and with different kinds of tool. In practice they must be reconciled in order to act, but agreements never entirely obviate the differences of view thereby brought together.

13. Compare Goodwin, "Professional Visions."

14. See Chumley's *Creativity Class* for a discussion of the role of dress in self-presentations of individuality and creativity (13–14).

15. Elsewhere, in "Where Knowledge Meets," I have discussed in more detail the role that places and buildings play in mediating meeting dynamics. My account also draws inspiration from Yaneva's description of building professionals involved in "renovation in the making." In "How Buildings 'Surprise,'" she argues that "a building is a complex mediator that skillfully redistributes the agency among human and non-human participants in renovation, provokes contextual mutations and transformations in social meaning" (8). Rather than a passive receptacle of meaning, buildings actively constitute social relations and knowledge: "By challenging the participants in its renovation, the building's capacity to act succeeds in redefining their social connections and their definitions of the world of architecture" (11).

16. Grasseni notes that "cattle breeders, archaeologists, laser surgeons, even police consultants . . . do each have a different world in front of their eyes, because they were each trained to see it differently" (introduction to *Skilled Visions*, 3). Likewise, those involved in site meetings do not see "the same" building differently. Each sees a different kind of building, because each makes the building into a different kind of object. These differences are the product of professionally trained ways of thinking and acting, embodied and performed through specific interactions with sites and buildings.

17. In *Architecture*, Crinson and Lubbock note that architecture, at least since the heyday of modernism, has been a relatively weak profession, vulnerable to encroachment from the other interests and professions that architects must deal with: "Many different people and factors are involved in building: clients, landowners, developers, planning laws and regulations, engineers and other professions, builders, manufacturers and financiers, and last but not least the form of the existing town and its inhabitants into which all new buildings must fit whether badly or well" (2).

18. See Till's *Architecture Depends* for a detailed discussion of these factors.

19. In *Why Architects Draw*, Robbins connects "a new architectural division of labor" (15) to the mid–sixteenth century when the split between architect and builder was enabled and fixed, in part through the development of orthographic projection: "Drawing would be . . . a critical instrument that architects would appropriate in the process of making themselves predominantly designers and mind workers. The drawing would be

utilized to separate the architect from those who realized the design through their hand work" (16). Representational developments were associated with social changes and transformations in the division of labor. Detailed plans allowed the architect to remain on-site without actually being there.

20. In *Construction Workers, U.S.A*, an ethnographic account of US construction workers, Applebaum highlights how the nature of construction sites gives building work a particular quality. Because the work is fixed to a site, it is decentralized, meaning that monitoring can be difficult. Its site-specific nature means that mass-production techniques are precluded, and a relatively high level of skill is required. Sociologist Thiel makes a similar point in "Class in Construction," a study of builders in London, linking the decentralized nature of the work, and the relative skill required, to a culture of autonomy that has been eroded in other working-class occupations by mechanization and mass production.

21. Till, *Architecture Depends*, back cover.

22. A detailed discussion of construction is beyond the scope of this book. Recent ethnographic work has helped to reveal the complexity of the construction industry as a social and institutional space, notably accounts by Lyon ("The Labour of Refurbishment"), Thiel ("Class in Construction"), Bresnen ("Living the Dream?"), and Pink et al. ("Ethnographic Methodologies for Construction Research"). Collectively these highlight the considerable fluidity of the workplace: materially as sites are constantly transformed through the work of building; socially as different trades and organizations are assembled and disassembled through this. Correspondingly these ethnographies foreground how knowledge is improvised to deal with these circumstances, less as a set of formal procedures than through the tacit and embodied skills that are acquired through communities of practice.

23. Hallam and Ingold well capture the dynamism of a process that has often been understood as "mere" implementation: "A famous modern architect designs a building, the like of which the world has never seen before. He is celebrated for his creativity. Yet his design will get no further than the drawing board or portfolio until the builders step in to implement it. Building is not straightforward. It takes time, during which the worlds will not stop still: when the world is complete, the building will stand in an environment that could not have been envisioned when it started. It takes materials which have properties of their own and are not predisposed to fall into the shapes and configurations required of them, let alone stay in them indefinitely. And it takes people who have to make the most of their own skill and experience in order to cajole the materials into doing what the architect wants. In order to accommodate the inflexible design to the realities of a fickle and inconstant world, builders have to improvise all the way" ("Creativity and Cultural Improvisation," 3–4).

24. Cited in Robbins, *Why Architects Draw*, 42.

25. Catherine Alexander notes, in the context of contract negotiations relating to IT provision, how parties to a contract bear differential costs as projects unfold. In "Legal and Binding" she argues: "It is with this displacement of transaction costs in mind that some companies are prepared to make concessions as a 'loss leader' in order to win contracts, knowing how difficult it would be for the other party to seek restitution or enforcement if they fail to comply with contract strictures" (480). Likewise, building contractors quote low, in order to gain the contract, knowing they will be in a strong position to negotiate if the contract is awarded their way.

26. In "Legal and Binding," Catherine Alexander describes how classical theories of contracts have involved a series of linked oppositions: the distinction between *Gemeinschaft* and *Gesellschaft* (Tönnies), like that of status and contract (Maine) and of mechanical and organic solidarity (Durkheim), assumes a difference: that transactions between people are either embedded in a network of social relations and hence personalized, or

operate as impersonal exchanges between two parties who are otherwise unconnected and may therefore be seen as autonomous actors. My account of the work of contracts in architectural practice owes a particular debt to Alexander's own more ethnographic perspective on this: "By considering the contract as opening an arena of negotiation, rather than circumventing the actions defined within it, the role of trust becomes more evident. The written contract is both more and less than the bond described by Maine. It is more in the sense that it gives external, material form to a relationship between two parties; it is less in the sense that it cannot contain all possible futures, and cannot operate without the web of social obligations and mores in which it is caught" (482). I draw particular inspiration from her conception of these interactions, characterized by forms of indeterminacy, framed and enabled by the determinacy of textual contracts.

27. See Callon, "Embeddedness of Economic Markets."

28. This description is partly inspired by Callon's discussion in his "Embeddedness of Economic Markets." He highlights how commodities of all kinds are created through the act of dissociating: the object to be transacted from producers, users, and prior contexts of production. Things can exist in this form only to the extent that ties can be cut to other things and people.

29. In *In Praise of Bureaucracy*, DuGay likewise describes how bureaucratic conduct operates as an imperative and procedure to enable the separation of "personal" relations and professional conduct (esp. 56).

30. Architectural historians Crinson and Lubbock describe how this ideal and practice of "professionalism" emerged in nineteenth-century Britain. In *Architecture*, they write: "If the seventeenth and eighteenth centuries can be characterised by the variety of routes of entry into architecture, the latter period can be seen as one of successive arguments and debates leading to the eventual triumph of a professionalised vision of the architect that was both narrowly focused and extraordinarily powerful" (38). In part a response to specialization and the desire to protect architecture from encroachment by other building professionals (particularly engineers and building contractors), education was increasingly formalized. Skills including drawing and design were claimed as belonging specifically to the architect, as distinct from the manual work of artisans, but also from the technical skills of engineers and surveyors. From the outset the ideal of professionalism existed in uneasy and unresolved ideals of the nature of architectural practice. Influential members of the arts and crafts movement were vociferous in their rebuttal of the "professional" ideal, which they saw in a range of linked respects to be inimical to architecture as art and practical craft: "In various ways all these resisters wished to re-establish continuity with craft traditions and building lore, to heal the division between design and building and to return in some form or other to the building lodge, both as the way in which building and architecture were practiced and as the framework in which people learnt to exercise their craft or profession" (39). In *The Image of the Architect*, Saint articulates a more contemporary ambivalence that resonates with discussions in the office of MHW: "Having neither the spiritual appeal of art nor the worldly lure of profit, professionalism has always been weak. Once institutionalized, professionalism quickly passes over into mere protectionism. At its best it prevents architects from becoming preoccupied with any one of the constituents of good architecture and reminds them of the necessity of others. But at its worst, professionalism unites the exclusiveness of art-architecture with the greed of commercial architecture" (164).

31. See Cuff, *Architecture*, chap. 2.

32. In *The Making of a Building*, Yaneva describes this "anticipatory" quality of architecture: "The emergence of the building is expected and foreseen in advance; it is strictly planned and architects are prepared for it. They know what is necessary for the building to happen, without relying on unexpected and randomly occurring events to intervene

accidentally in design" (159). In "Different Presents in the Making," Anusas and Harkness describe how the anticipatory logic of product design involves a similar teleology of "the project."

33. In "Different Presents in the Making," Anusas and Harkness describe the experiences associated with what they term the "close time" of the project in the context of commercial product design. Here "specific time intervals are continually discussed as practitioners coordinate their work" (59); the close present is "sustained as a force of both pressure and tension, with a regularity of verbal expressions concerning how time is in short supply and not felt to be under the practitioners' control" (59). While architects at MHW likewise articulate ideas about good design being "head down," "focused on the task," they also articulate ambivalences about this way of working, through ideas about futures of a more open kind. These are more akin to the kind of future Anusas and Harkness attribute to Earthship builders in the UK and Mexico, a more "free" time that is "burgeoning with the possibility of difference" (62). In other words, the temporal contrast they draw is encountered at MHW as a temporal ambivalence.

34. My discussion is broadly inspired by recent anthropological discussions of modern time, specifically the *JRAI* special issue *Doubt, Conflict, Mediation*. In "Doubt, Conflict and Mediation," the introductory essay, Bear highlights how the apparent singularity of modern time elides how it is practically constituted at the intersection of a series of circulating representations, social disciplines, and technologies. The act of working in and on time involves "an encounter with the material world; the limits of the body; multiple tools; and co-ordinations of diverse rhythms and representations" (20).

35. The constitution of time through meeting is central to a 2017 edited volume, Brown, Reed, and Yarrow, *Meetings: Ethnographies of Organisation, Bureaucracy and Assembly*, which highlights how the internal dynamics of meeting order and organize time. Meetings create specific kinds of future (for example as "actions"), which orient future practices and then provide benchmarks against which institutional outcomes are retrospectively accounted for.

36. Compare Anusas and Harkness, "Different Presents in the Making."

37. In "Building Stories," Murphy argues that "because buildings essentially progress from nothing to something, architecture is an inherently teleological endeavour. Architects, working in the present with drawings (plans and elevations) and computers, are always directed toward an imagined future building, and as such tend to labour in temporal flux" (246).

38. Latour describes the process by which scientists turn the complexities of the world into representations of this world. In *Pandora's Hope*, he describes the alchemy of a seemingly paradoxical endeavor: How can the complexity of the Amazon rain forest be encompassed in texts and other artifacts, a fraction of its size? Tracing the practical way in which ecologists achieve this, he suggests there is no singular gap between the world on the one hand and representations of this on the other. Instead scientists encounter a series of gaps, characterized both by radical incommensurability *and* by literal connection. The construction of buildings is likewise characterized by the stabilization of some elements in the face of radical transformation of others, but here the process of materialization is, as it were, in the other direction: from "small" to "big"; "representation" to "reality."

39. Hallam and Ingold, "Creativity and Cultural Improvisation," 2.

40. Hallam and Ingold, 19.

41. See Yarrow, "Retaining Character," and "How Conservation Matters," for discussions of the work of "keeping things as they are" in relation to conservation professionals.

42. After Schon, *Reflective Practitioner*, 19.

PART FIVE: PRACTICAL COMPLETION

1. My analysis is inspired by recent anthropological discussions of "ignorance." In "Making Ignorance an Ethnographic Object," Mair, Kelly, and High suggest that scholarly assumptions about the virtues of knowledge have led scholars to overlook the range of ways in which other people orient themselves to the unknown: "Anthropologists have too easily attributed to the people they study the same unambiguous desire for knowledge, and the same aversion to ignorance, that motivates their own work, with the results that situations in which ignorance is viewed neutrally—or even positively—have been misunderstood and overlooked" (1). From this perspective they suggest, "Under certain circumstances ignorance has a substance of its own, as the product of specific practices, with effects that are distinct from the effects of the lack of knowledge" (3).

2. *Translations from Drawing to Building and Other Essays*, 162.

3. Crinson and Lubbock, *Architecture: Art or Profession?*

4. Schon, *Reflective Practitioner*, chap. 1; Collins and Evans, *Rethinking Expertise*, introduction.

5. Schon, chap. 1; Collins and Evans, introduction.

6. In the terms developed as a general theory by Bourdieu in *Distinction*, and as elaborated most extensively in relation to architecture by Stevens in *The Favored Circle*.

7. Collins and Evans, *Rethinking Expertise*, 139.

8. Schon, *Reflective Practitioner*, vii.

9. Even in their differences, theorists have often shared the goal of encompassing explanation: either creativity is individual or else it is social; designs emerge in the thoughts of specific people, or else they are a result of interactions between people and things. Conventional architectural theories echo Western folk concepts of what buildings are: stable and fixed forms that persist through time, testaments to the genius, folly, or even mediocrity of the person who designed them. More recently, the challenge to this position has produced its own orthodoxy and its own kinds of interpretive certainty: behind this façade lurks the reality that buildings are in fact malleable, changeable, forever in the process of becoming something else. Most of these theories have some descriptive value. But none of them exhaust the descriptive possibilities of architecture as I observed it in practice, even within the radically confined space of just one office.

10. See Till, *Architecture Depends*.

11. Pandian and Maclean, *Crumpled Paper Boat*; see also Murphy, "Imagination as Joint Activity," 243, for a related discussion of "the possible" within the "actual" of architectural practice.

CODA

1. Back, *Art of Listening*, back page.

2. This approach has some affinities with "public anthropology" as described by Robert Borofsky in his paper "Public Anthropology," distinct from "popular anthropology," if that term is taken to imply the effort to convey the same ideas in simplified form. Anthropologists have made various recent calls for the discipline to speak more often and more persuasively to audiences beyond fellow academic professionals. Keith Hart, for example, has recently suggested that "if anthropologists are to pioneer a bold path forward, we will need to think a lot more deeply about the art of writing. . . . Since the boom years of the 1970s, many of us have got stuck in a groove of writing for other anthropologists and their students; and then we complain that the general public is indifferent to what we write. There is no shortage of powerful topics . . . but if we don't smarten up our literary skills and clarify our intellectual purposes, all that painstaking fieldwork will go to waste" ("Anthropology of Debt," 420). He and others, including David Graeber, have been par-

ticularly successful with their interventions into a range of public arguments. They have used comparative ethnographic discussion to make powerful arguments of broad interest, mostly through a rather didactic form. While I see these efforts at relevance as wholly positive, I suggest there is also further scope for the development of forms of writing that speak more broadly *through* description. Notwithstanding some notable exceptions, widely read accounts of just this kind of ethnographic sensibility have more often been written by authors outside the professional discipline of anthropology. I am thinking, for example, of John Berger's *A Fortunate Man*, a powerfully affecting account of a general practitioner, Geoff Dyers's *Another Fine Day at Sea*, a vividly evocative description of life on board a US military aircraft carrier, and Alexander Masters's *Stuart*, a subtle, sensitive biography of a homeless man in Cambridge, England.

References

Alexander, Catherine. "Legal and Binding: Time, Change and Long-Term Transactions." *Journal of the Royal Anthropological Institute* 7, no. 3 (2001): 467–485.

Andrews, Molly. *Lifetimes of Commitment: Aging, Politics, Psychology.* Cambridge: Cambridge University Press, 1991.

Anusas, Mike, and Rachel Harkness. "Different Presents in the Making." In *Design Anthropological Futures*, edited by Rachel Charlotte Smith, Kasper Tang Vangkilde, Mette Gislev Kjaersgaard, Ton Otto, Joachim Halse, and Thomas Binder, 55–69. London: Bloomsbury, 2016.

Applebaum, Herbert. *Construction Workers, U.S.A.* Westport, CT: Greenwood, 1999.

Back, Les. *The Art of Listening.* Oxford: Berg, 2007.

———. "Journeying through Words: Les Back Reflects on Writing with Thomas Yarrow." *JRAI* 20, no. 4 (2014): 766–770.

Ballantyne, Andrew. "The Nest and the Pillar of Fire." In *What Is Architecture?*, edited by Andrew Ballatyne, 7–52. London: Routledge, 2002.

Bandak, Andreas, and Lars Højer. "Introduction: the Power of Example." *Journal of the Royal Anthropological Institute*, 2015: 1–17.

Barber, Karin. "Improvisation and the Art of Making Things Stick." In *Creativity and Cultural Improvisation*, edited by Elizabeth Hallam and Tim Ingold, 25–41. Oxford: Berg, 2007.

Bell, Sandra, and Simon Coleman. "The Anthropology of Friendship: Enduring Themes and Future Possibilities." In *The Anthropology of Friendship*, edited by Sandra Bell and Simon Coleman, 1–19. Oxford: Berg, 1999.

Berger, John. *A Fortunate Man: The Story of a Country Doctor.* Edinburgh: Cannongate Books, 2015.

Boellstorff, Tom. "The Digital That Will Be." *Cultural Anthropology*, March 24, 2016. https://culanth.org/fieldsights/819-the-digital-that-will-be.

Borofsky, Robert. "Public Anthropology: Where To? What Next?" *Anthropology News* 41, no. 5 (2000): 9–10.

Boyer, Dominic. "The Corporeality of Expertise." *Ethnos* 70, no. 2 (2005): 243–266.

———. "Thinking through the Anthropology of Experts." *Anthropology in Action* 15, no. 2 (2008): 38–46.

Boyer, Dominic, James Faubion, and George Marcus. *Theory Can Be More Than It Used to Be: Learning Anthropology's Method in a Time of Transition.* Ithaca, NY: Cornell University Press, 2015.

Bredekamp, Horst. "Frank Gehry and the Art of Drawing." In *Gehry Draws*, edited by Mark Rappolt and Robert Violette, 11–28. Cambridge, Massachusetts: MIT Press, 2004.

Bresnen, M. "Living the Dream? Understanding Partnering as Emergent Practice." *Construction Management and Economics* 27, no. 10 (2009): 923–933.

Brown, Hannah, Adam Reed, and Thomas Yarrow. "Introduction: Towards an Ethnography of Meeting." In "Meetings: Ethnographies of Organizational Process, Bureaucracy, and Assembly," special issue of the *Journal of the Royal Anthropological Institute* 23, no. S1 (2017): 10–26.

Callon, Michael. "Introduction: The Embeddedness of Economic Markets in Economics." *Sociological Review* 46, no. S1 (1998): 1–57.

Candea, Matei. *Comparison in Anthropology: The Impossible Method.* Cambridge: Cambridge University Press, 2018.

Candea, Matei, Jo Cook, Catherine Trundle, and Thomas Yarrow. *Detachment: Essays on the Limits of Relational Thinking.* Manchester: Manchester University Press, 2015.

Carrier, James G. "People Who Can Be Friends: Selves and Social Relationships." In *The Anthropology of Friendship,* edited by Sandra Bell and Simon Coleman, 21–38. Oxford: Berg, 1999.

Carrithers, Michael. "Anthropology as Irony and Philosophy, or the Knots in Simple Ethnographic Projects." *HAU: Journal of Ethnographic Theory* 4, no. 3 (2014): 117–142.

Chumley, Lily. *Creativity Class: Art School and Culture Work in Postsocialist China.* Princeton, NJ: Princeton University Press, 2016.

Collini, Stefan. "Who Are the Spongers Now?" *London Review of Books* 38, no. 2 (2016): 33–37.

Collins, Harry, and Robert Evans. *Rethinking Expertise.* Chicago: University of Chicago Press, 2007.

Crinson, Mark, and Jules Lubbock. *Architecture: Art or Profession?* Manchester: Manchester University Press, 1994.

Crook, Tony. *Exchanging Skin: Anthropological Knowledge, Secrecy and Bolivip, Papua New Guinea.* London: Oxford University Press, 2007.

Cuff, Dana. *Architecture: The Story of Practice.* Cambridge, MA: MIT Press, 1996. First published in 1991.

——. "The Social Production of Built Form." *Environment and Planning D: Society and Space* 7, no. 4 (1989): 433–447.

——. "Through the Looking Glass: Seven New York Architects and Their People." In *Architects' People,* edited by Russell Ellis and Dana Cuff, 55–63. Oxford: Oxford University Press, 1989.

Daston, Lorraine, and Peter Galison. *Objectivity.* New York: Zone Books, 2007.

Denzin, Norman. *Interpretive Biography.* London: Sage, 1989.

Dingwall, Robert. *Essays on Professions.* Aldershot, UK: Ashgate, 2008.

DuGay, Paul. *In Praise of Bureaucracy: Weber, Organization, Ethics.* London: Sage, 2000.

Dyer, Geoff. *Another Great Day at Sea: Life aboard the USS George H. W. Bush.* New York: Pantheon, 2014.

Ellis, Russell, and Dana Cuff, eds. *Architects' People.* Oxford: Oxford University Press, 1989.

——. Introduction to Ellis and Cuff, *Architects' People,* 3–14.

Englund, Harri, and Thomas Yarrow. "The Place of Theory: Rights, Networks, and Ethnographic Comparison." *Social Analysis* 57, no. 3 (2013): 132–159.

Evans, Robin. *Translations from Drawing to Building and Other Essays.* London: Architectural Association, 1997.

Fanthorpe, U. A. 2010. "Atlas." In *New and Collected Poems.* London: Enitharman Press.

Forty, Adrian. *Words and Buildings: A Vocabulary of Modern Architecture.* London: Thames & Hudson, 2004.

Frampton, Kenneth. *Modern Architecture: A Critical History.* London: Thames & Hudson, 2007. First published in 1980.

Furedi, Frank. *Where Have All the Intellectuals Gone?* London: Continuum, 2004.

Girado, Diane. "The Architecture of Deceit." In *What Is Architecture?,* edited by Andrew Ballantyne, 63–71. London: Routledge, 2002.

Goldblatt, David. "The Dislocation of the Architectural Self." In *What Is Architecture?*, edited by Andrew Ballantyne, 153–172. London: Routledge, 2002.

Goodwin, Charles. "Professional Vision." *American Anthropologist* 96, no. 3 (1994): 606–633.

Grasseni, Cristina, ed. *Skilled Visions: Between Apprenticeship and Standards.* New York: Berghahn Books, 2007.

——. Introduction to Grasseni, *Skilled Visions*, 1–19.

Greenhouse, Carol. *A Moment's Notice: Time Politics across Cultures.* Ithaca, NY: Cornell University Press, 1996.

Gunn, Wendy, and Jared Donovan. *Design and Anthropology: An Introduction.* Farnham, Surrey, UK: Ashgate, 2012.

——. Introduction to Gunn and Donovan, *Design and Anthropology.*

Gutman, Robert. *Architectural Practice: A Critical View.* New York: Princeton Architectural Press, 1988.

Hallam, Elizabeth, and Tim Ingold. "Creativity and Cultural Improvisation: An Introduction." In *Creativity and Cultural Improvisation*, edited by Elizabeth Hallam and Tim Ingold. Oxford: Berg, 2007.

Harkness, Rachel. *Thinking, Building, Dwelling: Examining Earthships in Taos and Fife.* Aberdeen: University of Aberdeen, 2009.

Hart, Keith. "The Anthropology of Debt." *Journal of the Royal Anthropological Institute* 22, no. 2 (2016): 415–421.

Harvey, Penny, and Hannah Knox. *Roads: An Anthropology of Infrastructure and Expertise.* Ithaca, NY: Cornell University Press, 2015.

Hasty, Jennifer. *The Press and Political Culture in Ghana.* Bloomington: Indiana University Press, 2005.

Holbraad, Martin. *Truth in Motion: The Recursive Anthropology of Cuban Divination.* Chicago: University of Chicago Press, 2012.

Houdart, Sophie, and Minato Chihiro. *Kuma Kengo: An Unconventional Monograph.* Paris: Éditions Donner Lieu, 2009.

Ingold, Tim. *Making: Anthropology, Archaeology, Art and Architecture.* London: Routledge, 2013.

——. *The Perception of the Environment: Essays in Livelihood, Dwelling and Skill.* London: Routledge, 2000.

——, ed. *Redrawing Anthropology: Materials, Movements and Lines.* Farnham, Surrey, UK: Ashgate, 2011.

Ingold, Tim, and Jo Lee Vergunst. Introduction to *Ways of Walking: Ethnography and Practice on Foot*, edited by Tim Ingold and Jo Lee Vergunst. Farnham, Surrey, UK: Ashgate, 2008.

Iser, Wolfgang. "Interaction between Text and Reader." In *The Reader in the Text: Essays on Audience and Interpretation*, edited by Susan Suleiman, 106–119. Princeton, NJ: Princeton University Press, 1980.

Jackson, Michael. *Between One and One Another.* Berkeley: University of California Press, 2012.

Jones, Sian, and Thomas Yarrow. "Crafting Authenticity: An Ethnography of Heritage Conservation." *Journal of Material Culture* 18, no. 1 (2013): 3–26.

Killick, Evan. "Whose Truth Is It Anyway?" *Anthropology of This Century*, no. 9 (2014).

Knox, Hannah, and Antonia Walford. "Is There an Ontology to the Digital?" *Cultural Anthropology*, March 24, 2016. https://culanth.org/fieldsights/818-is-there-an-ontology-to-the-digital.

Laidlaw, James. "For an Anthropology of Ethics and Freedom." *JRAI* (n.s.) 8, no. 2 (2001): 311–332.

Latour, Bruno. "On Recalling ANT." *Sociological Review* 47, no. 1 (1999): 15–25.

———. *Pandora's Hope: Essays on the Reality of Science Studies*. Cambridge, MA: Harvard University Press, 1999.

Leach, James. "Creativity, Subjectivity and the Dynamic of Possessive Individualism." In *Creativity and Cultural Improvisation*, edited by Elizabeth Hallam and Tim Ingold, 99–116. Oxford: Berg, 2007.

Loukissas, Yanni. *Co-designers: Cultures of Computer Simulation in Architecture*. London: Routledge, 2016.

Lowenstein, Oliver. "An Architecture of Elsewhere." In *Architecture in Scotland: 2006–2008*, edited by Morag Bain and Oliver Lowenstein, 10–25. Glasgow: Lighthouse, 2009.

Lyon, Dawn. "The Labour of Refurbishment: The Building and the Body in Space and Time." In *Ethnographic Research in the Construction Industry*, edited by Sarah Pink, Dylan Tutt, and Andrew Dainty. Abingdon, UK: Taylor & Francis, 2012.

MacFarlane, Robert. Introduction to *The Living Mountain*, by Nan Shepheard. Edinburgh and London: Canongate, 2011.

Mair, Jonathan, Ann Kelly, and Casey High. "Introduction: Making Ignorance an Ethnographic Object." In *The Anthropology of Ignorance: An Ethnographic Approach*, edited by Casey High, Ann Kelly, and Jonathan Mair. New York: Palgrave Macmillan, 2012.

Massumi, Brian. "Line Parable for the Virtual (on the Superiority of the Analog)." In *The Virtual Dimension: Architecture, Representation, and Crash Culture*, edited by John Beckmann, 304–321. Princeton, NJ: Princeton University Press, 1998.

Masters, Alexander. *Stuart: A Life Backwards*. New York: Delta. 2007.

Miller, Daniel, Elisabetta Costa, Nell Haynes, Tom McDonald, Razvan Nicolescu, Jolynna Sinanan, Juliano Spyer, Shriram Venkatraman, and Xinyuan Wang. *How the World Changed Social Media*. London: UCL, 2016.

Miyazaki, Hirokazu. *Arbitraging Japan: Dreams of Capitalism at the End of Finance*. Berkeley: University of California Press, 2013.

Mol, Annmarie. *The Body Multiple: Ontology in Medical Practice*. Durham, NC: Duke University Press, 2002.

Murphy, Keith. "Building Stories: The Embodied Narration of What May Come to Pass." In *Embodied Interaction: Language and Body in the Material World*, edited by Jürgen Streeck, Charles Goodwin, and Curtis LeBaron, 243–253. Cambridge: Cambridge University Press, 2011.

———. "Imagination as Joint Activity: The Case of Architectural Interaction." *Mind, Culture and Activity* 11, no. 4 (2004): 267–278.

———. *Swedish Design: An Ethnography*. Ithaca, NY: Cornell University Press, 2015.

Murphy, Keith M., Jonas Ivarsson, and Gustav Lymer. "Embodied Reasoning in Architectural Critique." *Design Studies* 33, no. 6 (2012): 530–556.

Nadaï, Alain, and Olivier Labussière. "Playing with the Line, Channelling Multiplicity: Wind Power Planning in the Narbonnaise (Aude, France)." *Environment and Planning D: Society and Space* 31, no. 1 (2013): 116–139.

Nielsen, Morten, and Morten Pedersen. "Infrastructural Imaginaries: Collapsed Futures in Mozambique and Mongolia." In *Reflections on Imagination: Human Capacity and Ethnographic Method*, edited by Mark Harris and Nigel Rapport, 237–261. London: Routledge, 2015.

Paine, Robert. "Friendship: The Hazards of an Ideal Relationship." In *The Anthropology of Friendship*, edited by Sandra Bell and Simon Coleman, 39–58. Oxford: Berg, 1999.

Pandian, Anand. *Reel World: An Anthropology of Creation*. Durham, NC: Duke University Press, 2015.

Pandian, Anand, and Stuart Maclean. *Crumpled Paper Boat: Experiments in Ethnographic Writing*. Durham, NC: Duke University Press, 2017.

Parry, Jonathan. "The Marital History of 'a Thumb-Impression Man.'" In *Telling Lives in India: Biography, Autobiography, and Life History*, edited by David Arnold and Stuart Blackburn, 281–318. Bloomington: Indiana University Press, 2004.

Pendlebury, John. *Conservation in the Age of Consensus*. Abingdon, UK: Routledge, 2009.

Picon, Antoine. *Digital Culture in Architecture: An Introduction for the Design Professions*. Basel, Switzerland: Birkhauser, 2010.

Pink, Sarah, Elisenda Ardevol, and Debora Lanzeni. "Digital Materiality." In *Digital Materialities: Design and Anthropology*, edited by Sarah Pink, Elisenda Ardevol, and Debora Lanzeni. Fakenham, UK: Bloomsbury, 2016.

Pink, Sarah, Kerstin Leder Mackley, Roxana Morosanu, Val Mitchell, and Tracy Bhamra. *Making Homes: Ethnography and Design*. New York: Bloomsbury, 2017.

Pink, Sarah, Dylan Tutt, Andrew Dainty, and Alistair Gibb. "Ethnographic Methodologies for Construction Research: Knowing, Practice and Interventions." *Building Research and Information* 38, no. 6 (2010): 647–659.

Rabinow, Paul, and Anthony Stavrianakis. *Designs on the Contemporary: Anthropological Tests*. Chicago: University of Chicago Press, 2014.

Rapport, Nigel. "The Consequences of Anthropological Writing." *JRAI* 21, no. 3 (2015): 680–683.

——. "'Imagination Is in the Barest Reality': On the Universal Human Imagining of the World." In *Reflections on Imagination: Human Capacity and Ethnographic Method*, edited by Mark Harris and Nigel Rapport, 3–21. Farnham, Surrey, UK: Ashgate, 2015.

Reed, Adam. *Literature and Agency in English Fiction Reading: A Study of the Henry Williamson Society*. Manchester: Manchester University Press, 2011.

RIBA. *RIBA Business Benchmarking 2016*. Report prepared for the RIBA by the Fees Bureau. https://www.architecture.com/-/media/gathercontent/business-benchmarking/additional-documents/ribabenchmarking2016executivesummarypdf.pdf.

Riles, Annelise. "[Deadlines]: Removing the Brackets on Politics in Bureaucratic and Anthropological Analysis." In *Documents: Artifacts of Modern Knowledge*, edited by Annelise Riles. Ann Arbor: University of Michigan Press, 2006.

Robbins, Edward. *Why Architects Draw*. Cambridge, MA: MIT Press, 1997.

Rose, Gillian, Monica Degen, and Clare Melhuish. "Networks, Interfaces, and Computer-Generated Images: Learning from the Digital Visualisations of Urban Redevelopment Projects." *Environment and Planning D: Society and Space* 32, no. 3 (2014): 386–403.

Runciman, W. G. *A Treatise on Social Theory: The Methodology of Social Theory*. Cambridge: Cambridge University Press, 1983.

Saint, Andrew. *The Image of the Architect*. Wallop, Hampshire, UK: Yale University Press, 1983.

Samimian-Darash, Limor, and Paul Rabinow. Introduction to *Modes of Uncertainty: Anthropological Cases*, edited by Limor Samimian-Daresh and Paul Rabinow, 1–12. Chicago: University of Chicago Press, 2015.

Sandler, Jen, and Renita Thedvall. *Meeting Ethnography: Meetings as Key Technologies of Contemporary Governance, Development, and Resistance*. New York: Routledge, 2016.

Schon, Donald. *The Reflective Practitioner: How Professionals Think in Action.* Farnham, Surrey, UK: Ashgate, 2013. First published in 1983.

Schwartzman, Helen. *The Meeting: Gatherings in Organizations and Communities.* New York: Plenum, 1989.

Sennett, Richard. *The Craftsman.* St Ives, UK: Penguin, 2009.

Smith, Rachel Charlotte, Kasper Tang Vangkilde, Mette Gislev Kjaersgaard, Ton Otto, Joachim Halse, and Thomas Binder. *Design Anthropological Futures.* London: Bloomsbury, 2016.

Sneath, David, Martin Holbraad, and Morten Pedersen. "Technologies of the Imagination: An Introduction." *Ethnos* 74, no. 1 (2009): 5–30.

Stengers, Isabelle. *Another Science Is Possible: A Manifesto for Slow Science.* Trans. Stephen Muecke. London: Wiley, 2018.

Stevens, Garry. *The Favored Circle: The Social Foundations of Architectural Distinction.* Cambridge, MA: MIT Press, 1998.

St John Wilson, Colin. *The Other Tradition of Modern Architecture: The Uncompleted Project.* London: Black Dog, 2007.

Strathern, Marilyn. "Audit Cultures." In *Audit Cultures: Anthropological Studies of Accountability, Ethics and the Academy*, edited by Marilyn Strathern. London: Routledge, 2000.

——. *The Gender of the Gift: Problems with Women and Problems with Society in Melanesia.* Berkeley: University of California Press, 1988.

——. *Partial Connections.* Savage, MD: Rowman & Littlefield, 1991.

Taussig, Michael. *The Corn Wolf.* Chicago: University of Chicago Press, 2015.

Thiel, Daniel. "Class in Construction: London Building Workers, Dirty Work and Physical Cultures." *British Journal of Sociology* 58, no. 2 (2007): 227–251.

Thurley, Simon. *The Men from the Ministry: How Britain Saved Its Heritage.* New Haven, CT: Yale University Press, 2013.

Till, Jeremy. *Architecture Depends.* Cambridge, MA: MIT Press, 2009.

Turkle, Sherry. *Life on the Screen: Identity in the Age of the Internet.* New York: Simon & Schuster, 1995.

Vesely, Dalibor. *Architecture in the Age of Divided Representation.* Cambridge, MA: MIT Press, 2004.

Viveiros de Castro, Eduardo. "Perspectival Anthropology and the Method of Controlled Equivocation." *Tipiti* 2, no. 1 (2004): 3–22.

Wilf, Eitan. "The 'Cool' Organization Man: Incorporating Uncertainty from Jazz Music into the Business World." In *Modes of Uncertainty: Anthropological Cases*, edited by Limor Samimian-Daresh and Paul Rabinow, 29–45. Chicago: University of Chicago Press, 2015.

——. *School for Cool: The Academic Jazz Program and the Paradox of Institutionalized Creativity.* Chicago: University of Chicago Press, 2014.

Willerslev, Rane. "'To Have the World at a Distance': Reconsidering the Significance of Vision for Social Anthropology." In *Skilled Visions: Between Apprenticeship and Standards*, edited by Cristina Grasseni, 23–46. New York: Berghahn Books, 2007.

Yaneva, Albena. "How Buildings 'Surprise': The Renovation of the Alte Aula in Vienna." *Science Studies* 21, no. 1 (2008): 8–28.

——. *Made by the Office for Metropolitan Architecture: An Ethnography of Design.* Rotterdam: 010 Publishers, 2009.

——. *The Making of a Building: A Pragmatist Approach to Architecture.* Bern, Switzerland: Peter Lang, 2009.

Yarrow, Thomas. *Development beyond Politics: Aid, Activism and NGOs in Ghana.* London: Palgrave Macmillan, 2011.

———. "How Conservation Matters: Ethnographic Explorations of Historic Building Renovation." *Journal of Material Culture*, April 29, 2018. https://doi.org/10.1177/1359183518769111.

———. "Retaining Character: Heritage Conservation and the Logic of Continuity." *Social Anthropology* 26, no. 3 (2018): 330–344.

———. "Where Knowledge Meets: Heritage Expertise at the Intersection of People, Perspective and Place." *Journal of the Royal Anthropological Institute* 23, no. 1 (2017): 95–109.

Yarrow, Thomas, and Sian Jones. "'Stone Is Stone': Engagement and Detachment in the Craft of Conservation Masonry." *JRAI* 20, no. 2 (2014): 256–275.

Index

abstraction, in design, 101–2, 136, 170
administrative work, 221–23, 227;
    contract management and, 195, 204–7,
    212–13, 226–27; vs. creative work,
    149–50, 227–29
aesthetics: and architects' elite status, 31,
    236–37; architectural training and, 47,
    120; clients', perception of, 127, 129; vs.
    practicalities, 174–75
Alexander, Catherine, 259n25, 259n26
Alexander, Christopher, 87
analog media: and digital design tools,
    relationship between, 120–21;
    nostalgia for, 119; virtual capacities of,
    254n44
Andrews, Molly, 250n23
anthropology: and description, return
    to, 242, 263n2; ethical turn in, 246n4;
    ontological turn in, 245n9; public,
    262n2. See also ethnographic approach
Anusas, Mike, 261n32, 261n33
anxiety, in architecture, 160–62;
    expansion of practice and, 156;
    manifestations of, 223; time pressures
    and, 146–48, 223; uncertainty and, 162
Applebaum, Herbert, 259n20
apprenticeship, architectural training and,
    41, 55, 248n1
architect(s): authority of, 184–86;
    and builders, relationship of, 199,
    201, 258n19; as choreographer,
    184; competition among, 143–44;
    construction problems and, 195; as
    contract administrators, 195, 204–7,
    212–13, 226–27; good, attributes of, 125,
    126; income of, 2, 29, 127–28, 248n20;
    as mediators, 204, 206, 212–13; as
    receptor responding to design, 111–12;
    residences of, 1–2, 128; as therapist, 128.
    See also staff, at MHW
architectural assistants, 29; challenges for,
    34–35; transition from university to
    work, 32–33
Architectural Association, 46, 48
architecture: all-consuming nature of,
    41–42, 51–52, 53, 69–70; anticipatory

quality of, 216, 260n32, 261n37; as
    career choice, 39, 46, 54–55, 58, 59, 62;
    contextual, 60, 87; contradictions in,
    19–21, 31; ethnographic approach to, 3,
    9–10, 241–42; ideals about, 16, 39–40,
    47, 50, 247n8; individual creativity
    and, 153, 154; instinctive (intuitive)
    approach to, 58, 105–7, 109; interstitial
    spaces in ("spaces between"), 19–21,
    235–36; language and, 59, 82; literature
    on, critical thrust of, 31; mainstream,
    disillusionment with, 47–48, 58, 60, 61,
    239; parochial approach to, 24; and self-
    exploration, 47, 49–50, 70; sociological
    approach to, 10; specialization within,
    233, 236, 248n21; as vocation, 21, 41–42,
    48, 49, 53, 61, 69, 70; vulnerability to
    encroachment, 258n17
Area of Outstanding Natural Beauty, 76, 97
arts and crafts movement, 63; collective
    endeavor in, 141–42; vs. "professional"
    ideal, 260n30
assistants. See architectural assistants
authority, architectural, 184–86, 236. See
    also expertise
AutoCAD, 115. See also CAD

Back, Les, 3, 241
Bandak, Andreas, 248n18
Barber, Karin, 252n23, 252n24
barn conversion, 96–98, 172
Bauhaus ideal, 40
Bawa, Geoffrey, 84
Berger, John, 69, 254n50, 255n62, 263
betweenness, in architecture, 19–21;
    Eisenman on, 246n1. See also space(s)
    between
biographies, 46, 53–54, 249n10; middle-
    class vs. working-class, 250n23;
    personal vision statement, 54–55;
    professional, 62. See also self-narratives
blockages, 224–25; collaborative solutions
    to, 33, 146; reasons for, 169; switching
    tools to solve, 115
Boellstorff, Tom, 11, 253n43
Borofsky, Robert, 262n2

CPSIA information can be obtained
at www.ICGtesting.com
Printed in the USA
FFHW012150310519
52746009-58277FF